MAYBE IT'S BECAUSE I'M A LONDONER

BERNARD LOCKETT

Published by

MELROSE BOOKS

An Imprint of Melrose Press Limited
St Thomas Place, Ely
Cambridgeshire
CB7 4GG, UK
www.melrosebooks.com

FIRST EDITION

Cover designed by Geoff Hobbs Design

ISBN 1 905226 26 8

Printed and bound in Great Britain by:
Bath Press Limited, Lower Bristol Road,
Bath, BA2 3BL, UK

Dedication

I dedicate this book to my late Nan and Grandpop who brought me up and who were always there for me.

Acknowledgements

My heartfelt thanks to my publishers, Melrose Books, the Editor, Ross Hilton and the entire team.

My writing would not have been possible without the support and encouragement of my dear wife, Lea.

Chapter 1

1945 And The Beginning

The mid 1940s and London had been and continued to be grim. The life for so many of its citizens and for the country as a whole; indeed Europe and most of the civilised World were united in a similar vein. There had, after all, been over five years of war with so many untold hardships, depressions, fears and accompanying changes to virtually all aspects of known and, for so long, trusted lives and times. But – yes, it really was so that in January 1945 there was some reason to savour the winter sunrise and begin to see more than the light of dawn - the Allies were advancing through Europe and pushing the enemy back further and further. Finally, there was reason to hope and to begin to believe in a coming possible peace, negotiated too from the position of the potential glorious victor.

Here, then, an opportunity for the end of hostilities in Europe and more especially for relief from the torment of bombings and endless air raids to the very heart of everybody's local world and home streets. Soon the chance would come to finally begin to rebuild lives and to set upon the task to rebuilding and renovating towns, cities and the country as a whole. Soon too would be the time to welcome the return of many loved ones, family and friends, with eager expectations for a happier, more secure and better future. Of course, it was a reason to hope because the immediate past had been so bad and it didn't take too much of an optimist to think that anything coming must surely be better.

There had been the horrendous bombings, the night after nights spent during the time of the London Blitz, endless fires, the damage of the buildings, frequent demolitions, time when people had lived with constant power loss, burst water mains – simply times when normalities of life had ceased to exist And, if that was all, then relatively people thought they were almost lucky. For many, it was not only the loss of homes but, worst still, the loss of life of friends and loved ones.

Everybody was ready to believe that the end of hostilities was surely in sight. Never to give up, that was not the London character; the sheer will and determination was to succeed, but even so people were tired and wanted the better times and once again to see optimism.

In so many ways 1945 was pivotal. The old and the horrible, so much in evidence and, in contrast, the better aspects of life and country's traditions, the Nation's Heritage, were somehow still visible and very often intact. How the people of the East End had been so heartened by the visits and support of Their Majesties, King George VI and Queen Elizabeth: there when they were most needed, bringing understanding and solidarity in the times of so much suffering.

With the scope and prospects for peace soon to be realised, then the work and endeavours to build for a hopefully positive future could begin with a will and in earnest After all, what had the years since 1939 been other than a fight for ideals, a bid to rid ourselves and others of the curse of oppression and tyranny, then so to secure and prepare for a better and safer life, trustingly with fairness and prosperity.

1945 then, a significant year of change – out with the old, in with the new as chorused every New Year but this time with every valid reason. The traditional singing in the many pubs that previous New Year's Eve had been with extra verve and significance. Relatively, this may be when taken in a generalised nature, but for me it was more than that.

For me, 1945 was fundamental – it was the year I was born!

Let me now not be too grand by evoking the illustrious author styles of our forefathers by beginning with the immortal phrase: 'Our Hero' was born.

Suffice to say, 'I,' 'Little me,' 'That' or 'It' entered the world in January, 1945, but again I'm not sure that this alone would have been the reason for the war soon to end unless the enemy simply gave up. Here was I, sleeping, burbling and gurgling simply oblivious to the troubles that had been, and were still surrounding the grim East London hospital and similarly unaware of the joyous peace soon to be declared in Europe in the coming May of the same year.

So here, born in Bow and with the essence of a Cockney surrounds, even ignoring the fact that the said 'Bow Bells,' other than the local pub of course, were, in fact, some three miles away in the City of London, so already from the start an almost loss of a claim to fame.

My surroundings in that January though were very much a reflection of the immediate state of life - born in a relic hospital which could be called almost Dickensian in every respect, with long, poorly lit corridors, cold and lofty wards with bare hanging lights and the knocking, swinging doors to the big outside world. The constant noise of the passing trains, the electric

Underground and the steam trains hissing to and from Southend, meant that everybody was constantly aware of that outside world. That, though, was a touch of a nicer reality; the sounds and devastation of the Doodle Bug bombers was not – would we be hit this time was the worried question and frown upon everybody's faces. Had their own homes and families been affected; where was the damage this time?

All this and in the grim inner-City style surroundings of East London, and not the coastal City of the same name in South Africa either. This hospital could only have been said to be modern to Victorian eyes and was an Institution, both in grim reality and also to the life of the local populace. It doesn't help to think that the same hospital has continued to carry on to serve the same area into the 21st century, a reflection not of the greatness and vision of the Victorian times and effectiveness of the builders but rather as a sad reflection of this country's National Health Service.

Being rather small at birth, around 4lbs (in old money) and probably with a brain that has remained equally small as a result, my earliest days were at the courtesy of the said Hospital and, obviously, right from the start a drain on the resources from which they have never recovered. I can therefore, because of being cocooned within the hospital walls, with reason, claim to know absolutely nothing about the momentous world events happening all around me.

My immediate family life was overshadowed and dominated by the fact that my mother was ill most of the time and frequently in and out of hospital herself. She had been a victim of a bomb blast, which she suffered when working with the Woman's Voluntary Army Corp in 1944 causing injuries, lung difficulties and the onset of various respiratory diseases.

Father was, by his nature, a rather distant and emotionless parent with the result that my main family, the heart of my early years and indeed for a substantial part of my later life, were my Grandparents on my mother's side - Nan and Grandpop to me and, to all intents and purposes, my real 'parents' in every respect.

Home was to be the centre of my universe - at least that was how I saw and felt the true situation. And, of course, I was right to think so. I lived in Bow, which itself was the 'capital' of the district of Poplar and the town hall and local council offices were situated not too far away from our house; Bow was in London and London is the country's capital so I was capital based in every sense. Not for me to claim to be a suburbanite, let alone a country-boy, I was introduced to the world at the very centre, a 'capital' situation. Didn't Charles Dickens so frequently write 'Capital, Dear Boy?'

The home too was equally very special - not for me the usual living arrangements of a normal house or flat in an area of similar and uniform accommodation, I had to be different. Oh no, my home was rather a detached double-fronted house centrally, located on the very main street of the very central Bow - indeed a 'capital' position in every sense of the word.

'A double-fronted, detached house?'

Yes, but here's the rub.

My grandparents, my mother's parents and with whom my parents lived, were caretakers and our part of the 'big house' in my imagination, was the basement flat – and the grand upstairs were three floors of offices!

'18 fireplaces,' I would hear my Nan and Grandpop say, referring to the fact these were the total number of fireplaces that they needed to scrub and polish every day to keep them pristine, not to say the numerous windows needing washing on a regular basis in an effort to rid them of the notorious London smog and grime.

These infamous windows had already caused untold mayhem into the home life long before my 'arrival.' In the early 1940s war years, my Nan and Grandpop had both spent a day on a real luxury cleaning and polishing of the windows, admired their considerable efforts, only for a bomb blast in the notorious blitz to blow out every single, and spotlessly clean, window! Once all the damages and repairs had been completed, there was nothing for it than to start the job all over again hoping against hope that 'lightning does not strike twice in the same place.' Fortunately, it didn't and all was well!

The house was late Victorian, rather imposing to the eye. First to note were the impressive pillared steps leading up to the main entrance – 'front door' or, rather, front double doors to be precise and to be even more grand. Each side of the entrance were large, equally imposing, bay windows on all but the top floor which itself was not just an attic but with full height, straight windows on all sides. To top it all were sets of very decorative chimney pots and a black tiled roof. Oh yes, it was the way to gain entry to our living area in the basement and this was the grand way to come; otherwise I should also say that there was a direct doorway to the basement off a corner road to the side of the house and not nearly so grand, but the address was only on the main street so that made everything alright.

The house still stands today, but now totally as offices and the basement reduced to the ignominy of a store. The fact that the house is still there is yet another testament to the Victorians as builders, it having survived all the war time bombs (apart from the 'blasted' windows, of course!) and it even withstood 21 years of me, and that's an achievement in itself!

Our basement home was in effect really rather basic and not in any way in tune with the view of the grand exterior. For us, my parents, grandparents and me, were two bedrooms, both continuing the theme of bay windows, which at basement level gave a wonderful view of car wheels and the feet of passers-by on the distant pavement? That, in itself, gave the opportunity of being aware of change of fashions and times in footwear!

There was an extremely large living room with a kitchen corner, at the back of the house and therefore somewhat quieter, plus a bathroom which initially was without the luxury of an actual fitted bath; that would come later. In the meantime we enjoyed the daily ritual of a fabulous tin bath, carried in appropriate ceremony to be placed in front of the warm kitchen range, there to be filled with endless buckets of piping hot water. What a twosome job it was to carry the tin bath outside again, once finished, and full of water, to be emptied and gurgled down the outside drain! Next, the bath was cleaned and dried off, and hung up in pride of place ready for the next time.

Keeping the best of the house 'til last, finally there was a large hall with a rather very grand staircase, both stairs and wooden banisters highly polished, leading to the upper floors, and to a different world; all very 'Upstairs/ Downstairs,' in every respect. Later on, and in time for me when I was a little older, a store room would be converted and renovated and I would get my very own room and thus a three-bedroom town dwelling was created, then very much reaching the heights of luxury and the whole property itself so 'desirable.'

Outside, beyond the back door and a second introduction to the big world, was a walled yard, which no doubt in 21st century estate agent speak would be called 'a town house courtyard' and not then as it really was – a good social gathering place for all the local cats and dogs to sniff and happily howl the time away. On clear nights though – and by that I don't mean when there were no animals around - away from the dazzle of the street lights, the yard was an amazing place for star and night sky watching and dreaming.

Naturally, upstairs the rooms were grander and taller and, because they were used as offices, they were quite empty at evenings and weekends. So whilst our actual living accommodation was small and basic, there was plenty of room to expand upstairs. In any case, with much evening and weekend work to be done there, it was the norm, that for me, time was often spent on 'tour/walkabout' in the big house. Each main office floor had four very large rooms plus a couple of smaller rooms with an assortment of store rooms, toilets and cooking areas. I was too young then to have delusions of grandeur by sitting 'boss-like' at the big desk or, rather, at several of the big desks.

Nan and Grandpop had not wanted by choice to be the caretakers of an East London office building. Yes, they were both Londoners and proud of it and they initially came from that area, very foreign to me, of North London, Tottenham in fact. Grandpop was born in 1888 and Nan in 1890, true Victorians, and they met in 1912 in a pub with the glorious name the 'Jolly Boatman,' especially apt when considering that Grandpop was in the Navy and too was a very happy personality.

Marriage for them came in 1914 and Grandpop continued in the Navy throughout the First World War and for some years after during which time he had some exciting trips to China and the Far East During his time there he sent some very evocative postcards home to Nan, details of his travels and places his ship was visiting and the life he was seeing. The most marvellous aspects of the cards, though, was that they always ended rather wonderfully with the phrase:

'My Dear Lal, I have the honour to remember you and to be, Yours ever, Jack.'

Really lovely and what a decent age that has been, in those earlier times.

When he left the Navy in 1920, Grandpop joined his father's small business as a painter and decorator. Nan had been a 'seamstress' – a wonderful title for some hard and endless work in a dress factory in Stoke Newington, North London, surely the forerunner of a Far East sweat factory but in a skill and tradition for which the areas of north and east London can be justifiably proud.

They moved for the first time to Bow in the late 1920s, living in a small terrace house in one of the maze of streets off the main road and both carrying on in the same line of work. This was the time too when Nan, to get extra money into the home, took on an additional job, cleaning offices at the house in Bow which would later be home.

Fortune came into their lives in the mid-1930s when after so much work and efforts so normal for their generation, Nan and Grandpop achieved the immediate prospects and fulfilment of a better life by saving enough money to put down as a deposit on a new bungalow at Leigh-on-Sea, in Essex, close to Southend. With this move came too the opportunity for Grandpop to start his own business as a painter and decorator, setting up in the Southend area in nice surroundings, clean air and, with plenty of new building, a ready-made market requiring decorating services.

It is easy to imagine what must have been their sense of pride to have made the move away from London and to be living in Leigh, so close to Southend, an area which generally was the real 'Utopia' of life to countless Londoners experiencing many day trips and indeed, holidays in the bracing air there. Southend was truly the fresh lung of grimmer London – the sea breezes – oh yes; the sea really does come right in twice per day even if at low tide you need strong binoculars to actually see it! On top of this, the local delicacies of cockles, whelks, and fish and chips in endless abundance. In fact, all in all, the true recipe for everything good in life missing from the inner City areas of London.

Looming war during the late 1930s, however, soon put an end to Nan and Grandpop's ideal. There was not any more so much business around, people not wanting to spend money 'in case of the approaching hostilities.' If that wasn't enough, on top of that the failure of a corporate customer to pay their due bills (so, nothing different then to now) forced the closure of Grandpop's enterprise. Unfortunately, there was no alternative for them other than to sell their house, suffering the consequences of a severe loss in the transaction because of the slump in house prices as a result of the approaching war, then with heavy heart return to London and back to Bow. There they were fortunate, if 'fortunate' is the right word, as they had been able to make contact with Nan's old firm and get the job of full-time caretakers there and with accommodation thrown in.

Proudly though, they took immense heart that they had made the effort in the first place, tried, alright failed, but they could cover their debts, enough to settle the outstanding mortgage payments from the proceeds of the house sale, but with nothing left to begin again except with heads held high. The house in Bow, though, must have been a bleak contrast to their own bungalow with garden in Leigh and surely meant very heavy hearts for a long time to come.

During the Leigh years, my mother too, then unmarried, naturally for those times lived with her parents especially so as she was the only child of the family. She was herself one of the pioneering early breed of commuters travelling each day to London as millions have done since. For her then the journey compared rather favourably with today's travels – not so very much slower and certainly far less crowded plus the comfort of an actual seat, and the reality prospect of actually getting to the destination on time!

My mother was a journalist and she thoroughly enjoyed her days at both The Daily Telegraph and with Reuters, where she spent sometime working on the South African desk. Both jobs were very much London based and this was well before the time of extensive travel in the field. After her return to London, mother naturally followed on with her career, but now with the reduced journey just from Bow to Fleet Street, courtesy most times of the big, red London bus except in times of strikes or the dense London fogs when there was nothing for it but to walk the four miles each way.

It was on her return to London living, which sounds rather much grander than simply to say 'Bow living,' that mother first met my father.

Father's family were Bow based too, although with much higher feelings of grandeur because their house was set in the more respectable and off centre area known as Bromley-by-Bow. Perhaps it would have been even grander still had the Tudor name of 'Bromley-atte-Bowe' still been in existence and accepted. Their superior sense stemmed also from the historical fact that their house was built upon the site of the area that had once been Henry VIII's Hunting Lodge. Father's family made continued regal process throughout their future lives as a direct result of their auspicious beginnings!

Father's family had been large by modern standards and was even large by mid 20th century values. In total, there had been nine children, four boys and five girls, one of whom had died in childhood and they all lived together in their big house. One of the brothers, my namesake in fact, had been killed in war action in 1941, but this still assured me of seven aunts and uncles as direct relatives plus their own families too.

My paternal grandfather had died in the 1930s thirties, having picked up a slow and lingering illness during the time when he served with the British Army in India some years before. He was born in Norwich and had been a coach-maker by trade in his early life, joining his own father in that profession. Family photographs show the wonderful and detailed creative work that he did and all with an obvious sense of pride and achievement as a real craftsman.

Because it was always the case that father's family did not talk about private issues to anybody, even me, as if I was an actual outsider to such matters, it would have been thrilling to know more about that background. But that was how they were and it was not 'done' to be otherwise.

The matriarch of father's family, my paternal and therefore 'other' Grandmother, was of Irish descent, her own grandparents having been born and brought up in Ireland. They came from County Cork in the West of Ireland and came over to England at the time of the potato famine. They lived first in Hackney, just north of Bow and still very much part of East London. Their move to Bow came in the early 1900s, where they set up home in what was an equally imposing rhree-storey house close to the church in Bromley-by-Bow.

Always I found it to be very difficult to become part of, or feel so very attached to, father's family, very difficult you see to penetrate their outward aloofness. It is therefore little wonder that my main affinity was always to be to my mother's side and to Nan and Grandpop. Father's family at all times had a degree of coldness and being at a distance from their surroundings. Very middle-class Victorian in their values, in fact, but for them it was what they felt was to be 'proper' and to be distant from familiarity which to them, and for them, was an enigma.

Grandmother from father's side could never be 'Nan' to me – that was simply not possible – it was a 'Grandmother,' a distant acquaintance and never to be a life's rock or saviour, rather a formidable and austere figure. Certainly, a person to be respected but at the same time to observe the Victorian maxim about children – 'to be seen but never heard!'

Father's family took the approaching war as a signal to leave Bow – oops, sorry, 'Bromley-by-Bow,' which is just as well as their former house was later to be the victim of a direct bomb hit. They dispersed with marriage and in today's upwardly mobile style to suburban Essex. That area was certainly a place in which to have 'arrived' in the late 1930s with recently introduced modern underground and rail connections to support everyday life. Places such as Wanstead, Buckhurst Hill, Romford, Wickford and Laindon, and that in the pre-Basildon days, of course, were set to feature as aunt and uncle locations for me in my upcoming formative years.

My parents had married in 1940. Mother and father had lived initially in various suburban locations so as to be near to father's relatives, how nice that must have been for my mother – no doubt she worked additional overtime in those days to be longer in London! However, with father then participating in the war effort and doing his bit for King and Country, they came back to London and Bow to set up house with Nan and Grandpop. Obviously, father was away from home for much of the time, although he was to serve only in home-based army posts and never go overseas.

Although my mother continued to work at her journalist job in the war years, travelling daily to blitz- affected London and Fleet Street, without incident, it was her involvement with the Woman's Voluntary Army Corp which was to be instrumental to her destiny, to some years of illness and an early death. She had, however, recovered sufficiently to allow the process of my being, although it was as a direct result of her injury and ensuing illness that I arrived early in 1945.

This, then, is the immediate scene of the family and life to which I became part of in 'central' Bow, and the house and environment to which I was introduced once the hospital had finally thought that I was capable of surviving in the hostile world.

Peace has been declared, the 'blasted' windows replaced, and I can gurgle, make noises and begin to take stock of my immediate surroundings. I am me, I am one, I was to have no brothers nor sisters – a dreaded 'only child' – a phrase in later years so often very relevant and with a valid meaning especially so in my selfish moments when 'throwing toys out of my pram' even when in my 50s. Oh, for the potential of development and possibilities missed!

Chapter 2
1945 – 1950

I was introduced into the world in Bow and that and the sense of being in London were then firmly my roots. That was not only my roots but the roots too of virtually all my known family and everybody that I knew or who were part of my life in my early blossoming world.

In fact this part of the world, the centre of my known universe would be the base for life and adventures for me for many years to come even though my family, based on their earlier and happy experiences, yearned with a wish to move somewhere 'better' sooner rather than later. Defining 'better' is not so very easy although it was obvious in this case it meant a return to the sea and Southend, away from caretaking and the inner City environment. This dream would, however, take many years before realisation.

Whatever the immediate outcome, such dreams do, however, always serve to concentrate the mind and to set the mind in motion for a splendid result – something to aim for and to excite for what soon may be. To me, at the very early age, I was naturally oblivious to such thoughts and ideals and in these earliest times the immediate surroundings of my home were paramount and I would for the time being be supremely satisfied merely to be looked after, kept warm and to be fed and watered, inner City or not.

Bow, London, indeed like anywhere in the known world at that time, was where families began to return to 'normal,' although what was in fact 'normal' after six years of devastating war and life changing circumstances? Stoic resolve though, was, in evidence and, with commitment and dedication everybody would pull together and lives and work patterns were resumed with a vengeance.

For my family, there was not too much talk of war exploits and even if there had been, I would not at that stage have understood very much anyway. The background was though that Grandpop had more thoughts of 1914-1918 and his own active service in the Navy; for my father and uncles the war years had been entirely in England and then mainly in London. Duties such as the Home Guard, Night Watch and Fire Watch in the mighty Royal Docks of the East End were the scene of family efforts plus, of course, my mother's contributions to the Woman's Voluntary Army Corp.

This is not to be in any way denigrating to the family war efforts. Any such local involvement was of the utmost value and importance, which in its way contributed on the home ground to support the heroic efforts at various fronts. Like all families at the time, there were many war time stories and exploits to remember and relate and we were no different.

Nan and Grandpop remembered all the air raids, the mayhem and noise, the constant worry of where and what would be devastated next. Mother had made daily visits to Fleet Street for her job, saw and heard all the horrors. Father – he was very much quieter – simply kept it all to himself and wasn't going to tell anybody.

War time life and events crossed all levels and whilst at the one extreme were epic national exploits, at the other extreme were the personal and local elements which were as much part of that war time fabric.

Nan would always go out after an air raid to look for any stray dogs. So, to our infamous back yard would be brought a variety of homeless four-legged friends, there to stay until such time that a new home was found. This activity would go on to a lesser extent even after the end of hostilities so I would grow up always used to the company of dogs, maybe one or two. You see, as would occasionally happen, if no other home became available or could be found, then our own dog population would increase accordingly.

The family home at Bow therefore settled into a new regime with me ensconced and enjoying all that would be taken as home comforts based on 1945 post-war style. We would be warm, thankfully there was enough coal for that, food would come enough via the ration book with some ingenious cooking and recipe enhancing when Nan would bake daily various breads, puddings, cakes and general 'goodies.' Accommodation was stretched at first and the living room with the kitchen corner began to live even more up to its name 'living' and the centre of all day-time activities.

I was there, beginning to take it all 'in,' as the only child and obvious centre of attention (well, 'obvious' to me, anyway!). Here must then have been the very first instances of my rattling my cage and 'throwing the toys out of my pram'– just as I would continue to do later in life if things did not go in exactly the planned way!

Because my mother was to be so often ill, frequently in hospital for long periods, to me it would be Nan who became the true mother figure in my eyes and the person to whom I would always turn and bond. For her, and Grandpop too, it must have been a somewhat awesome undertaking to begin at the age of 55 but I would never hear them complain or make heavy work of the task – 'Set to and take it in their stride.'

This must have been the motto.

Nan was a lovely, jovial lady with a round and smiling face. She had working hands and a never-fading energy – nothing was too much and every challenge in life was one to be faced and resolved. In so many ways she was a typical East Ender except that she revelled and took example from her very positive and strict late Victorian upbringing for her family and home values. This meant to dress well, to have proper meals, for the home to be tidy and as pleasing as possible and to have hobbies and pastimes, like music and reading, as very much part of everyday life. In that respect, Nan's style and values were could be equally in place wherever she was living – she did her best and was always there to help.

It was mainly Nan who cared for me, as a mother figure. She was the one who cooked, cleaned, did everything and brought me up.

To see Grandpop was to immediately see an 'old' sailor and here 'old' means typical. Even though some twenty years after being away from the sea, he still seemed always to stand as if being prepared for the ship's roll as a result of a Force 8 gale. It was similar when he walked, or rather very slightly rocked. What a jovial and kind man he was too, always seeming to be content with life, calm in whatever situation and a trusty pipe always by his side or gently puffing, ready to face any problem life may throw at him. Grandpop had an almost bald head which I took great pleasure of gently patting and stroking which I later learnt that my mother had done when she was younger. That gave him so much pleasure too.

Poor mother – she was very pretty and almost delicate in a china doll fashion. So often suffering from illness and so despairing at being so frequently in hospital and even when at home to be uncomfortable and in pain. There was tremendous spirit still there though and she so tried to give of her best and to do and be a caring mother to me. So often, even though the will was there, the strength simply was not. If all that was not enough to suffer, then she so missed not being able to continue any more with her job in journalism, which she had so enjoyed and which she had done so well. Nan and Grandpop too had been proud that their daughter had done so well in her work and for them too it was so disheartening and sad to see and realise how things and events were now for her.

And father – well father was so very different. Very upright, almost a re-incarnation of a Victorian gentleman, even complete with a distinctive moustache – a very frightening and extremely grim figure in every conceivable way. During all my youngest years I was always completely frightened of him, his unpredictable temper, very difficult mood swings, his sulking and not really talking for days on end if he was displeased about something. It would be difficult to imagine two people to be so different from each other as my mother and father. Simply I do not know how mother coped with him – I never was able to do so myself.

Whilst Grandpop was always there to lend a hand and help, my own father would, by his own nature, be somewhat distant and was not, I must say, ever comfortable in the true position of a father role in the early years, although he was slightly more relaxed when I was many years older. How it would have been had my mother been fit and well is probably another matter but overall the fact cannot be overlooked that not only father, but all of father's family had a degree of coldness which, as I said earlier, tended to be 'proper' in their minds – and this was just their way which absolutely nothing would change.

Of course, by now, early 1945, father's family had all moved away from Bow to the leafy and green fields of suburbia. Brenda, with her husband Dick, were at Buckhurst Hill, on the edge of Epping Forest and some ten miles – which must have been tens of thousands of miles in terms of style and difference – from Bow. With them too lived my paternal grandmother, the sister Irene and her husband, Pip. Indeed, quite a full load for a comparatively small two-bedroom and box room end terrace house but nevertheless a very 'proper' address for very 'proper' people.

The other principal relatives looming large in my life as the pages unfold were father's sister Ethel, with husband, Bill, who lived in Wanstead. This, dare I say, could only be looked upon as pseudo-gentile suburbia as it had an East London postcode, not even Essex. The saving grace was, however, that Wanstead was linked in its Parliamentary seat to its Essex neighbour – Woodford – and the Member of Parliament for Wanstead and Woodford was no less than Winston Churchill. Naturally, respectability was given to their address after all.

Romford and Laindon, both again in Essex and some twelve and twenty miles from Bow, respectively, and indeed the true forerunners of today's 'Essex Boy and Girl,' were the base for others of my father's clan whilst others dispersed further afield – well to Sussex anyway, which apart from being south of the Thames really was in another continent to my limited (then) horizons. Little wonder then that I hardly remember seeing or being in any way or any more aware of that side of the family.

Those uncles, Bill and Dick, who had the privilege, having passed the extensive and mandatory entrance examination needed to enter a 'proper' family, had both until the war years been living too in Bow. Not though in the 'hub' or main street location the like of which was my domain – no, no, but in a back street area immediately off from the Roman Road street market.

Dick's family had moved from Buckinghamshire in the mid-1930s to Bow. The wonderful and evocative expression 'in service' describes their country years and most of them, other than Dick, of course, were to return there after the war and to live back in the country from then on. This would prove to be a great future opportunity for me, the inner City boy, to see and experience some real countryside in what is a truly rural ideal of 'chocolate box'-style cottages and villages with the very beautiful scenery of farms, rolling fields and the Chilterns.

Bill's family had uprooted from even farther afield before coming to Bow, when Bill's father joined the Metropolitan Police Force. They came from Devon and, interestingly, from a village not too far from the Devon Bow of the same name. Perhaps it was this similarity that gave them the home comforts to make such a move; other than that the difference is mind-boggling!

Living close to each other, and forging an early friendship, they were no doubt street-wise boys of their day and not amiss to searching out the local 'prospects.' Dick was first to become aware, and obviously bowled over, by the enchanted world of my father's sisters at the 'big house' in Bromley-by-Bow. He obviously was quick then to tell Bill of the delights awaiting him and available in that house or residence as befits a 'proper' family' so both Dick and Bill, having gained their acceptance, were accordingly quick to claim their prizes.

* * * *

Soon after my arrival into the world, but not, I am sure, because of mine specifically, peace in Europe came in May 1945 so the time really came for everybody to pick up their lives and move forward, especially so for my family now with an extra mouth, forever open in the nest, to feed.

Respectability was immediately gained for the whole family by my father joining the Civil Service – a Civil Servant no less to surely make an establishment position for my family. Did I sit in the pram announcing to the world

'I am the son of a Civil Servant?'

Probably!

His first position was that of a Clerical Officer at a coal supply depot in the far-off reaches (from Bow, anyway) of West Kensington. Such respectability! What a contrast – Bow versus Kensington – no contest, surely!

To my awakening eyes it did surely seem exciting that each working day my father needed to travel to some of the farthest reaches of the Underground's District Line – that green line on the London Tube map from the eastern suburbs through to the west, with central London in-between. Not just to Whitechapel, that gateway to the East End, but far, far beyond to Tower Hill, Victoria, onwards still farther through Sloane Square (and how's that for a comparison with Bow Road), beyond even Earl's Court until finally reaching West Kensington. To my early childhood mind this was an adventure tale that, had it been then broadcast, would have been worthy of a special David Attenborough series delivered in hushed, reverent tones

After all, it was all of twenty stations each way – amazing – the New World! What aspirations and thoughts must have passed through father's mind and thoughts when making that daily journey? Surely he dreamed of an address in Sloane Square rather than in Bow. Naturally for him, he never said nor did he indicate such thoughts and being an avid reader he would probably been too engrossed in his book to harbour such thoughts.

There at the Coal Depot, father set to in trying to achieve the impossible in the immediate post-war years to make sure that adequate fuel supplies were made to all the key Government Offices as the country got back to work.

Grandpop continued with his work as a painter and decorator and with the devastating condition of so many buildings after the war, there was once again no shortage of work. In fact, with so many renovations, Grandpop developed a panache for not only plain painting and decorating but also for furniture restoration, and the repair and repainting of objet d'arts, memorabilia and various items of antiques in all shapes and sizes. How exquisite an old fireplace would look after he had made some carvings and general enhancements, topping everything off and outlining with gold detail. Perhaps not so much value then, though, but what a change to Grandpop's fortunes there would have been had it been possible to time-warp his efforts forward to the more discerning and receptive market of the beginning of the 21st Century. 'Antiques Roadshow' could have been broadcast entirely from Bow.

Each evening, Grandpop would rush home from his various projects and join Nan in carrying out their various caretaking duties, some of which she would be doing herself all day. And if that was not enough, Nan had the usual household duties and the looking after of mother and me as well.

Evenings meant therefore all washing and cleaning, polishing to be done throughout the building – the stairs, offices, halls, not forgetting the servicing and stocking of all those fireplaces. At least though now the windows could be cleaned without fear of bomb blasts. These toils would take up a good deal of the evening which was finally completed with the carrying of bucket loads of coal up from the basement cellar to distribute around the variety of fireplaces.

I suppose that, on top of all that, I had created some of my own mess too!

Ours was never too often a complete family because of my mother's frequent spells of illness for which she would often be away in the hospital – tests, more tests, the occasional operation, therapy – it was a never -ending round and extremely draining on all the family. Nan was always there for me and did everything that a small boy would expect or want but nevertheless there was always a natural void. Obviously, my mother would re-appear into my life from time to time, even, perhaps, for a few weeks but more often just for a couple of days before returning once again to the alien hospital leaving a gap and insecure immediate space in my world so difficult to understand.

Sometimes I must have initially wondered who was this person, my mother, who suddenly re-appeared; then to become acquainted and used to the mother touch and feel again then for her to disappear from my life after a short while and just at the moment when I had again become familiar with her. It was necessary to have to learn to cope with this as part of my young life and it was to Nan that I by nature turned for love and support.

When I was around two years old, and a little more aware of life, I was often taken to the hospital where my mother was but because of the no children visiting policy then in force, I could only be outside. Father, in a thankful sense of momentary humanity, would point to the window; sometimes mother would look out and wave but more often than not it would be Nan who would be at the window when mother was too ill even to look out.

Thankfully, I never fully understood the significance nor enormity of the event.

On reflection it is, of course, totally inappropriate and rather terrible to talk of such visits as a 'highlight' of my immediate life, but I suppose that, in my mind, I was out with my family, would perhaps have the occasional chance of seeing mother no matter how briefly and, finally, the visit was to an area with an enormous park. Here were swings, sandpits and playgrounds – wooden horses to ride. Then beyond the play area was the almost savannah expanse of grasslands edged in the far distance by majestic trees going back, in my eyes, to an endless horizon. By a miracle the place had been spared the ravages of the war-time. This place, Victoria Park, still remains the same today as a great open space in East London, a true breathing space for this area of London. 'Savannah' though it is not, my thoughts and ideas of 1947 is relative only to that time – I should have visited an African Game Reserve for a fair and true comparison.

Come 1948 and mother was very much better, even though then I did not know that it would not be permanent. She was home for initially a longer period and then, real joy, actually home to stay. Soon she would have sufficient strength for us to have outings all together which indeed was a first for my young life.   We were a complete family at last. Or rather, as complete as it was possible to be with father always a distant and completely cut-off character. He was never there for my mother, never there to support and even when she was in hospital, his visits would be purely restricted to the weekends. His evenings were always pre-occupied elsewhere, always home from work too late for time to go to the hospital. The effort could have been made and his was his choice and his decision not to. It was not that he had a sparkling social life, he just wanted to remain distant and aloof, not his concern. For family matters my father had no feelings nor emotion.

Apart from the visits to my aunts – and by that my introduction and, dare I say, indoctrination into suburban Essex, we would go to Southend-on-Sea, where I would get my first ever view of the sea – let's assume here that the tide *was in* on that day! Here too, to experience the delights of the frills of day trips – endless supplies of ice cream from a delicious Italian shop on the front. I wasn't similarly thrilled about cockles though – I don't like them any the more now and so not then either!

Grandpop had a small car for a while then, a black Morris with cold, red leather seats I fondly remember and to this the family would encamp for excursions, although not usually father who would somehow find some other more pressing engagement. So it would be the 'arterial road,' no less, to Southend – all very grand and exciting. If the green of the District Line on the underground map was firstly said to be 'grand,' what then could possibly be said of the 'arterial road' – all the way, yes all *the* way to Southend and the sea.

Such was the bubbling excitement to be actually going out for the whole day. A real, almost magical and unimaginable adventure that began with the very journey itself.

Through the immediate East End streets to the first greenery of Leytonstone and the expanse of common beyond the 'Green Man' pub, on past evocative place names to test the imagination –'Gant's Hill,' 'Newbury Park,' 'Gallows Corner' (ugh!) – Yes, now we had made it to the 'arterial road' so it was time for a stop for petrol.

'Four dollars worth of petrol, mate' Grandpop would say, meaning one pound's worth of fuel, the dollar being worth five shillings at that time.

Perhaps at this point the engine would need a 'breather' before having to encounter the vigour's of the 'arterial road' or, perhaps, because, like me, it was simply overawed by the occasion. A short break to halt the journey process but not to dim my excitement!

'What's that place there?'

'Where is that car going?'

'How much longer – where's the sea?'

And so on – excitable mayhem truly reigning.

With the car nose pointed eastwards, on we would go then into the first real countryside with farms and cows. Further on the journey would be marked by the passing of pub landmarks – 'Halfway House,' 'Fortune of War.'

'What's a public house?'

'Ah, well, that's a place for people to meet and have a drink.'

'Why?'

'Have a sweet, love' – and with that I would happily shut up – until the next time.

So the journey went on right to the outskirts of Southend. Naturally all the family were quiet at Leigh especially as we had to drive right past the former home and thoughts must have been of shattered dreams and what might have been. Spirits were soon revived though with the first sight of the sea at Chalkwell and the descent to the seafront Esplanade.

Was the sea in or out?

But did it matter if it seemed to be mud all the way across the Estuary to the distant Kent shore – the excitement was boundless!

'Mind the bloke in front' I would cry out with the trusted experience of a back seat driver when Grandpop came to park the car.

'Of course, boy,' he would reply whilst negotiating with the space.

Why, you must wonder, could there even have been a parking problem even on those days too – well, no not really but we had to park in a space with a sea-view!

There would be ice cream, sandwiches, cakes, sweets, tea for the elders, and juice for me. The sea horizons, ships to and fro – sometimes, excitingly, one of the big P&O Liners heading out from London or Tilbury *en route* to the Far East, or Australia, upside-down world destinations. Then that long, long pier which would, in any state of the tide, be a link to the sea. And on the pier – a train – can you imagine a real train gliding over the sea (oh, alright, initially over the mud flats at certain times of the day, but don't let us spoil the illusion!) and travelling right to the very end of the pier. Around the pier some amusements – rides, merry-go-rounds, helter-skelters. More ice-cream perhaps to be followed by a slightly sickly feeling resulting from the combination of too much food, excitement and fast-revolving rides!

Time then to return to the car, probably me being pushed along in a chair by then or, at the very least, quieter. Grandpop would be able to negotiate pulling away from the car park without my back-seat comments. Thoughts of the day would take away the edge of the excitement of our retracing our path along the 'arterial road'– my dreams would run riot:

'Where was that P&O ship now? – what far-away world port had it reached?'

The fact that the vessel would be on its voyage for some five or six weeks didn't occur to my mind – having seen the ship at midday then by the evening, I thought, it must be in some exotic place, not just off Dover!

* * * *

Fortunately for those immediate years, in 1948/9, mother's health continued to improve sufficiently so that a real holiday could be considered and eventually planned. Now the broadening horizons would shoot even beyond Southend, indeed westwards for unbelievable miles towards the West Country, indeed Devon and Torbay.

Starting off from Bow, first to the centre of London and to a really big railway station – Paddington – the hissing of steam engines, the distinctive smells of the long-distance trains, people hurrying to and fro with luggage and similar young children like me in tow and, generally, the romance and excitement of travel still very evident then if not so today. People were travelling and going to places, and I was one of them!

The romance and supreme excitement of the 'Torbay Express' its powerful Castle-class engine with gleaming headboard to tell the passing world where I was going, the smart brown and cream liveried coaches, all so much more exciting that today's transport offerings.

Quickly, the gathering speed through west London and on into Berkshire and to place names so completely strange to me, accompanied by a panorama of fields, farms and villages. On further to Westbury, Taunton and Exeter and soon we would finally be at the sea as the train sped along the sea front and past the towns of Dawlish and Teignmouth. I marvelled at the Devon-red sea cliffs, perceptive boy wonder that I undoubtedly was!

'We'll soon be there won't we?' I said with mounting excitement!

'There' was near Paignton, in Torbay, overlooking the sands at Goodrington, a fine recipe for a family holiday from a child's point of view – miles of sand for endless sand castles and a real sea that was visible at the shore-side all the time (sorry, Southend!); the creamy ices, clotted cream and scones, even in post-war rationing times; donkey rides.

'What's a donkey, mum?'

More rides, games and no grimy cities in sight. We stayed at a Holiday Camp in a 'chalet' but I was oblivious to the accommodation, I only had eyes for the seaside and its activities.

It is always said that you only retain the best memories of early holidays – halcyon days indeed – and 'that it was not really like that at all.' To me, though, these thoughts were very special, it was a real family holiday, my mother was there with us and she was almost well again and I was not to know that this was not always to be so.

After all, this great outdoors, Southend, Devon . . . gosh, how my world was expanding!!

* * * *

I was very fortunate from a very early age to be taken to see all the main London sights and to be told and feel a part of the great traditions and heritage of the capital. Here began an appreciation from which I would enjoy and benefit for all of my life. It was all there – St Paul's Cathedral, Buckingham Palace, all the glorious Royal Parks, the Houses of Parliament, the Tower of London – all the places were part of my own territory, my 'home patch.' But closest to home and life's centre for me was Bow.

Bow and the very Bow Road where we lived, was surely the hub of the known universe – well, my known universe. The endless hub of traffic, constant noise, the busy to-ing and fro-ing of people going about their daily lives.

There were big red trolley buses, and the traffic junction in Bow Road became the place and centre for hours of endless amusement for me to watch as the trolleys – 'hands' to me – would always be jumping from the wires with the result that the immobile vehicle would then block the road. The frustrated conductor would jump out, red-faced, cap pushed to the back of his head, completely flustered and alarmed even thought the occurrence would probably happen several times during the working day. He would then collect the long rod kept at the side of the trolley-bus – and I always thought that the rod was there to be used for fishing at the weekends. The 'hands' would then be ever so delicately placed back on to the connecting wires – the trolley was mobile once again.

Even with the lesser traffic volumes of the 1940s, there would sure then to have been a significant snarl-up of traffic which would barely clear before a similar trolley incident would occur to start the process all over again.

The many shops and markets lying off from the main Bow Road added to the cacophony of sights and sounds, the vivid scenes of a bustling, shopping world. 'Best King Edwards – tuppence a pound'

'Pound of apples, six oranges, couple of nice bananas – come on – Yours for a tanner – you can't do better than that now – what do you want me to do – give it away?'

'Get your fish here – all fresh and just straight from the sea today!'

'Come on, Missus – you know you really want them – so come on now.'

'Stop me and buy one!'

One what? It didn't seem to matter because everybody seemed to stop and buy!

The post-war years were still the time for those strange little books with perforated coupons – the ration books. These were vital and absolutely necessary if you were going to be able to purchase from the shops those valuable pieces of meat, mouse-trap size cheese or even the occasional fresh eggs.

In our home, though, fresh eggs were so rare that I grew up hardly knowing what a fresh egg was – not for me any 'soldiers' for tea!

Devon's Road, the scene of all the bustling shopping opportunities, reminded me of the first family holiday in Torbay and I would let my imagination run completely wild thinking that, if I went far enough along that road, I would surely reach Goodrington Sands! Rather not though but you would find a butcher, a couple of grocers and vegetable shops and – oh the luscious smells, a fabulous fried fish shop. Going further along Devon's Road would lead to that Dickensian Institution of my birth but hospitals generally, and their association with my mother's illnesses, were not places that I wanted to see.

The Dairy, just off Bow Road and very close to our house, was the place where I, as a growing child, could safely be sent on my own, and therefore was the momentous scene of my very first solo assignment and outing. Here was a mission full of unparalled responsibility as I set forth clutching the money lest I lost it and reciting in my mind the precise order lest I forgot it. Strangely upon arrival, I always remember the place to be empty, nobody to serve, no other customers, just various milk barrels lying around, never any bottles or cartons since you had to take your precious container (had I remembered it, yes, it was in my left hand, oh good!); always an eerie silence broken only by the distant hum of some refrigeration motor.

'Give a shout, love' Nan would instruct me to do on entering the Dairy to attract attention.

Me – shout aloud in an empty space to attract attention – some hope for that which would have been far too adventurous and forceful.

First, I would quietly 'A--hem,' cough or make some other completely insignificant and inappropriate sound. Of course, nobody would come; they were always busy about their work somewhere upstairs so how could they possibly have heard my mouse-like efforts – so the feeble 'A–hems' would need to get louder. If that didn't work, then a very small, oh so small stamping of the feet would be the next degree of approach and attention seeking to my plight. Sometimes I had spent so much time in my fruitless efforts that another customer would come in and bellow out a thundering shout accordingly. Saved! Then all I would have to do was hand up my container to make my valuable and precious purchase; then, which was of supreme importance, remember, as Nan had instructed, to give our dividend number:

'Seven hundred four eighty.'

Fine, I could then be sure, and report back accordingly, that we would get our allocated points for the much sought-after yearly rebate!

All this safely accomplished, there was nothing left other than to quickly run home with the milk container which could then be stored safely and cool in the cellar. 'Fridge' – what was that, surely a bucket of cold water kept in a cool place?

Soon though I would be made redundant by events from this seriously important task – the milk delivery round was once again re-introduced in Bow with the battery vans doing their bit for traffic congestion. Now, we had bottles to store in the cold water buckets.

Locally, the big market place to go to was at Roman Road which is very much the same place today as it was then.

'Up the Roman,' as called by everybody around about.

With our local Devon's Road, this was not the place for us for everyday items but for something more individual – household curtains, towels, linens, even the odd pieces of clothing:

'Come on, get your best remnants here, you can't beat me on price!'

If the weather was good – of course the weather is always good in the golden days of childhood memories – the trip 'up the Roman' could be extended afterwards to a part of Victoria Park, my vista of endless savannah fame, and a chance for some games and getting generally messy playing in the sand pit. Probably after that I was indeed in need of some of the clothing offerings from the market!

In all my early years I had always been taken to see the main London sights, firstly, of course, with the young eyes not taking in too much, but gradually – being such an intelligent chap – becoming much more aware. Remembering the opening words of the old East End music hall song:

'I'm following in father's footsteps; I'm following dear, old Dad.'

So I too set out to travel on the District Underground line from Bow Road but probably not so far as Kensington, but rather to emerge at Charing Cross (and before you rush to check the underground map, it was 'Charing Cross' in my time, the name was changed to 'Embankment' much later on!). Then, across the road from the station there to see the River Thames, the exciting Captain Scott's 'Discovery' (no, I didn't have long-distance vision, the ship was moored on the Thames then and not at Dundee as now!), and the other moored ships and Thames traffic plus the distant views to the Houses of Parliament. Next would be to walk up to Trafalgar Square, for Lord Nelson and to be amongst the pigeons, along the Mall for Buckingham Palace and to see the Guards, finishing off in St James's Park to feed the ducks.

For me, naturally, St Paul's Cathedral and the City were much closer to home and, apart from the Underground, could easily reached by bus. My favourite, and aforementioned, trolley bus would take us to the edge of the City, to its terminus at Aldgate which was also a gateway point just up from the Tower of London and Tower Bridge. But is was the bus 'the 98 horsepower omnibus' of music hall fame, which was the chosen mode of transport for journeys beyond the bounds of Aldgate, in fact through the City to the West End and even beyond.

The number 96 would go onwards to Putney, in the far-flung corners of the Empire!

'One and a half, all the way, mate,' my Grandpop would say to the Conductor and I could then be content and confident to then spend the next hour or so viewing all before me, naturally from the very front seat on the upper deck, the journey making a regal procession through first the City, then on through parts of the West End, past Green Park and Hyde Park Corner to Knightsbridge and Kensington before reaching Fulham and to cross the friendly old Thames again at Putney before finally arriving at the terminus – Putney Common – a south west London landmark to rival my savannah expectations of Victoria Park.

And, if this wasn't excitement enough, there was then `the journey back home to look forward to, this time to experience everything in reverse. It did not occur to me that, on this return trip, we would start with the best, only to go steadily downhill expectation-wise when finally again reaching the home streets of the East End. But then I was tired and hungry and expectations of tea far outweighed aesthetics!

These were good days and added bus trip itinerary locations included travelling by bus one way to Victoria seeing Oxford Street *en route*, then down Bond Street and around by the gardens of Buckingham Palace – would I be able to see anything looking over the wall from the top of the bus? The return would be by No.10 through Lambeth and parts of Southwark, over London Bridge with sights of the Tower of London, Tower Bridge and the freighters berthed in the Upper Pool. Oh, and to accompany the crossing of London Bridge would, of course, need to be my rendition:

'London Bridge is falling down, falling down . . .' probably much to the annoyance of everybody else on the bus!

This London, the London beyond my Bow was surely a big place and I was making all efforts to be part of it. It was grand and I echoed the immortal words of Dr Johnston 'a man' (or, in my case boy), 'who is tired of London is tired of Life.' I was not tired.

* * * *

After all these expeditions and voyages of discovery, there was home and that very special place for anybody to be and to claim roots. There were toys, dogs, people, and especially so in my case when considering the increase of our house population every day with people coming to work, always family around and so a full house. There were not so many young personal friends in those early days, in fact none of any recalling significance before school days which, on reflection, was obviously bad and resulted from our living in an area without any immediate neighbours; all the closest houses were in commercial use and, unlike us, did not have any caretakers living in. On top of that, I was an only child and all aunts and uncles were childless and it was only to be a distant nephew of my Nan who would later on have two sons. Whatever, I can honestly say that I was never lonely, in fact happily contented and did not knowingly suffer at this early stage of life from isolation but perhaps later it could be a reason to be selfish and a tendency to be a loner.

It was a case of what I never had experienced, I never missed.

At home, the upstairs offices, empty in the evenings and weekends, were enormous places of excitement and scenes of adventure for me. Rooms to run around, chairs in which to swing, corners filled with strange pieces of furniture called 'filing cabinets' – surely they had no other use than as places to hide behind! Then in-between the rooms, corridors, different doors, some rooms with desks topped by large, cumbersome and black typewriters:

'Don't touch, or I'll clip your ear' – oh, well better not then!

Bigger rooms had bigger desks, therefore must have been for bigger bosses! Dipping fingers could go gloriously from one ink well to another with consequent messy results – goodness, how Nan and Grandpop must have blessed my 'help!' Here too, upstairs, were the loftier windows from where I was able to look down on those trolley-bus wires rather than looking up at the wheels or at the feet of passers-by from our home windows. Upstairs was truly a different perspective on life!

Toys were restricted exclusively to the home basement – it would not have done for the big bosses to come into their work ready to make big business decisions only to find themselves surrounded by various pieces of Dinky-toys!

Whilst bought toys were great fun, but filled with imagination from the outside world, a whole host of special enjoyment was possible. Chains from the hanging light fittings became make believe electric tube trains, pencils would become the tunnel walls, a saucer the station – imagination running so easily wild. One thing also, I was assured of endless scrap paper for drawing coming from the waster paper bins from the offices upstairs, long before that age of shredders! Never to be an artist though, strictly lines and squiggles for which there was unfortunately no Turner prize in my time, otherwise I might have started off famous.

Soon we would have our own telephone – even I had seen 'odd things' before on the office desks in the upstairs world. Big and black, with a heavy handset needing two little hands to lift and hold it before attempting conversation. Just think, today, these very phones sell for a fortune in a bric-a-brac shop. We could dial direct for local calls (so now, perhaps, I could call the dairy in advance to tell them I was coming) but for anything outside the confines of East London, then calls were via the operator – an imaginary voice coming from the wall 'Number please – and your number' whenever wanting to call the aunts and uncles in the far-flung reaches of Essex.

Radio would be on most evenings:

'Good Evening, this is the Home Service' – you mean a service just for home, how fantastic! – the message would vibrate around the house. No television yet for our family in the early years, just books, puzzles, talking, and simply to do things together and so entertain. Even though Nan and Grandpop were from an ordinary background, absolutely nothing grand, they had an upbringing in their families to enjoy piano evenings and recitals at home and their impromptu Sunday concerts at home were the highlight of their early lives. But circumstances meant that the piano had never come to Bow. This did not stop singing and our own music hall was often to visit us in our basement corner, although 'Maud' never did come into our garden!

Sundays were always to be special in the early years. Church was not regularly on the agenda except for Christmas, Easter and significantly important family events and anniversaries when we would all be dressed in 'Sunday-best,' hats for the ladies, trilby hats for gentlemen, cap for me, umbrellas at the ready, to all process along the road to St Mary's Church, imposingly situated on a central island in the middle of Bow Road. Otherwise, and importantly though, Sundays meant no caretaking work and even no house cleaning, so a time for better clothes even in the home. During the morning there would be massive lunch preparations with the most appetising and appealing cooking smells as Nan would make and bake with help from mother if she was well. Normally, one would understand the beauty of baking wafting from the kitchen but, since our kitchen was simply a part of the living room, we were permanently engulfed by the aromas, sitting with mouths watering waiting for lunch:

'Can I taste a bit, please Nan?'

'Best wait, love, otherwise you won't eat your lunch,' was the reply. Ah well, better luck later.

A huge roast would be the norm – and this would feed us in various guises – you know cold meat, Shepherd's Pie, stews, etc. for most of the week. It was a true 'Sunday roast' – always superb roast potatoes, yorkshire puddings, root and green vegetables ex-Devon's Road fresh, home-made gravy and sauces, the lot. Finally, to round it off, freshly baked fruit pie or puddings with lashings of thick, creamy custard. No wonder some would then want to sleep for a while in the afternoon, especially so when knowing tea would follow, but I would be in my make-believe world of chains and pencils and very much oblivious to another Sunday tradition – the radio afternoon play. So to Sunday tea, very traditional East London with Southend influence –

shell-fish, prawns, shrimps and never without cockles, limitless brown bread and a big cake at the centre of the table, enough to keep all fed throughout the rest of the evening.

A few Sundays in early life, but many more in later life, would involve spending the day with father's relatives. Even though the day would include the adventure for me of the ride on the Central Line tube train into suburban Essex, these Sundays were never nearly as wonderful as being at home. Firstly, the family was not complete – Nan and Grandpop were never invited, oh no, a very much them and us situation with father's family adopting the superior stance. These days were always cold and severe, I had to be careful and mother was never relaxed or cheerful there, always on tenterhooks, perhaps wary in-case I accidentally broke something, caused a noise or other disturbance in what was a very severe regime.

Here, father was in his perfect element and immediately took an even more commanding and a thoroughly unhealthy, domineering stance with my mother to which she didn't resist. I suppose that with his sisters and mother there, he felt even more the need to show his authority but it was all a very chilling and most unhappy experience.

'He has had enough, don't let him eat any more or he'll be sick all over the table,' was the message ringing in my ears.

'Yes, he's had enough – Robert's right,' said my aunt, Brenda, backing up my father.

Mother will quietly look and me and will me to obey, just to keep the peace.

The lunch safely over, father would then dive into his book to read, mother would chat with me or perhaps volunteer to go to the kitchen to help clear away.

'Don't you bother, Marjorie, just you go and sit down – we can do everything here.'

The atmosphere was so difficult, so straining and I could tell that mother was most uneasy – I was the same – very uneasy and nervous too!

I did so look forward to returning home from those Sunday visits, to leave behind the woods of Essex, and for the train to dive into the tunnel at Leyton making for my home territory of East London. That tunnel was so symbolic and the perfect divide between that frightening world of my aunt's home in Essex and my own home in the safety of the City.

At the times when mother was in hospital, the Sunday routine was much sadder. There would still be the huge and traditional Sunday lunch, but immediately afterwards we would head off for the bus (Grandpop had by then given up the car, my father had no interest in cars or driving), then walk to the hospital and the special visit before returning home, often rather sombrely to carry on with the Sunday traditions and that special tea. It was then so obvious that all concerned around me had their minds, naturally, on my mother and the hospital situation with the result that the evenings then tended to be rather gloomy even though Nan and Grandpop would put their thoughts aside and make efforts to cheer me up with games and pastimes.

Whatever those circumstances, overall home was a very happy and contented place for me in my childhood, with my chains for make-believe trains, plus the usual assortment of toys and then, gradually the ability to put more than two words together to make sense became apparent to me and so my life was enhanced initially by comics and simple books – naturally simple books for a simple soul!

My fondest memory of the late 1940s was the superb 'Rupert Bear' series, the annual volume of which was to be the most eagerly awaited and treasured Christmas gift. Surely Father Christmas's sack must have been so very heavy filled with masses of these volumes for every child in the world, I believed. In addition to the annual, the stories also appeared everyday in the *'Daily Express,'* so as a youngster I would have rushed for the paper every morning to read the latest Rupert instalment and not because I was a budding childhood genius keen to catch up on the world news or on the latest stocks and shares. Yes, the *'Express'* did have that sort of latter information in those days!

Gosh, how involved I felt with the Rupert stories, identifying with all the adventures, the family and friends and I felt part of the circle too. I suppose that this feeling was in some ways similar to how today 'soaps' are so much a part of life – but what a difference in the spirit and gentle nature of the events and story line, no 'What's 'appening' or 'What's it all about' in these storylines! Had I then known that the creator of Rupert had come from Canterbury, then I am sure that I would have been a new 1940s style pilgrim on a hurried 'progress' to that City, if not to the Cathedral!

The approaching change of decade from the 1940s to 1950s so found me in a reasonable and happy life, made even more contented by the fact that about this time my mother was beginning to enjoy better health, albeit on a temporary basis, was at home, reasonably fit and part of everyday life again. As a family we were then lucky too; those who had to work had plenty to do and did so without interruption; life was steady and whilst we were by no means well off, there was money enough for life's basics and always plenty of food, and good food too, on our daily table. In addition to my simple hobby and playtime pleasures, I appreciated and was able to enjoy too, all that was offered in my immediate home territory of Bow, a background which I would value even more in later life.

I saw London and its many attractions with early and growing eyes, saw the changes and have the benefit of hindsight now to critically evaluate the good and the bad of developments. The countryside and sea were not alien to me and for a child being brought up in the immediate aftermath of the war; I counted myself fortunate in having also experienced a holiday by the sea. Of course, it was also a very much closed upbringing with little outside contact nor mixing with many of my own age until school came later. On reflection, of course, this was not good but in my young and therefore unaware eyes, I harboured no such negative thoughts.

Life, though, cannot remain the same for ever and so too was the case for me. I had heard of, and had been ever so gently told about, a place called 'school.' At the time I didn't connect that the place could possibly have any relevance for me nor that it could ever happen to me. It was something that I felt that I did not have to consider.

That illusion was soon shattered in late 1949 when Nan took me (mother wasn't well and, naturally, father was not there to do any family things) along Bow Road and into the mighty and very imposing Town Hall. Here was a building so official looking and with so many more offices and more imposing than my own home. We went along endless corridors, stairs, and more corridors and finally to a room marked 'Education Officer.'

Into this room we entered, me by now clutching Nan's hand ever more firmly.

'Name?'

'Turner,' Nan replied, 'But this is my grandson and his name is Robert Livsey..'

'Age?'

'Four.'

'I'll be Five in January, wont I Nan,' I said, trying to rise importantly to the occasion.

The Officer looked severe, very foreboding in fact. He so reminded me of my father.

'I see – we'll put you down to begin next year then, probably in September but that could change if a place becomes available in January.'

'Do you mean the coming January, just a few weeks away?' Nan said.

'Yes, it could be possible – but – we'll let you know.'

That was it then – I was accepted – but accepted to what I began to wonder!

Chapter 3

The School Bell Tolls!

Even in 1950 most children would begin school in September and so would enjoy a summer holiday of freedom beforehand, but I had to be different. Having been to register in good time, our efficiency was awarded, as the Education Officer had predicted, by a place becoming available to start immediately after Christmas in January 1950, which was a true Christmas present indeed, certainly one to rival the 'Rupert' Annual in enjoyment terms!

My upbringing gave me very little idea or preparation as to what to expect. Also, the total lack of mixing with, or knowing others of the same age group was detrimental and an obvious disadvantage. There was absolutely nothing easy about this transition in my life and the red of my cold winter's cheeks was matched only by the red of my tearful eyes.

There was a similarity between my feelings and the weather on that very first morning – it was cold, drab and everything clogged in thick, pea-soup-like London smog. The task of taking me to school on the first day of this new adventure in life, fell to Nan as mother, even though she was at home, simply could not go out in that sort of weather. Father was off to work in his usual way and probably not too bothered either, just being 'proper 'Be good, Boy' Grandpop said as he left for work,

'We'll have some special games tonight, you'll see,' he continued to encourage me.

So we left home, Nan and I, hand-in-hand to walk along Bow Road passing all the well-known and familiar sights – even the trolley bus jumped the wires as usual, in a form of a salute, I thought, which gave me a sense of well being. I knew then that all these familiar sights and sounds of my known life would carry on and be there for me even if I was going to have to spend five days per week inside a strange and, at that time, hostile, place. Soon we turned into the equally familiar Devon's Road and – yes – the market was open with all the usual shouts and bustle there to support me embarking on this new life. I was able to re-assure myself that life was really going on.

Then Nan guided me to the right and into a brand new street –so this was it – the school street – I dazed. There ahead of us was a single-storey building – St Botolphs, the local junior school. Oh good, I thought, at least my home compared favourably to this establishment – we had four floors in total, which made home far superior to school. Already a big plus point.

St Botolph's School was from Victorian times – what is it with me that I was forever becoming involved with buildings from the Victorian age, which always seemed to be a fundamental part of my early life? Was I re-incarnated? The buildings stood on three sides of the rectangular piece of land, with the road on the fourth side and a large playground in the centre. The familiar church spire of Bow Church could be seen in the distance, towering over the corner of the building; the noises of Devon's Road market could be vaguely heard above the din.

So many people and so much noise outside the school. Various elders with offspring in tow, some of the one or two obvious new ones seeming as bewildered as me, whilst the 'regulars' were just confidently running around and screaming and shouting. The gates opened, the bell rang and it was time to go.

Hugs and kisses from Nan.

'See you at lunchtime, love – don't worry, be good dear!' she called, and so the school world began.

What a long day that first day at school seemed to me – indeed many ensuing days in those early terms seemed to be endless although there would always be the heaven-sent break at lunch-time with a return home to my real world for 45 minutes bliss of normality and. delicious snacks to revive me for the afternoon session.

School was the initial scene to me of strange people and new faces – of noise, shouting, some tears and general commotion. By comparison, home was a haven of calm, familiar, safe and secure. It was not surprising therefore that the very first day at school should be a day of complete haze to me – the heavy fog and my mind were in one tune, together in dimness!

In 1950's Bow, the 'school run' was the school walk every day and at 'bell time,' before lunch and at the wondrous end of the afternoon, the school surrounds were jammed with people with shopping bags as opposed to what today would be a fleet of cars! Class doors would open direct on to the playground (nothing as sophisticated as corridors) so the class itself was always well air-conditioned in the winter! With the opening of the doors, out I and all my class mates would quickly run, to breathe in the immediate air of freedom, then off to return to home security.

So the days of early 1950 moved on; the smog finally cleared and I began to get more used to the new life – No, I am not going to say yet that I actually liked it but more so now that I began to cope and also, which was particularly good, began to make some new friends.

Every day when the school doors opened it would be:

'Good Morning, Miss Baker.'

'Good Morning, girls and boys' would be the (reasonably) cheerful reply.

Having Miss Baker as a teacher was an amazing coincidence for me as she had been the very same teacher who had first taught father's younger sister, Ethel, some 40 years previously. Poor lady – how could the same person have to suffer two members from the same family – she should have been awarded a medal! Unfortunately, Miss Baker did not seem to appreciate or realise her extremely good fortune and she was rather prone to make unfavourable comparisons:

'I remember Ethel; she was so bright and quick to learn.' Meaning that I wasn't, I suppose!

'Ethel got a prize from me with a personal recommendation.' Needless to say, I didn't. Similar style remarks seemed to follow me throughout my school career, which even if it was a reflection on my ability, meant that overall I was not too especially enamoured with school time. Teachers as bullies – I wonder!

Anyway, the time soon went and the summer holidays of 1950 were soon reached with a return to freedom and the usual mix of outings and home fun. Victoria Park, those London bus rides, accepting with more understanding the London sights, seeing for the first time some of the museums and being in seventh heaven playing with all the gadgets and displays in Kensington's Science Museum. That year there was to be no holiday (lack of money I suppose, but not because of my school fees which were 'courtesy' of the LCC! 'London County Council,' many years before Mayoral days) but I am sure I returned refreshed and rejuvenated to the school in September, with brain cleared and ready to be in receipt of learning – some hopes for that!

* * * *

The early 1950s were, even more than the very first years of my childhood, a more positive and concentrated time of life's development with so many changes and improvements to London life happening all around me coupled with my growing ability to 'take notice' and to be aware. Many thoughts and minds were concentrated to the forthcoming 'Festival of Britain' Exhibition in 1951 to rival the Crystal Palace Exhibition of exactly one hundred years before.

Often I would be taken to see the developing site across the River Thames opposite Charing Cross (Embankment) tube station. The impressive Festival Hall was the centrepiece and once opened, the exhibition site generally was a very exciting place for me to be. Naturally, we visited as a family and it was also the scene of my very first school trip with a very fidgety and flappy Miss Baker. I so remember the thrill of climbing aboard that magnificent steam locomotive – 'Britannia' – resplendent in shinning British Railways green livery. How my imagination, always at fever pitch, ran riot, when with one tiny hand, I actually clutched at the controls and would have demolished the nearby Hungerford Bridge had the engine been fired up and moved! Many boys become interested in railways, at least in those years when they were rail systems with flair and which actually worked and provided a valuable service. I was no exception, my interest was kindled and I would be train daft over many years, you know the real forerunner of an 'anorak.' The Festival of Britain was responsible for this, whether that was in their overall remit or not. You can imagine the publicity headlines when it comes to the next one in 2051 – 'Young Bow lad made train daft at the South Bank, 1951!'

Whilst the Festival of Britain was paving the way for the new about the same time during 1951 also marked an equally important end in the transport era in London – the last tram. Although we never had trains in Bow (but we had trolley-buses and – no – I won't go on again about those wretched wires), there were a number of routes in other parts of the capital. My favourite was the route that travelled in the tunnel under Waterloo Bridge, up from the Embankment to Aldwych and beyond, in fact the same general way that is partly now a road tunnel. My imagination would always run riot in a tunnel!

So it was a great thrill, even if a somewhat sad occasion, when one Saturday, whilst I was resting from the rigours of the school week (ah!), Grandpop said:

'Get ready now, we're going out, Boy,' so off we went to London and a suitable tram stop near to Holborn on what was to be the very last day of the service – I was on it! What a thrill – sitting upstairs, naturally, in my favourite front seat. How proud I was of the ticket issued, which I clutched tightly in closed hand and which I would take excitedly to school on the Monday, for once looking forward to the start of the 'working week.' I was even 'invited' to address the whole class to tell them about the event me at the very centre of attraction and a very first opportunity to 'hold the floor.'

Without any doubt, one of the most fortunate of my childhood experiences was to be introduced to the theatre at an early age, but not as a theatre-goer. Obviously the musical significance of Nan and Grandpop's own upbringing and family musical evenings at home, plus their regular interest in the Music Hall at the Hackney Empire or People's Palace in Mile End, near Bow, played a part. They wanted to be sure that I too could gain an interest from an early age. Needless to say, I certainly did.

My memory of the very first show is as vivid now as it must have been when leaving the theatre after the show. The production was 'Oklahoma,' with Howard Keel at the Theatre Royal, Drury Lane and what could have been a finer setting for my first show. This was truly to experience the bright lights of London and, significantly, the bright lights returning to the capital lifting the darkness of the war years, becoming the new future so to speak. The musical certainly lifted the spirits and kindled my enthusiasm.

The whole outing was an occasion in itself. Everybody would sure to be dressed in their very best clothes. Nan, in a smart dress with formal coat and, a little blue hat with such an ever so small veil. Grandpop, in his best, perhaps his only suit, with crisp white shirt, a hefty mackintosh and his very best checked cap. Luckily, many times mother was then well enough to come to and she would immediately look much better, delicate still, yes, but very nice in a tweed suit and pretty blouse. Then there was me – me in a little grey suit, white shirt too and bright red tie, my hair neatly parted and 'glued' down with plenty of hair cream for good measure, cap in hand in 'case of the cold later in the evening! And father – of course, he was not many times with us but if he did come, then he would walk a few paces away from us, look very severe and thoroughly wishing not to be closely associated.

Our little group would walk proudly along Bow Road, perhaps having brief words on the way with some passing acquaintances:

'All off out are you?' somebody would say in a friendly fashion but obviously full of question.

'We're all off to the West End for the evening to see a *show,'* Nan would happily inform.

'Ooh, ain't that nice' would be the passers-by reply 'Be Sure you all enjoy yourselves then. Don't the little one look a picture,' referring to me 'Quite the little old man cut down!'

Smiles all round, some embarrassment from me and from father – he would simply be off to look into some shop window and completely distance himself from such displays of friendliness and familiarity.

Once at Bow Road Underground Station, we would take the faithful District Line train to the Centre, then walk the final distance to the theatre and be part of the throng of theatre goers. Me – a 'theatre-goer – wide eyed and in short trousers and cap!

Inside the theatre, Grandpop would admire the decoration with an extremely critical eye, the others would be studying the programme and explaining the various details of cast and plot to me, and then perhaps all would be involved in people watching:

'Isn't that … over there?'

'That's right, so it is — who are they with?'

For me, I was simply overawed by the occasion and would be busy to take everything in – the bright stage footlights, the huge and magnificent curtains, the orchestra tuning-up, mounting excitement as the house lights dimmed and the show began. Three hours then of supreme magic – songs, verse, dance routines, the melodies, costumes, scenery and lights effect all in abundance. Then, if that was not enough to overfill a small boy's excitement, there was one more extra – a big tub of ice-cream during the interval! It would be even fun to queue for the ice cream in the centre aisle, feeling very important and as if the spotlights were trained just on me. Normally, the queue was so long and by the time I had found my way back to the seat, the house lights were already beginning to dim, the orchestra getting back into place and the show ready to continue.

It really was a star evening, nothing at the time could come to be nearly so special and, once we had returned home, the sleep would be very hard to come as the day's events filled my mind. To prolong the excitement and to commit details to mind, the very next day I would set about building my own model theatre – books to form the stage and sidewalls, a magazine for the balcony; a handkerchief would have to make do for the curtains and a pocket torch for the spotlights; the stage would be set with empty match boxes and for the actors – well, matches had to do for that and the rest had to be imagined but the whole exercise kept me very much amused.

Fortunately, the theatre would be very much a focal point in the family life, which was especially so in the winter months. Theatre seat prices were much more economical in those early years, even when compared to the obviously lower wages of the time. This must have been the case when thinking that we were certainly a family with limited finances and visits could be on a reasonably regular basis. Probably the London theatre then had to rely mostly on the home audience as opposed to the large tourist numbers which they cater for now, with consequent explosion in seat prices that one needs a mortgage extension for a night out!

A feature of every winter, and very much a fixture in the theatre round, was the traditional and magnificent pantomimes at the London Palladium, such a glorious theatre and with all the added excitement of Oxford Circus and Regent's Street so close by. Often, the pantomimes would run from Christmas to Easter, so popular they were. Some of the verses about Father Christmas and snow seemed a little out of place with the Easter Eggs and spring sunshine but, whatever, this was magic and such liberties are surely allowed in make-believe.

Importantly, I would be given a programme which I studiously looked at, chiefly to see how many scenes were to be in the show. This was because at the side of the stage was an illuminated sign to show which scene was playing.

'Oh, good, Scene 11,' I would say, very quietly, 'That means there's another eight scenes still to go,' I continued excitedly. They were long shows and everybody certainly got their moneys-worth, to put it commercially!

As much as theatre was an established winter tradition and a feature to relieve the torment of the school years, then early in the 1950s an equally important summer tradition was happily introduced – the day trip by 'steamer' from Tower Pier, by the Tower of London on the River Thames, all the way down river to the sea at Southend and then across the estuary to Margate on the Kentish side, and then coming all the way back.

With thrill and excitement the day would begin. In order that we could be first in the queue so as to ensure a good place on board, we would need to leave home just after 7.00am and take the underground for the six stops to Tower Hill to be at the pier in good time. The bustle of the early morning activities at the Tower of London would provide plenty to pass the time whilst we waited for the pier to open and we would be allowed to board. What ship would it be (a ship – yes – never a boat, this was a real sea voyage!) – 'Royal Sovereign' or 'Queen of the Channel' probably not the older 'Golden Eagle' then nearing retirement. Once on board we would rush to our favourite seat on the top deck perhaps in the Observation Lounge if the weather looked 'suspect,' or to sit by the look-out rail on the open, top deck on a fine, sunny day, of which, of course, there were many!! On the open deck I would stand on the seat in order to be able to see over the rail but quickly jump down to the deck when the ship's horn sounded lest I would get blown, in my mind, into the foaming sea!

So, punctually at 9.00, the voyage would begin and for this adventure, 'voyage' is not too grand a word. The very first highlight was that Tower Bridge would have to open to allow our passage – oh, the thoughts of traffic mayhem that there would be at that time of the morning as a result of the bridge closure to road traffic – these trips should be re-created now to create a real snarl-up which would probably last continuously from one day to another!

Soon followed all the familiar sights of the East End (and having been born, brought up and living on the north side of the river, I did not consider it right to look too often to the south bank!) – there was Wapping and all the old riverside wharves, this long before the days of the rejuvenated Docklands.

'That's the 'Prospect of Whitby' over there,' Grandpop would say pointing to the old, riverside pub which did not mean much to me at the time.

On then past the Isle of Dogs before a brief stop at Greenwich – oops, sorry –that's a southbank place but the buildings of the Royal Naval College are magnificent and fully justify my gaze. Next would be the mighty Royal

Docks, cranes reaching to the sky, hard working and full of cargo ships trading with destinations all over the world. The river would now get much busier and Grandpop would then reminisce, thinking not of the Thames, but of the far-off Yangtse and of his navy exploits there some 40 years before.

So to Tilbury and the chance for some Liner spotting and the many dreams that they would inspire:

'Port out, Starboard home,' Grandpop would say, referring to the best cabin locations on the P&O ships to and from India, a comment made all the more relevant by the sight of one of the P&O Liners tied up at the Tilbury Landing Stage waiting for its passengers; there would be a passing salute from our own ship, making me feel very important.

Thoughts of Charles Dickens and 'Great Expectations' would be provoked as we sailed past the flats of the Essex and North Kent marshes; finally the Thames would widen and looking much less like a river open out to the beginning of the Estuary accompanied by the freshening smells of the approaching sea. Ahead to port — oh, yes I must get into the nautical mode – was the distant views of our coming 'old friend' – Southend – and some minutes later we would be tied up at the end of Southend Pier, a familiar sight now seen from 'the other way.'

With the salute of the bell and the clanging of the engines, we would cast off now to begin the real sea voyage part of the adventure – across the ever-widening estuary and, perhaps if the weather was cloudy, there would even be one point when it would not be possible to see either shore – alone on the mighty ocean, indeed. By about 2pm we would this time be off the Kent Coast and finally arriving at Margate. We would not get off the ship but rather stay on board to enjoy a short cruise. The ship would then make off from Margate to North Forland and to see the distant approaches of the English Channel.

'That's the way to the Mediterranean, India and China,'

Grandpop would say knowledgeably and then my imagination would really run riot. If Southend was only a couple of hours away behind us, then surely Bombay could not be too far ahead, I thought!

Back then to Margate, more passengers coming on board to return to London, and the homeward voyage would begin with everything to see all over again. The coming of the evening meant a visit to the ship's restaurant and that very special Fish and Chips tea. To eat at sea and looking out of the window, this really was grand. Finally, happily full after the meal, it was time to be back on deck, whatever the coolness of the summer evening, ready to see the ship turn in the river at Greenwich then to steam stern first up river – our vantage point would therefore then too be in the stern so we could see where we were going and be ready to see the lights of Tower Bridge and the mighty arms opening to allow 'my' passage.

What a day that was!

'Did you enjoy it, love?', Mother and Nan would ask.

'Oh yes, yes!' I cried. 'Can we go again, tomorrow?'

'We'll see, love, about sometime later' was the reply and perhaps, just perhaps, there would indeed be a second trip before the end of the season. After all, this was the time without any main holidays away and these day trips were a fine substitute.

What a great shame that similar trips are not run on a regular basis today. Surely it would be popular with both locals and tourists alike and it's a great opportunity missed – anyway I would go, and more than once!

Just to balance the geography, we would sometimes go up river too although this, for me, did not have the same degree of excitement. We would set off from Westminster bound for Richmond or even on to Hampton Court, the Palace and the Maze in which, naturally, I would always get lost. These boats were naturally much smaller – notice the word 'boat' as opposed to 'my steamer' to Margate!

The trip passing Chelsea, Putney and Barnes was pleasant enough but probably more so for adult eyes keen on home spotting in these classic parts of London. For me the highlight of the trip was the passing through the various locks, the gurgling and pumping of the water, the boat rising or falling accordingly and the exposed, slimy green walls of the lock as the water receded leaving us, and the often accompanying myriad of small boats ready to go on our way as the lock gates opened.

Whilst on this nautical theme and exploits of 'an old sea dog' on the river, I must not forget the London river cruise from Westminster or Charing Cross, to the Tower and sometimes onwards to Greenwich, this last part literally being in the wake of my much loved steamer cruise. Views of the Embankment, Blackfriars and towards St Pauls, standing out and reflecting the inspiration of the years of the Blitz, were all the same as now with the occasional exception that, in many cases a clearer view was more possible then, given the absence of so many high-rise buildings. The Upper Pool of London, between London Bridge and the Tower was much busier then than now with the variety of cargo boats unloading at the various quays and I always remember the sight of loads of bananas (in the middle of the City of London!).

Familiarity meant that I really began to know this route and all the sights. The crew would give a commentary, which being a brilliant young boy (!) I could almost later recite and they would always end with the message:

'This commentary has been given entirely voluntarily so any contributions in appreciation will be gladly accepted by the crew.'

And with that, the hat would be passed around.

One extra special outing of especially great excitement occurred during the summer holidays from school in 1951. Without any hint, I set off with Grandpop to the tube station in the usual way and we travelled not only through London but then on to Hounslow before he told me we were going to see the new 'aerodrome' near Hounslow called Heathrow which we finally reached by bus. It was then a collection of army-style prefabricated huts alongside the main Bath Road, very basic, very small. Then to top it all, Grandpop then said we were going to go on a sightseeing flight which, excitedly, we did in a small bi-winged plane with just eight seats.

A co-pilot opened the door and very officially showed us to our seats – there were eight in all, ranged four each side behind each other down the plane. It was an open view to the cockpit and to the two Biggles-like pilots who talked in hushed tones and took frequent radio messages.

We were off – just a short hop along the runway and we up in the air and heading eastwards towards London. Oh what fabulous views of all the London sights, the blue sky and fluffy white clouds – it was so lucky to be such a clear day that I saw for miles, not only London but the distant Downs of Surrey and Kent to the south and the Chilterns to the north. What an experience! – and how different to visit Heathrow now to then. Terminal five – there wasn't even what could be called a Terminal 0.1!

I was so over-excited when I got home, simply bubbling over to tell of my trip. Mother and Nan knew of Grandpop's plans but had been sworn to secrecy so that I would have had no inkling of the proposed event. Lovingly they listened to my bubbled excitement before saying:

'Every time that we heard a plane overhead, we ran out to the yard to wave!'

'Did you see us, wave?' mother said endearingly.

What a pity the plane had not flown over East London.

During the early years of the 1950s, new buildings would not only emerge throughout London to change my known landscape, but development was taking place in Bow too. Soon there was a whole range of high- rise homes – 'flats' – how very strange I thought, how could the name 'flat' be given to such buildings when they were so high and had so many floors!

At school, I had become very good friends with Michael whose family owned a large grocer's shop in Devon's Road. At the time it was not a place where Nan usually shopped but, diplomatically and to show kinship, she did begin to buy some of our regular weekly shopping there – the bacon was terrific, as too were the magnificent cheeses, cut to order from massive, round whole cheeses. Smells from the shop would waft tantalisingly upstairs to the flat above during the times of my many visits and fortunately there were always tasty bites to hand!

The small, individual shop philosophy of Devon's Road mirrored a similar style in so many areas of the country then and was simply carrying on with a way of life that had always been. After all, wasn't it Napoleon who had commented that we were a nation of shop-keepers! Thoughts of supermarkets, shopping centres and 'under one roof shopping generally' were still a long way off. It was, and is, a style I like and offered good quality for all its quaintness. The grocers wore white aprons, the butcher and fishmonger wore a straw hat – yes, even in Bow, and the flavours, smell and variety of freshly baked bread from the local baker was enough to still conjure up mouth-watering reflections even today.

A 'take-away?' – Well, yes – one which was, of course, a fried fish shop with so many varieties of fish from basic cod to skate and dover sole all with the very tastiest fried chips, all served from a magnificent coal-fired stove and fryer. The shop had even been referred to in an old music hail song 'Old Mother Butlers,' notoriety and a fine reminder of that fabulous shop. Music Hall, incidentally, was something which I never did experience in my years in the East End but I would have loved to have done so. Gosh, the fish and chips were good and worth the visit even if it did mean taking nearly ten minutes to run home trying to keep the package as hot as possible – or perhaps time was lost by the occasional stop to have a bite of chips *en route*!

On Bow Road itself, with the big house, there were only just a couple of shops in our immediate neighbourhood although we were, rather grandly, in the centre 'of the commercial district,' how incredibly metropolitan! There was the small corner shop, a real 'open all hours' establishment that sold everything, most of which would today been called very well past the sell-by date – not here the Devon's Road quality. The other shop – very necessary – was for sweets and ice creams, you know the absolute essentials for young life and, oh yes, it sold newspapers too but to me at that age, newspapers were just for wrapping fish and chips in!

Participating in sport was never high on the agenda in our family and therefore not on mine either. This was compounded by the fact that in my primary school there were no sporting facilities and it was not the culture there either. However, let me immediately stress that this did not in any way mean that there was no exercise or that we were, using today's expression, 'couch potatoes.' Walking was the culture instilled to me in our house. Always we would walk whatever the occasion and, even if having a trip by bus or underground, there were numerous times that we would walk to the next stop to board later on and save money by missing one fare stage. Of course, in the notorious London smogs of the 1950s, there wasn't much alternative other than to walk in any case! Then there would be the lengthy walks of expedition around London or wherever else we visited so fear not for idleness. And if all that wasn't enough, the family themselves, particular Nan and Grandpop, had more than plenty to do all around the house.

Whilst not being sports active, this was not to say that Saturday football was not important because it was – very – not to see a game, something in fact, strange as it may seem today, I never did – nor even to hear on the radio (I'm not even sure that there was even a broadcast in those early days and if there was then we did not listen to it). No, the importance of football became apparent every Saturday purely because of the family's entry of the Football Pools done with religious conviction week in, week out.

Early in the week, Grandpop would study the form, make his match result predictions scientifically and fill in the coupon. Nan's method was less scientific – she merely 'did' the same numbers all the time, a style which Grandpop frowned upon and couldn't understand why she should want to waste the opportunity. Mother and father were just occasional observers although, secretly, I know that father used to have an occasional try 'on the horses' but with varying degrees of misfortune.

The coupon safely completed, a collector would call every Thursday evening .to collect it, together with the money! The process would then be under-way for another week and tension would steadily mount right through to Saturday late afternoon.

Every Saturday winter's evening at five o'clock, a hush would therefore fall upon the household. I would be given whatever was felt necessary to be kept quiet and suitably amused – 'seen and not heard' would be the most appropriate phrase! Then quiet whilst Grandpop with sheer dedication would take down all the football results from the radio broadcast, often with an exclamation 'no,' 'can't be' or, more positively 'oh, that's good.' With all the results in would come the moment of reckoning whilst the list was checked off against the coupon.

Silence.

Glances from Nan and Mother; Father probably reading and completely oblivious to the mounting tension and drama unfolding in the very room.

'Not this week, mate,' Grandpop would announce to Nan to accompanying sighs all round, with dreams once more put back on hold until the following week. School again on Monday!

To finalise the ritual, unless we were to go out on one of increasingly regular theatre visits, Saturday evening would be the time for Grandpop's analysis of the result, what went wrong and initial forecasts and predictions for the next week's round of matches. Perhaps I would be sent at speed to the beloved fish and chip shop or we would have a very special Saturday tea cooked at home such as smoked haddock and for those who wanted it, but not me(!), poached egg on top.

Chapter 4

Mother

Mother's health continued to be a problem again during the early spring of 1952 and for a while was really very unwell and once more needed to spend some time in hospital. One day, when I arrived home from school, having known that mother was seeing her doctor during that day, Nan and mother both asked me to sit with them.

'Listen, love,' mother began, 'You know that mummy has not been so very well lately and I have been to see the Doctor today. He thinks that I should have some special hospital treatment and that will be best for me'

'Will you be going to the hospital for long, then?' I asked without really being able to absorb the news just then.

'We hope not, love,' said my mother. 'And Nan and Grandpop will be here and looking after you. Be a good boy and soon we'll be all together again.

'Now that I'm older, perhaps I can come and see you every evening and not just at weekends, like before,' I said trying to put a brave face on the situation.

'Well, love, I'm sorry, but it is going to be rather different this time. I have to go to a special hospital in the country and there is no chance for any evening visits.'

This was too much for me and I began to cry, in fact there were several tears all around.

'Love,' said Nan, 'try not to be too upset. Mum will get better quickly and although it is very hard now, soon she will come home again, you'll see,' she continued.

'Your Nan is right,' mother said 'I do not want to always feel so ill and by going away now I hope to get better and feel well in time for the summer. We don't want to miss any of our summer trips and lovely times together, do we? Just think of the boat trip to the sea – we'll be together to enjoy that, you'll see,' mother said confidently.

We all sat calmly together, me especially trying to come to terms with the situation. I felt so especially sad when mother had seemed at first to be getting better and her health decline seemed all the more unfair as a result.

Later that evening, when father came home from work, even at my then young age, I really regretted that he was such a cold and distant person, so completely detached.

'Oh, it's for the best, Marjorie,' was his only comment when mother told him the news. He'll (meaning me) be alright with your parents to look after him, so you don't have to worry about that.' Even at that sad time, it would never have occurred to my father that he should take responsibility to be there for my welfare. He was really a most difficult man.

I learned that my mother was to go to a special hospital for lung complaints at Braintree, in Essex and about 40 miles away from our home in Bow. As she had said to me, this meant that visits could only be made once during the week (although not for me as I was, of course, at school) and then we could all go together on Sunday.

A few days after the news had been broken to me, mother left with Nan by taxi for the trip to the hospital. By the time that I got home from school that afternoon, Nan had returned and said that my mother was safely settled in, that it was a very pleasant hospital with some beautiful grounds. Of course I was glad that the place sounded nice but it did not take away the feeling of being so very much cut off from my mother, much more so than when she had been in the local hospital, in walking and almost sight distance from home.

When the time came for Nan's mid-week visit to see mother in the hospital, I could not go home from school for lunch in the normal way but instead went to visit one of Nan's best friends who ran a Drapers Shop in Devon's Road. I enjoyed those visits and the fun of spending 45 minutes experiencing the life of a shop whilst tucking into lunch. It was fun to see and speak to all the customers coming in and out of the shop, many knew me and my family and they asked me kindly about mother and how Nan was as well.

Without a car for the hospital trip, the return journey would take most of the day. First to take a bus to Chelmsford and then a further two connecting buses to Braintree and the hospital. I do remember the rural ness of the surroundings and the then most pleasant real countryside well before the time of major housing development in the area. Even Chelmsford then was not much bigger than a Market Town. All was an enormous contrast to Bow and for mother, at least for a time, the cleaner air and treatments did give her some benefits.

* * * *

By summer 1952, when mother was again home and a little better, concerted efforts and piggy-banks were raided to have a real holiday again that year although it was felt that a return to Devon would be too long a journey for my mother. Brochures were perused for alternative and more suitable areas closer to home and Folkestone, on the south coast of Kent, was chosen, it being only about 70 miles from London and an easy journey. More brochure checking and a small hotel was then selected, endearingly called a 'private hotel,' which was a far more respectable name for a guest house (more eloquent too than the older style 'boarding house'). Whatever, what it actually meant was that we were going to stay in a small seaside hotel without bar facilities, not that my family drank so much anyway!

August 1952 then, and the holiday began in style with a taxi, collecting us from the front door, followed by the ride from Bow through Central London and to the railway station at Charing Cross. All the family were laden with cases and bags full of clothes for all weather eventualities; I, though, was just optimistic for the sun and carried my bucket and spade with supreme importance. The bustle of the station, the hissing of the mighty steam engine and the gleaming green carriages, our reserved seats, would all add to the excitement of the occasion.

All safely settled in the train and the whistle would blow and we would be off, steaming across Hungerford Bridge and looking down on to the River Thames and seeing all the familiar river sites from this different perspective.

On through that 'foreign territory' (to me) of South London and then leaving the City well behind reaching the North Downs and the rolling countryside. Kent had for many years been the destination for hoards of East Enders who would by tradition spend their late summer holidays hop picking in the county. We, however, were speeding through the Weald of Kent, past all the hop fields, intent on making for the coast. Soon it would be Sandling, the small railway junction near to Hythe and the coast all accompanied by the first sound of seagulls and the distant smell of the sea. Finally, after only some 80 minutes after leaving London which in terms of change of environment could have been 80 hours; we were in the different world of Folkestone and our holiday by the sea.

Luckily we were travelling in the early 1950s because if we were taking the same journey some 50 years later, it would then take 20 minutes longer – but that of course is like for like progress!

Once at Folkestone Station, we joined the throngs of many other people similarly arriving for their holidays. We all went to the taxi queue and father, happy for the chance of getting away from us for a few minutes, would go off to the station office on the mission of reserving seats for our homeward journey. Funny how that task always seemed to take ages and he would finally turn up at the hotel about an hour after us!

There can surely be no better place for a social study evocative of the 1950s than a decent English seaside 'private hotel,' such as where we stayed in Folkestone. A beautiful Victorian House set in nice gardens and standing gleaming white in the bright, clear sunshine. The bay windows reminded me of our home but after that the similarities ended – this was a pristine place standing in quiet and well manicured surroundings of the seaside.

Excitedly, we went in, made introductions and were shown to our rooms, all at the front and with glorious views to the sea. Furnishings were typical small hotel, all rather big and somewhat old fashioned, but still very nice for all that and happy as a place to call home for two weeks. Immediately it was time for lunch after which a chance for a quick look round the place that was to be our temporary home for the next two weeks. That initial walk gave enough appetite for more food so we made our return for tea.

The Tea was the time for social study! The genteelness, the proper ritual of a full afternoon tea with delicate sandwiches and the scones and cakes neatly displayed on silver cake stands, all taken in the comfort of the sea facing lounge filled with huge and supremely comfortable armchairs and sofas. The polite and almost quiet conversation.

'Nice day again, isn't it?'

'Oh, yes, very nice indeed and such lovely sunshine.'

'Perhaps a little too warm though!'

'Are you staying long?'

'Yes, for two weeks, and we just arrived — it's our first day, you see!'

'Well, we do like it here – and we are sure you will all like it too!'

Perhaps hardly the right scene for a small boy, but I was very content and, hopefully, was on the very best behaviour.

'Please may I have another piece of cake?'

'When we have finished, please can we go and have a look at the sea?'

And that is exactly what we did so that by the end of the very first afternoon we all felt very much at home – that is except for father who obviously suffered immensely from the enforced family time. Still, it was already arranged that he would stay with us only for the weekend and would return on Sunday evening to London and go back to work. I really wasn't too sad about that as I felt much happier to be just with mother, Nan and Grandpop.

The whole operation and running of the 'private hotel' was supreme properness, beginning with breakfast promptly at 8.30am when we would be summoned by the gong to the dining room. Lunch at 1.00pm, the aforesaid afternoon tea around 4.00pm with the final meal, dinner around 7.00 pm, all adding up to a very 'feastful' day! The ritual would hardly seem to leave time for any other activity but because everything was done in the height of efficiency it would be possible to be out of the dining room in about 30 minutes except for the more leisurely dinner-time. Of course, breakfast would be especially quick because the proprietors would be intent on 'losing' their guests as quickly as possible so that they could begin their cleaning tasks and food preparations.

The English seaside resort of the 1950s in no way resembled what is on offer for the most part today. Of course, now there are the Brighton's, Bournemouth's and Blackpool's, for example, that flourish and have progressed but in the 1950s even the smaller resorts like Folkestone were a hive of activity which supported not only 'private hotels' but even rather grand establishments now long gone or converted to apartments. During the day the beach areas would be busy, people enjoying sea bathing, masses of ice cream and tea/coffee stalls, Punch and Judy for the children, amusement and games areas, boating pools, sea trips from the shore, plenty indeed to excite and thrill especially for a small boy away from the City for a treasured two week break.

On top of all this were bustling shops in the town and, in the evening, a choice of a couple of Variety Show theatres and one traditional repertory theatre for plays. That was certainly all very adult and the family would take it turns for these evening outings with one staying behind with me to baby-sit. I was normally so tired, after all the day's happenings, by that time and so soon fell into sleep!

This was certainly the time of the English seaside resort at its best years prior to the overseas holiday package tour and places were happily busy.

Every good day, and, of course there were many, was spent by the sea. Making endless sand castles on the one sandy beach, specially filled with sand as opposed to the normal south coast pebbles; enjoying and taking part in the bustling activities of the fishing harbour, all rounded off by the daily opportunities for sea cruises running directly from the beach:

'Come on, sailing in ten minutes, hurry up now' – was the boatman's shout.

We would rush on board only to sit for at least another half-hour hearing the same message continually shouted to round-up more prospective customers! Finally, we would set off for a sea trip lasting about 90 minutes during which time we would sail to the main shipping lanes of the Channel and see the passing big ships, trading to and from exotic places of the world.

The beach amusements area was great fun for me – the boating pool with the small self-drive motor boats made me feel very important as a 'captain' steering confidently round and round; then to try the helter-skelter and to go with Grandpop on the dodgem cars to see Nan and Mother turning the other way. By this time, father would have left us to return to London and work only to come back for the last day or so – never for him too much family time!

What did father get up to all the time in London, I would wonder in a very innocent mind. Frankly, though, it didn't bother me too much, I was happier that he wasn't with us.

Already becoming rather mad about trains, I found it very exciting to go to Folkestone Harbour to see the boat-trains arriving from London and also to see the excited throng of passengers boarding the ferry and the excited imagery in my mind of France and travel to foreign destinations. The whole harbour was a hive of activity with at least two trains coming to and from every ferry sailing, and around six/seven sailings during the day time with the time in port much longer than now with all loading/unloading operations done with large cranes. I loved to see the cars loaded, precariously lifted and deposited in the ferry's hold. 'Roll-on/Roll-Off' was just a figment of somebody's imagination then!

Then the ship would finally cast off with hoots both from its own horn and from the harbour itself, and made out to sea where, in clear weather, you could see it making its way to France for some time to come. Not long, and another ferry would arrive from France and all the happenings would begin again in reverse, to end with the departure of the boat-trains to London. Certainly, fun-filled times for me, not just simple pleasures but rather an inquisitive mind thrilled and excited by all these happenings.

The cliffs top area at Folkestone, known as 'The Leas,' had always had a very gracious air and for example in Edwardian times there would be a patrol to ensure that everybody 'promenading' was well dressed enough f or the occasion. Did my 'school-boy' outfit of shirt and shorts fit the bill, I wondered. As far as mother, Nan and Grandpop were concerned; they always had their 'Sunday-best' when being on the holiday, so they would be allowed to promenade.

Even in the 1950s, The Leas was a place to be seen and the best location to stay in town – that's why we were there of course! It was, and still is, a wonderful place to walk to enjoy both nature and the sea and to see the passing ships in the busy shipping lanes of the English Channel, topped on clear days by views of the French coast itself, a sight which filled me with absolute awe for the very first time.

'Look, love – that's France over there' my mother would say to me.

'Fancy that,' Nan would reply in equal amazement as me, I suppose.

It would be a very excited little boy that returned to the said 'private hotel' after such experiences.

My childhood was very fortunate from the point of view of always being taken to new and different places, also for the chance to explore generally although, relatively speaking to the present day, the scope of exploration was very much in the small geographical area of 'my local patch.'

So to, when on holiday in Folkestone, time would be taken to see more of the surrounding area. Off, then, to see Dover Castle, Canterbury Cathedral and for some general meanderings by bus through the byways of country Kent, all very much in contrast to my normal 'hunting ground' of Bow. Selfishly, my favourite excursion was always to the nearby small town of Hythe and there to take a trip on the Romney, Hythe and Dymchurch light railway. These miniature full scale working steam trains ran then, as they continue to do now, across Romney Marsh and to the lighthouse at Dungeness. This really was seventh heaven to me and an unbelievably wonderful trip, even being allowed once to blow the engine whistle!

How quickly the two weeks would fly past and I got so used to the way of life which I did not want to change not only because of my own pleasures but also because at the first time it really did seem to improve mother's health so much. Anyway it was time to pack the cases, to clean the sand from my pail and spade in readiness for the journey home.

'We'll be back next year,' I would announce to the proprietors as we paid the bill and left for the station.

'See you then,' would be the affirmative reply. That's alright, I thought, all confirmed then as we left to return to the station.

To end the holiday in style there would be one more treat left to experience – that was lunch on the train during the journey back to London. We would go to sit in the restaurant car and be served with excellent, freshly cooked Dover Sole with a delicious pudding to follow. Once again, luckily for us that our holiday was in the 1950s; if you wanted lunch on the same train today, then you would need to remember to bring your sandwiches.

Back to Charing Cross and back to father who would be standing severely on the station to meet us.

'Good holiday then?' he said after shaking us all by the hand, including greeting my mother in exactly the same way. If he had any other sort of emotions, then he was most definitely not one for showing them in public.

Once more it was back to a taxi and the homeward journey to Bow. Oh dear, how drab everywhere looked after the two weeks at the sea, and the noise and bustle everywhere!

The end of the holiday marked the closing down of the summer season – gosh, that sounds rather grand! It also meant the temporary ending of freedom as usually school began within a few days of our return from holiday. The Bow routine, the school walks, lessons all soon replaced the trips and holiday thoughts but firstly it was always exciting to exchange all the news with friends and sure enough, the first school task would always be the essay – 'My holidays!'

The highlight of the beginning school year in September 1952 was that the whole school was leaving behind the Victorian St Botolph's and moving to a brand new, purpose building. The new school was built on an old war-time bomb site in the 'up market' Bromley-by-Bow area, in fact just across the road from the site (by then also bombed) which had been home to my father's family. The prodigal returns!

'Thank-you LCC' (London County Council, as then was).

The education system had been very fair to me donating the experience of a brand new school whilst at the same time ensuring that I could be continued to be taught by the said Miss Baker who, you'll remember, had already 'enjoyed' the experience of teaching some family members 40 years earlier. With the new school came a new headmistress drafted in from the foreign lands of South London, how very cosmopolitan I was to become! Therefore with all these events, some dedicated efforts to learning were obviously necessary and generally the first stage of schooling – the primary school years – passed without any undue problems scholastically and I was in a group of long-term and loyal friends.

* * * *

I felt so lucky to be growing up in the 1950s because it was the time to be able to enjoy and experience the very best of the fine, old traditions whilst at the same time able to become increasingly aware of the developing opportunities and improvements coming with the ensuing years.

For me, our house immediately leapt into modern times in early 1953 when we got our first television in readiness for the approaching Coronation of Her Majesty Queen Elizabeth II. The television, a 12 inch black and white set was placed in our living room/kitchen and had therefore to share a place at right angles to the gas cooker which, I suppose, was at times more interesting to look at in any case! 'Andy-Pandy' and 'Muffin the Mule' were the children's programmes that I watched avidly. Once, when suffering from a bad cold and being off school, I so remember a feature of 'Muffin the Mule ' when an announcement was made to wish better all children that were unwell – I felt so embarrassed because I really believed that broadcast was for me alone!

Being eight years old at the time of the Coronation, I was old enough to be aware of the happenings and to fully appreciate the events. I was given a model Coronation Coach and Horses which gave me a lot of pleasure only to be later stacked away in a toy box and sometime discarded. If only I had been in younger years a potential antique collector and kept the model coach to make a 'fortune 'in later life!

We had a large and boisterous party at the school – bunting, streamers, balloons, drums and spoons to make music – or noise at any rate. To add to the party atmosphere, there were jellies, hats, sandwiches, and lemonade – the lot. Even the normally restrained teachers entered into the part spirit but it did seem very strange to see them trying to behave normally!

On Coronation Day itself, father, in an absolutely uncharacteristic show of paternity values, took me up to London to see the parades and the procession itself. Nan and Grandpop stayed at home with mother then not well enough to come out and they watched all the happenings on television.

'I'll wave to you when I see the camera,' I said, little thinking that there would be anybody else other than me in the crowd!

Crowded as it was, but we stood in the Mall and father lifted me on his shoulders at the right time the procession was passing. My vivid memories were of the Queen of Tonga, looming large and smiling in that awful weather of pouring rain, and then of the Coronation Coach itself, glorious and golden with the Queen herself, smiling, waving and acknowledging the enormous crowds. The marching bands, the soldiers, the pageantry, again the crowds – it was good to have been part of the day and actually there, although the family at home saw more of the event on television than I had seen on the spot.

* * * *

Mother's health really did deteriorate badly throughout the summer of 1953 with frequent spells in hospital and whilst I did not understand nor realise at the time, everybody else knew the inevitable. A one last family holiday to Folkestone was hastily arranged for September after mother had come home from hospital and was sufficiently well enough to travel. This meant that upon my return to school after the summer break, I had to take a letter to the headmistress to seek permission to go away the following week on a holiday.

That was a nerve-wracking ordeal to have to ask and it took some effort to be allowed to go by the school, even though my circumstances were as they were.

'You want a holiday?' the headmistress asked me in her sternest possible stance.

'Yes, miss,' I replied.

'But you've only just returned to the school after the long summer break!' she said.

'Yes, miss,' my becoming stereotyped reply from my ever more nervous self.

'Whose holiday is it?' she continued.

'My Grandfather's arranging it for my …' I stumbled and was completely unable to get all the words out and to explain it was for my mother who was ill.

'Your Grandfather!,' her stunned response. 'Why can't he take you on holiday in the usual holiday time, not when it's term time at my school?'

'Don't know, miss,' was my increasingly weak reply. I simply could not bring myself to say directly to the headmistress that the rushed and unexpected holiday was being arranged for my mother, that she was ill and the family wanted for me to go to enjoy time together.

'Well, you had better just go then, but listen here, I am not happy and it will not certainly be allowed to happen again – not in my school!'

Anyway, with that ordeal finally over, we went and my memories of that holiday are mainly concentrated on being together (although, of course, no father) and of the usual happy events we did together. Folkestone in the late summer was equally as nice as for our earlier visit, perhaps better for me when there were no queues for the children's amusements, the boating pool or the other rides.

Poor mother could not do very much though, just managing to walk a short distance from the hotel to sit on a seat on the Leas. After a few days of the tonic sea air though she did seem better and we even managed a couple of excursions to the then becoming well known surrounding area.

Nan and Grandpop were on a constant vigil making sure that my mother was alright. I was really oblivious to the poignancy of the sad surroundings.

Back home and I returned to school, although very much aware that the doctor was then calling on a regular basis at varying different times of the day. My aunt and uncle, Brenda and Dick, by then had a car and would sometimes call; a most chilling experience as she always appeared dressed in sombre black, which really frightened me. At these times I would try to spend as much time as possible with Nan and Grandpop, for safe feelings and for a sense of family warmth, during their visits.

That awful evening in October 1953 when they came, I remember Brenda saying loudly to mother:

'Look, Marjorie, there's nothing for you to worry about – you are really quite fit and will soon get better. The doctor says there is nothing to fear.'

Nan was crying in the other room and I really then knew the worst. I was glad that Dick asked me to go with him in the car and we drove towards the City and to Aldgate and an all-night chemist where some prescriptions were collected plus a horrible big black cylinder of oxygen. When we got back home, I just wanted to play with my things and shut myself off from the situation. I was glad when Brenda and Dick had finally gone – I was with my family again even though the atmosphere was very subdued and mother was not able to talk to me other than a few gasps. We simply held hands.

Where was father during all this? Oh out, of course, late home from work as usual and even when he finally came in, he was more intent upon having something to eat rather than comfort mother or me. By now, the scene at home was very depressing and even with the help of the oxygen, my mother could do no more than manage a few breathless words.

Next morning I went to school in the usual way but very much conscious of the upset and desperate feelings back at home. At the mid-morning break, the headmistress called me to her office. There I found Uncle Dick – my mother had died at home about an hour before, he told me gently.

I left the school with Dick and we got into the car, but it was not to take me home but rather to Buckhurst Hill and there to stay with him, Brenda and the other members of that side of the family including, of course, my paternal grandmother.

This really was a most wretched time. Bad enough that my mother had just died, but then to have to stay at that house, which I hated in any case, when all that I wanted was to be with my Nan and Grandpop and in my comfortable and natural surroundings even though I realised the enormity of the situation at home and that my mother would never be there again.

Later I learnt that, in fact, Nan and Grandpop wanted me to be at home but my father had disagreed. He was at that stage of my life so uninvolved with me at most times other than to intervene in the most inappropriate way. I was 'in exile,' so to speak, at Buckhurst Hill and wasn't even allowed to attend my own mother's funeral. This really led to my having enormous fears at that time that I would be moved away from my beloved Nan and Grandpop, and my home surroundings of Bow, to have to live in that awful house and alien environment. My thoughts devastated me and I could not possibly have been more miserable as, obviously, Nan and Grandpop were nothing to my father and quite probably, I thought, he would want to settle with, or at least near to, his sister and family. My mind simply filled with these and other similar negative thoughts.

The gloom of that following week in Buckhurst Hill seemed endless and I was in no feeling to be aware of the suburban life nor to consider and compare them to my own surroundings of Bow. Bow was home and this was a strange and hostile world. I probably grew up enormously during that week, which is both good and bad. Good not to be forever a young child but bad to have sufficient awareness of events and the feelings to realise the magnitude of what could possibly happen. My life and world was upside down. I wanted to be at home and I wanted Nan and Grandpop.

A week after mother's death, and a couple of days after the funeral, I was finally allowed to return home. For how long, or for what the future may hold, I did not immediately care; only to feel an immense feeling of relief to get back to my roots and natural surroundings, to be with Nan and Grandpop, even to get back to school, just anything that that was my normal way of life. Of course, at home there was a very empty feeling and the loss of my mother was a devastating event.

Even though all through my young years she had been so often away from home, at least I knew then that she was close by in a hospital and also that I could often see her. Somehow, I made myself think that the situation was the same now and that the fact that she was no longer there was not immediately of such grave significance.

Full realisation would come later with a sense of such a devastating blow and loss.

Because of the way my early years had been, it was Nan who was my mother figure and to whom I turned in various lives's situations. Similarly, Grandpop was more of a father figure and role model to me than ever my own father, to whom I hardly had any real feelings and indeed who I frankly very much feared because of his strange coldness and sulking temper. It was to be in much later life before there was any true rapport between me and my father.

For now I was safe. I was at home in Bow and my frights would soon recede although at the time I was fortunately completely oblivious of the fights that would go on in the background over the immediate following months as my father had various schemes and plans to take me away from my cherished home environment. In retrospect it is possible, with a certain degree of humanity, perhaps to see father's side of the story. He was a widower at a comparatively early age of his late thirties; he probably did not want to go on living with his 'in-laws' but the fact was that that he had never the capabilities or inkling to be a family father figure to me. Frankly he wasn't too interested in paternal matters other than occasional involvements with me and would have been completely unsuited to managing an upbringing, let alone a family life on his own.

I must say that, despite the threats and obscure plans then displayed by my father, life did in fact settle down and would continue for many years completely uninterrupted in the most unlikely family unit of me, Nan, Grandpop and father all living together in, almost, 'perfect harmony.' Perhaps this is, indeed, a different and unique situation but the amazing thing is that despite the immediate storms at the end of 1953, it really worked and worked well. Simply, father had a degree of freedom whilst living at home with us. He was able to 'do his own thing,' be out whenever and to have the sense of freedom and non-commitment, obviously important to him, and knowing that I was being extremely well looked after, that would never have been possible had we been just our two selves. At the same time he had full opportunity to be involved and oversee my own upbringing even though, at his own volition, this was only to a small degree.

For Nan and Grandpop the arrangement was also the best solution under the circumstances. They had the awful experience of having lost their only child at the early age of 36, but they still had a family unit and since they had virtually brought me up anyway, it would have been too awful for them to contemplate had they lost me too at that time.

Life, though, could never be the same again and at a young age of 8, it was something that I had to get used to. Then, more than ever, I needed the benefit of a happy and secure home and fortunately that was possible whilst still living with Nan and Grandpop in Bow.

Chapter 5

A Changed Life

One most significant and immediate change to my life's routine after mother's death was that my cherished Sundays at home in Bow were never to be the same again. Sunday then came to be the day for visits to the aunts and uncles, with father, usually to Buckhurst Hill to see Brenda and Dick, Irene and Pip, who, of course, all lived together with their mother with whom I should have had the feeling of my 'other' Grandmother, but never did.

Any time alone just with father was trauma enough for me and I was very much afraid of him. On top of everything, I had the constant and underlying fear that soon I might be taken away from my home permanently perhaps just to live with him in some strange place. For the whole journey on the train he would read his paper or his book, never talk to me other than the occasional – 'Be quiet' – or other similar words of comfort! I simply just sat so miserably in the train, staring out of the window and thinking of times doing the same journey with my mother, and thinking of what I would have been doing if at home.

It didn't occur to me that the Sunday visit though was a small price to pay for being able to live all other days of the week with Nan and Grandpop in Bow and, in any case, why should an eight year old boy need to think so rationally. Many things I hated about the day, but my principal dislike was that the programme was so severe in a very grim household and without childhood, or even, adult fun – there were not even any make believe chains to play with!

Lunch was always less good and even Uncle Dick's regular quip every Sunday

'What, no Yorkshire' (. . . pudding) failed to lift the gloom because then Brenda would then barely talk to him for most of the day. That house then in those early years was always one of 'Ati's' (atmospheres) as Dick would call it. To make matters worse, after some months, the Grandmother died so that the Sunday routine would then include the trip to the Cemetery to tend the grave. Although I would never actually go in to the place, it was still a horrible visit for me to bear, especially so when it was the very same place where my own mother had been cremated.

The only possible saving grace for me, on those Sundays was that Dick had a car so there would always be a traditional Sunday afternoon drive, which was perfectly acceptable and a highlight for me when ignoring the Cemetery bit. My thrills of cars and driving were surely to stem from this time, so at least something good came out of it!

With this background then, it wasn't for me to notice or feel the obvious between my home area of Bow and the delights of Buckhurst Hill.

The gentle suburbia feel compared enormously to the grime, hustle and bustle, noise and industrial haze of Bow. In Buckhurst Hill, the uniformity of all the houses, row after row, pristine then but surely just the same as the City Victorian terraces would have been when new in East London and then destined for a similar 'used look' fate in later times. The gardens were all well kept and gave an air of prosperity, in fact looking much nicer then overall rather than now when the majority of front gardens have been removed to form giant car-parks. The small High Street shops, to me, were reminiscent of my familiar Devon's Road (Bow) although with greater and more affluent variety; there were more jewellers and perfumeries than I think we had in my home territory!!

Without doubt, the highlight of Buckhurst Hill was the skyline of the magnificent Epping Forest and the more immediate Knighton Woods. This was a place where later I could run and play, momentarily to get lost until finding another clearing and a sense of direction. How lucky then to experience the sense of freedom without alarm.

Even though barely ten miles from Bow, there were farms with real, live cows, open fields and the very pleasant river valley of the Roding, long before the arrival of masses of cars or of the ? The sound of push mowers, or the occasional passing of the tube train, there running over ground, would be the only noises to pierce the peace and general air of tranquility. Whatever though being there broke my home environment feel, the sense of safety and security and, most importantly, no Nan and Grandpop, hence, initially at least, my general morose and negative feel about those Sundays.

However, the day would pass and Sunday evening would be the time to return home and back to where I belonged with the happy realisation and a sense of relief that it would be a whole week before that day would come round again. Of course it was sad to have harboured such negative thoughts of a Sunday especially when the next day only meant a return to school again – but at least it was a return to normality, my world and the world of which I was a part. Positively though, the school environment and my friends there were very supportive during the times immediately following mother's death. Even Miss Baker stopped making snide remarks or negative comparisons between me and my aunts as her earlier prized' pupils – a plus point indeed!

* * * *

Birthdays were always made extra special for me and I received especially good presents from Nan and Grandpop which first began, and then continued to add to, my collection of model railways, my pride and joy. You see, by this time, the mid 1950s, I had grown up a bit from those 'chains' and was now into the real thing. Even in those days, model railways were expensive and very much out of keeping with what Nan and Grandpop could probably have afforded, and with this realisation I treasured them even more. At this time and age a reasonably simple track layout would suffice, although in later years the operation would become thoroughly more sophisticated with cross-over, electric points and signals, main line and local lines.

A party would be the Birthday highlight with several best friends from school duly invited to come around on the nearest Saturday afternoon – and on that day Grandpop would really have to go upstairs to the offices for enough peace and quiet to be able to hear and record the football results. Days of preparation would go on in the house before the event and the air would be full of delicious and mouth-watering baking smells, there would be endless rows of jellies and thick, colourful custards, extra bread for sandwiches, and stacks of plates brought out from the cupboard store.

After an excited and sleepless night before, the dawn of the chosen Saturday would finally arrive. The novelty of the day would begin with me firstly going off with Nan on the bus along the familiar route westwards through the City and on to Charing Cross where we would get off the bus and head for the J. Lyon's Corner House, then a veritable London institution, this one then situated close to the main railway station of Folkestone fame.

What an emporium of goodies was the Lyon's Corner House! Several floors, I remember and we would start first with a visit to the tea shop with its waitresses with white caps and aprons and black dresses. There we would revive with a superb toasted tea-cake, scones and jam and a big pot of tea with real tea-leaves –very adult, very grown-up. Happily refreshed, the work would then begin by visiting the food department – the Delicatessen – on the ground floor – Devon's Road was never considered good enough for my party.

What a stunning array of luxury foods! Round the shop we would go selecting different varieties of salads, stuffed tomatoes, dressings and mayonnaise, hams and cut meats, barbecued chicken pieces (remember this was in the 1950s, so all this a real luxury and novelty then in a era well before the time of endless take-away's and the Burger-Bar culture). Next for the 'attack' would be the cake and gateaux section and to complement the fruit cakes already made at home, we would buy some luscious cream cakes that would be painstakingly packaged and, most importantly I remember, the boxes tied up with ribbon – at least that would keep my sticky fingers at bay for the journey home!

Laden with boxes, then, we left for the bus stop by St Martins in the Fields, to queue for the bus home trying all the time to risk the temptation of an impromptu tasting. The precious smells would waft around the bus on the journey home.

'Cor, what 'ave you got there, Missus,' the conductor would shout to Nan.

'Something good for my Boy's party,' Nan would reply 'Do you want a sniff, 'cause that's your share,' she would continue.

By then the whole bus would be involved and all the passengers would know that I was going to have a birthday party.

'Happy Birthday, Boy, don't eat too much and get sick then' and other similar comments from the fellow passengers to ensure that the birthday party atmosphere would begin there and then on the bus home.

Such friendly exchanges amongst people not knowing each other was so typical then of the London, and especially East London atmosphere, and was most endearingly. This was well before the time when people were more concerned with mobile phones and other similar distractions!

As a special salute then to the birthday, wonderfully then finally on reaching Bow the bus would be made to stop right outside our home so that we did not have to walk too far along the road with all our parcels.

At home finally and then the rush to get dressed in the best kept party clothes ready to greet my guests who would all arrive similarly unrecognisable from the uniformity of the everyday school clothes. Our front room would be converted from a bedroom so it would be fair to call it a 'parlour' just for the day. A dream world was created with balloons, streamers and fairy lights all adding to the party atmosphere and all finally set off with various tables set up and laden with all the party goodies.

Everything in place and everybody ready, party time could finally begin – games, face masks, food, puzzles, more food, perhaps by then one or two slightly green faces and then the rings at the doorbell as parents called to collect the guests, but nobody leaving without still more food rounded off with a goodly selection of 'doggy-bags' to take home. So ended a day that always created so many happy thoughts and memories for some time to come – and I would walk on air accordingly – and it would be the talk of the class on the following Monday – I should have invited Miss Baker too and seen her in a funny hat!

The party was not the only important birthday event and around the time there would also be a special London visit – to a favourite museum, or the Tower, Madam Tussauds perhaps. Yes, as a quieter type of soul, I really was thrilled about these events, never dull, never boring and the pleasures would become even greater with older years.

Even the trip by Underground or Bus to London was a thrill, none more so than one particular time when as the train halted for some minutes at Whitechapel (and who would not want to halt at Whitechapel!) and Grandpop and I got out to see what was wrong. The driver, very flustered and frustrated by the delay, started to talk to us and then said:

'Bring the boy into the cab and let me show you both how things really do work!'

We did just that and me especially with hardly controlled relish! We travelled all the way to the end of the line at Richmond. I was absolutely thrilled to see the front view – the dark tunnels, the passing trains, the signals, the lights of the approaching stations, already so well known to me. When we finally came out of the tunnels, next was the over ground travel through West London and seeing places not so familiar for me.

At the end of the journey in Richmond, the driver kindly gave us some tea from his flask and we enjoyed the ten minute break talking about life on the Underground.

'How old do you have to be before you can drive a train?' I asked with obvious career intentions.

'Well, son, you are a bit young yet, maybe in twenty years time.'

'Oh, at least I have got some experience,' I replied putting rather too much emphasis on the afternoon!

'Come on, Boy,' Grandpop suggested, as we prepared to leave the train's s cab.

'Where are you going?' the driver asked. 'We're going back east now and my shift takes me to Earl's Court – stay with me until then.'

We did!

What a day! A rather long round-about journey to the time we finally got out at Charing Cross, which was our original destination, but a journey and day very much full of seventh heaven to me!

Whether I was with Nan and Grandpop or with my father who could by then just about cope with me for a very, very, occasional outing to London, or whether we were all together as a family, the magic would always be the same. It was a fortunate and valued childhood in that respect. I grew up with, and regularly saw, the Changing of the Guard, the Beefeaters and the Tower of London, the State Occasions, the processions, indeed everything of note. All this means that I have always, now and continue, to delight and appreciate all the wonderful aspects of our country's heritage and traditions with value and enthusiasm.

Soon, Kensington would not just be for me the Science Museum, for which, however, I would maintain a continued interest, but my net then spread further to include the Natural History Museum too – all the big animals, the exotic models of the world's creatures. Whilst perhaps the occasional visit to the nearby Victoria and Albert Museum was then a bit above my head and somewhat wasted on my younger eyes, it did nevertheless plant the seed of interest and I would reap with enthusiasm later benefits and appreciation of that fine museum too. In fact, when in later years if school visits were arranged, I do believe that I was more enthusiastic it than the accompanying teachers who, I suppose, had their work cut out attending to the hoards of noisy school kids – more interested on their sandwich packs than the exhibits!

'What have you got in your lunch box?'

'Spam sandwiches.'

'I like Spam, I've got egg, let's change.'

'No, I don't like egg and I don't want that.'

'Please, Miss, Robert won't let me have his sandwiches and it's not fair!'

'Give him some of your sandwiches, it's a reasonable exchange,' said Miss Baker. I might have known that she wouldn't take my side of the discussion!

* * * *

Some positive changes occurred to life in Bow and to our home in the years of my growing up in the mid-1950s. Whilst Nan and Grandpop had their same caretaking duties, Grandpop continued initially during the day with his painting and decorating work but in 1955 he officially retired from that role, only to take on odd jobs of a similar nature and more duties in the offices at home.

About this time too there was a change in the office occupancy, with one of the companies moving away and their place was taken by a paints and chemicals sales and development company. The ground floor became a sales office, and a small testing laboratory was set up in part of the coal cellar – we were moving into high-tech times in Bow! Fortunately for us, living in the house, there were no obnoxious smells even though a gruesome-looking paint testing machine was installed.

This gave Grandpop a new duty to check and record equipment at evenings and weekends - very impressed he was with himself with pad and pen checking dials and recording all the data. There was also a far less high-tech use for the laboratory – it proved to be absolutely perfect place to dry and 'air' (what, with all those fumes!) the washing and Nan's working day became supremely efficient as a result. There was still use for the fantastic old hand mangle which she lovingly operated to get at least some of the washing water out of the clothes and thankfully the old mangle wasn't redundant just yet. Still it groaned, slithered and shook, a massive and old family heirloom.

With all the talk about the Kensington Science Museum, I reckon that the mangle would have been a possible object worthy of display there! It was a great shame that, when we finally moved in later years, the old mangle was finally thrown out to be replaced by a spin dryer. What a marvellous bric-a-brac item that old mangle would have made today, a feature surely in a very up-market antiques shop and we would have been rich!

Soon an associate company of the Paint Group took over the middle floor as an administration office and one room was converted to a Board Room – gosh, how very grand and Nan and Grandpop needed to spend much extra time in polishing and cleaning that very room, directed, of course, by me from the Chair! This was the beginning of big business and our address was surely then on the London corporate map as opposed to the time when a charity organisation had occupied two floors. Our 'business centre 1950s style' was completed on the top floor by a local Government and Council office – that of the 'District Surveyor' – which I thought in my imagination must have been something like a throwback role from the time of the British in India – except that the staff did not wear plumed hats!

One fortunate result for us, especially Nan and Grandpop, by these changes of office occupancy was that a concerted effort was made by all the companies to change from coal to electric heating. The famous Boardroom even had something rather grand called 'central heating' – wow! So, no more fireplace cleaning or coal deliveries, nor the carrying of bucket loads of coal upstairs to be reciprocated by the carrying of similar loads of ashes downstairs. The working day was reduced by half as I suppose too were Nan and Grandpop's wages, but it was so much cleaner and, in our own small way we had finally moved from the Victorian industrial age to electronic 1950s.

These dramatic changes also meant that we lost our own fireplace in our basement home so that evening were spent staring at a lighted red bar for warmth as opposed to the roaring fire. What about the toast – that was a real loss, not to say winter chestnuts! The famous tea-cakes from J. Lyons never did taste the same afterwards.

Father had moved upwards in the Civil Service from the Kensington Coal Depot to the grandly termed 'Ministry of Works' and to a clerical position in a large office block on Lambeth, overlooking the Thames. I was, rather amazingly given our usual stand-off style relationship, taken there on several occasions and found it hard to believe that it was actually my father speaking when he said to others in his office:

'This is Robert, my son.'

He then proceeded to introduce me around to his work colleagues and overall to give the impression of the caring and responsible parent. It was a most weird experience for me – were he like it all of the time then I could have had a greater feeling and friendship for him at the time. Obviously, it made him feel good, and to be really horrible, it probably was done to enhance his position in the office. Once we were outside, he soon reverted to his normal self!

Overall though, the visit was good and it gave me the fine chance to marvel at the wonderful views of the river and across to the Houses of Parliament.

The seemingly strange arrangement of father living as a widower with his 'in-laws' fortunately for me, did appear to work and for him too it was obviously a reasonable solution which, despite my earlier fears, he did not seem, fortunately, to wish to change. Father was a somewhat 'free-spirit,' frequently out during the week after work and sometimes too on a Saturday but, unfortunately, never doing anything else on a Sunday that would prevent the ritual visits to the aunts. That he could live his life freely without the need to worry about me or my care was apparently good for him. It also meant that when, especially in later childhood life, he and I did have an outing alone together, whilst he would act in usual 'proper' way, there would at least be a small degree of understanding and rapport between us.

I knew that throughout the years, father did meet an occasional women friend – too strong a term to call a 'girlfriend' – normally through work, but nothing normally ever developed except on one notorious occasion about one year after my mother had died.

Then, I was told in the week by him that, whatever I was going to do on the following Saturday with Nan or Grandpop, I was to drop any plans as I was to go with him to Reading, about 35 miles west of London in Berkshire, to meet his new friend. When I told Nan and Grandpop, they were most alarmed and their concerns reflected my own bad feelings about what the trip could possibly entail. Naturally, Nan and Grandpop asked father what was happening. He was most evasive, saying that he only wanted me to meet his friend.

When the day came, I went with father to Reading, momentarily forgetting my alarm as we took the train from Paddington and thereby remembering my happy holiday memories of the travels to Devon. We went to a cafe near the station in Reading, strange not to a house, I thought, and there met father's lady friend.

She spoke in a very strange accent to my ears and I later found out that she came from Wales. Then it all clicked into place!

The lady had travelled from Wales just for the meeting and it was considered that Reading was a good place, although hardly half-way! It was a very strange sensation for me to actually see father being all sweetness and light to the lady and even speaking to me in much lighter tones. From the conversation, this must have been a very long-lasting friendship after all and the lady seemed to know so much about my life, where I had been and what I had been doing. I even was quizzed about the school and she knew about Miss Baker.

I was suitably filled with plenty of buns and cakes to keep me quiet whilst father and his friend exchanged some very friendly moments. I did not understand much about this event at all and it needed time at home to relate the day's adventures to Nan and Grandpop to realise where my father had been and what he had been up to at those times when mother was ill or when we were away on holiday without him!

Strangely, I must have had a very bad effect on the lady – I never saw her again and even if father somehow continued to meet with her, nothing came from the association!

It would not be until very many years later in different circumstances that there was to be a firm and permanent relationship in father's life. Until then, it was simply a case of occasional company without commitment, one so-called 'friend' following each other. 'Without commitment'– a phrase in itself which very much summed up my father, both in his friendships, and with me. Thankfully, life worked in the way that it did and my own life gradually became more secure and felt less threatened by the thoughts that perhaps one day I would be taken away from my home.

Coming up to the age of 10 then, I was feeling more secure in life and, as a result, more confident of various events. This even began to mean that I no longer felt so much foreboding about the Sunday's aunts' visits and that in itself was a triumph!

* * * *

Generally, the Bow of my growing up years was a very safe place, at least in my view, in which to live. Really, the gangland image of East London did not seem to be immediately around us, although in reality some pretty horrendous events did take place not too many miles away. That did not affect my life – I could go out safely as often as I liked, either on my own or with friends to the parks, to do shopping and, of course, alone to school once having settled in. I also remember that our side door at home was only locked at nights, at other times I and various callers came freely to and from at will.

The friendliness that I've experienced amongst the bus passengers was equally noticeable on the streets and the shops – everybody had time to talk, laugh, and help where help was needed and, whilst being generally rather poor, there were terrific values of life. An East Ender had the right touch to always be bright and breezy, ready to turn disaster into triumph, no matter how big or small the problem.

'Awful rain today, isn't it?'

'Yes, but it's good for the flowers.'

It was little to wonder that I and many others felt so safe. It was because of the number of helmeted and friendly policemen that were visible 'on the beat' at all times. Perhaps also it was because generally people felt and behaved so differently then. It was all a question of life-style and values and a general realisation and acceptance of what was obviously right, allowed and therefore permissible as opposed to that which was, equally obviously, unacceptable and against society.

By the mid-1950s, Bow was becoming much bigger, mainly because the older terraced houses were being replaced by blocks of flats and therefore a larger overall population. Yet still the basic character did not yet begin to change. We still had the specialist small shops, plenty of pubs (not that I then knew about the inside!) and an array of buses (soon, though, no more trolleys) plus the underground lines, all the key to past and future excursions. My favourite parks had expanded too, the mighty Victoria Park was always the same but a new, but much smaller, park was built, created from a former bomb-damaged site, not far from Bow Road.

Here were swings, round-about rides and a sandpit to remind me of days spent by the sea. This was the place where I met school friends, to generally run about and play and to build extravagant and massive structures in the sand only for them to be jumped on within minutes! The park too was the scene of a twice- yearly visit of a fair with larger and more varied amusements and rides – coconut shies with prizes as well, all very great fun.

Although Bow catered very well for the daily needs of life, for the more sophisticated requirements such as clothing and furnishings, by no means a too regular event, we needed to spread our wings further to the neighbouring borough of Stratford, not the one 'on -Avon' but rather the 'Stratford-atte-Bow,' to give the place its rather more sophisticated sounding name from the Tudor times. A shopping visit there would really be a treat – all of ten minutes away by bus – but worth it for the bigger shops and even a department store – this too was the scene on a very special occasion for lunch.

If we really felt like getting even more adventurous, we could go even further to Leytonstone, right on the very edge of suburban Essex and not really East London any more. This was really the very most dignified place to visit and even to mix with the up and coming Essex Suburban 'society,' all rather respectable for refugees' from Bow.

Nothing though could beat London's West End for the very special shopping outing and for that best coat or party outfit. Off we would go and begin at Oxford Circus, seeing both Oxford Street and Regent Street, which even from an early age I would visit with wide and open eyes, probably too because I wasn't paying for the purchases either!

For us the day began with the No 25 bus direct from Bow to Oxford Circus and from there, in the hub of the populace, to begin the shop round of the mighty department stores such as D.H. Evans, Dickens & Jones and Selfridges. Very specially too, Nan would buy an outfit, feeling very much a Duchess for those few moments and reveling in the occasion; there would be some shirts for Grandpop and Father and, no doubt, something for me too – certainly I would not be left out! This being the big day out, there would be both lunch and tea in the West End with at least one of the meals being taken in our favourite J. Lyons Corner Houses, of birthday party fame. Yet again, our return home to Bow would be under the weight of numerous parcels with me and the adults all having thoroughly enjoyed a commercial day out.

Strange, on reflection, to think that the London West End was the preferred shopping place of the family when the East End fashion markets were on our doorstep and where today it is very much worthwhile to visit for specialty clothing of decent quality and value, let alone the numerous factory shops now in existence. Obviously, for us in those times, it was the feeling of betterment that drove us westwards and also a typical case of 'the grass being greener.' I didn't complain – it was a good day out and a widening of my own personal horizons.

* * * *

By the mid 1950s, Uncle Dick changed his car to a big black Austin and with it came the chance for many more outings. I make no excuse, nor do I in any way feel bad about admitting that with those outing prospects and drives that I actually began to like the prospect of the Sunday visits. Of course, too, I by then felt much more secure about my own home life and realised that it was then absolutely certain that my father would not be taking me away from Bow.

Uncle Dick's new car had leather seats, heavy doors and disproportionately large wing mirrors – cars' eyes surely. The need in winter to sit with layers of coats, hats, scarves and gloves was later overcome with a modification to the car to include heating – or, rather, cool air blowing in air-conditioning style.

So in this very car, a stately progress would be made – Dick driving, Brenda in the back seat, very formally attired with hat and gloves and sitting regally next to father. Why did she not want to sit in the front with Dick? Perhaps she thought it more relative to her enhanced status to be in the back, chauffeur-style fashion!

Father sat in the back too, next to his sister, with kid leather gloves on, whatever the weather. Good – so that left the front seat free for me and I sat there very happily. Dick was a very kind person and made every effort to be nice and to look after me, although whenever he turned to talk to me, Brenda would command:

'Keep your eyes on the road, Dick!'

Father would nod in agreement. They were a real right pair to be brother and sister!

Dick had fitted an imitation, model toy driving wheel on to the front dashboard so that I could imagine steering and controlling the car, in fact copying all the driver's movements. What a sight that must have been to see a small pair of hands on the wheel with me barely tall enough then to be able to see out of the window, unless I was sat on some cushions.

No, I wasn't that small but the windows in that car were very high up!

What occurred as a very special event was a visit to Dick's relatives in Buckinghamshire which was something very much to look forward to. Firstly, it was a whole day away travelling by car and even at the very tender age of around ten, I had developed a liking of the countryside and loved to experience, if only briefly, that side of life – but not to be too far from the City though! These visits were based on the grown ideals of a true townie – lovely to visit the countryside for a change and even perhaps to imagine as a possible way of life for a few moments – all imagery and escapism because in reality it would always be the town for me – and that town would need to be London then and for wherever I went in future life too!

Naturally, the drive would begin from Buckhurst Hill and would be made in a kind of royal progress, the City and suburb types making an inspection visit to the country!

'Not too fast, Dick,' Brenda would command with regularity, although how it was possible to drive fast on 1950s-style small roads I am not altogether sure.

'Careful on the corners, then,' she would continue – Dick would grimace in the mirror, I would try to stifle my giggles and concentrate on my dummy driving wheel!

The route would take us from the suburbs of Essex and into Hertfordshire, first to St Albans with the fine Cathedral and there often to stop to have a look at the Roman remains of Verulanium. Soon afterwards we would reach the chocolate-box style villages of Buckinghamshire with such delightful names as Great and Little Kimble, Ashton Clinton and Stoke Mandeville.

Always the visit would be to Dick's own aunts and uncles living in a farm called Stockwell Lane. Off we would all troop in, an unlikely brigade, led by Brenda, always 'townie' resplendent with City hat and gloves, a fur coat in winter, very much inappropriately over-dressed, given both the poor state of the family and very down at heel cottage in which they lived but nevertheless adding to the characterisation of the event.

In the first home of the visit, there was a dim, dull kitchen with an enormous black and overpowering oven range. The range gave off a sort of smoky haze and, before long, the eyes would smart from both this and the difficulty of seeing in the dim overall light penetrating the room through the very small and rather dirty windows.

This would be the scene of our reception and location for a somewhat stifled and still conversation.

'How have you been keeping?'

'Oh fine, just fine, except for this cough, you know,' to the accompaniments of gentle nods all round.

'It's still too wet to plant the potatoes,' we would be told.

'Yes, I know – Dick can't trim our lawn either,' Brenda would reply trying to get in the same overall tone of country-talk conversation, and making herself sound so very foolish as a result.

Not at all surprisingly, father said nothing at all, looked generally gloomy and many times did not even bother to take off his bespoke kid gloves.

Other mutterings would follow before it was time to move on to the next 'victim,' but not before having collected some freshly new-laid eggs, and some mud on our heels, as proof of our visit to the countryside!

Less frequent visits to some of the other relatives would always cause problems; they lived in such remote and far-off corners of the county. I doubt if we would ever have found them at all were it not for the help of friendly, local policemen, to whom Dick was commanded by Brenda to ask directions.

'Down from London are you, fresh in these parts?' , but then kindly giving precise directions.

Little wonder for the difficulty when 'our royal party' finally arrived at the poor and unsuspecting relative – the home, set in a far corner of a field, was a converted old wooden railway carriage which, in itself, gave me untold delight! Inside were spirit lamps, an oil-stove and with an overwhelming musty smell. Imagine here the arrival of the hated and fur-coated Aunty Brenda with town shoes to match plus the kid-gloved father; what a sight it must have presented and a true regal progress to the country folk of Dick's relatives.

To end the round we would the drive through the beautiful Chiltern countryside to Bledlow, Chinnor Hill and Kingston Blount and the final relative victim of the day. Here at least was a house befitting Brenda's presence — modern (in an early 50s sense), detached with all 'mod cons' and extensive gardens and grounds backing on to the forest. They must have been Dick's relatives from the best side and their's was a bubbling, friendly household with always a huge home-made jam and cream sponge presented for tea, a guarantee as to the way to my heart!

Strangely though I could never understand why the lady always wore a hat inside her own house – perhaps it was to be in competition with Aunty Brenda's outdoor apparel. Still, it all made another element to the overall experience of a day out in Buckinghamshire!

It was quite a day – full of characters and people who, for me, spoke in rather strange accents but were very kind and homely. The real glory though was the chance to see and experience the beautiful Buckinghamshire countryside, a true feel of rural England at its best and a spreading of the horizons for a thorough City-boy!

*　*　*　*

So the year would move on, naturally interspaced with the inevitable school lessons, to the climax of Christmas, the winter holiday from school and the pantomime season. Nan and Grandpop would always ensure the very best possible Christmas season in our house.

For us, preparations began weeks before in October when Nan would make the Christmas puddings in which we would all take turns at stirring and 'having a wish.' In another month it would be time for baking the cake and making the fruit mix for the mince pies until the final hectic moments for the run-up to the great day – to the market for the freshest of vegetables, also to get a huge ham and to look for the turkey to take pride of place. For that, I often went with Grandpop direct to Smithfield Market in the City of London, where there were many poultry stalls and what a fine sight that was, butchers in straw hats and bright red aprons with row upon row of turkeys hanging from up high in the ceilings.

All this, and then the present buying and wrapping to add to the mounting expectation. Finally came the home decoration – always a proper and fresh tree, the fairy lights, paper chains around the room and from corner to corner with a huge lantern bell in the centre. Once again, the front bedroom was ready to be our 'front parlour' for the festive season.

However, before all the home festivities would be the school party at term end and a chance for all once again to tout their party clothes. Plenty of jellies, pies, cakes, games and funny hats with that rather unreal feeling when teachers tried to act jolly and 'normal' whilst being not too conspicuous in odd jolly hats, the over excited pupils dropping left-over jellies into the desk ink wells, there to remain congealed into the summer months. There, I've owned up now and its too late to get expelled!

All the growing excitement always made Christmas Eve a long and seemingly never ending day – I   simply could not wait to see what Father Christmas had brought me. The worries of whether he would remember to call and not forget the address were made even more frightening when we no longer had open fireplaces at home and even some of the chimneys had been blocked off.

'Grandpop, can you please make sure that the actual open chimneys are clear so Father Christmas won't make any mistakes when he's here?'

'Of course, Boy, we will light a small fire in one of the open chimneys on Christmas Eve afternoon, let it cool down in time, then he'll know where to drop the parcels,' Grandpop suitable reassured me.

With so many thoughts on the mind, it was of little wonder that I couldn't sleep! I own up to being rather old before I finally didn't believe in Father Christmas any more.

Somehow, the sleep finally came but I was sure to wake up early and later in life, when I knew that my 'night visitor' was Grandpop, who would always wear an overcoat and red hat, I would fein sleep during the presents delivery in a big sack, a left-over from the coal days (but cleaned, I hasten to add).

Then it would seem hours to wait until everybody had gone to bed before I could switch my light on and start to unwrap the parcels. What thrills! – always Rupert, some more books, some clothes, and, most importantly, some more new parts for my rapidly expanding collection of model railways. Only then would the excitement give way to sleep and, contented, I would slumber a few hours before awaking on Christmas morning and to all the pleasures of that special day.

With very early bustles in the kitchen, the turkey would be placed in the oven and the vegetables all prepared and ready to be cooked later. There was little time left in the early part of the morning to enjoy the new presents as first was the traditional visit to church. Home then by late morning in time for the visitation from Brenda and Dick, who would 'take tea' before continuing their regal procession elsewhere.

After that there was always an hour or so to try and test the new toys and pieces of model railway equipment until even I was hungry and ready for the superbly prepared feast that Nan would deliver to the table.

To begin, there would be a home-made soup, something like tomato or mushroom, to be followed by the smoked salmon course. Then the turkey, all lush and golden brown, accompanied by 'roasties' (potatoes and parsnips), sprouts and various stuffing's and sauces, and the ham. Finally, the suitably aged Christmas pudding, with enough brandy poured over to allow a 'flaming entrance,' all rounded off with the mince pies.

The meal was always timed to be over by 3pm, in time for the Queen's speech on television, the elders would toast the Royal Family, I'd follow the example with lemonade; we would all stand up for the speech in a fine tradition and Christmas afternoon highlight.

Back then to the games and setting up more of the model train sets; the others all disappeared to the kitchen for a game called 'washing-up,' but I didn't understand the rules of that game then so didn't want to take part, but was told that I would need to learn the rules for one day in the future!

Soon it was time for tea and the fabulous cake. Evening was reserved for games for all and father would enter into the spirit of the event – party hat as well. I can only reflect that, by then, he was beginning to be affected by some warming glasses of wine and festive cheer! Tiredness would by then overcome me and I would be off to bed, so missing the day's final ritual – turkey and ham sandwiches in the late evening but I would make up for that another day.

Later days of the Christmas holiday were traditionally spent with visits to the aunts and uncles with more turkey, more cakes and more food generally, although with Brenda and Dick that was questionable. Typical of their festive cheer was that they had a Christmas tree with battery lights so that they could switch it on just for the occasional few seconds!

My sights were set on the days to enjoy at home before the new school term began. That was the time to enjoy all the new toys, to visit friends and exchange Christmas recollections, toys and games. It was rather wonderful that, without envy, all of us school friends enjoyed the experience of trying and exchanging each other's toys – the same too with the model railway collections, which even in the 1950s were becoming so extensive and diverse that the variety available always ensured somebody would have something unique to the collection. The sight along Bow Road then was a constant crocodile stream of children running along to exchange toys and model train engines in the Christmas aftermath! Christmas 1955 was typical of the pattern spent in this idyllic way and the happy visit to the London Palladium for the traditional pantomime was my 'icing on the cake.'

* * * *

The return to school at the beginning of the following January was different – it was back to the primary school for the very last terms and time for the '11-plus' exams in the spring of 1956 to decide which 'lucky' secondary school would have the pleasure of my company for the ensuing seven years. Who would be the honoured receipt of my personal 'royal appointment?'

'Do your best, love.'

'Do well.'

Words of encouragement from Nan and Grandpop as I set out from home on the morning of the exam, even a 'Good luck' call from father as he headed off to the Underground and his daily journey to work at Lambeth.

Whatever the merits or otherwise of the '11-plus' exam, it did do something to concentrate young minds and it excited families with the thoughts of something positive to aim for educationally. I was no different in this and for once knuckled down to the scholastic challenge, which for me was a record in itself and proved the system!

Bow was really quite fortunate with several Grammar schools, always the parent's preferred choice, in the immediate catchment area and, in addition, there were a couple of half-decent secondary Schools. At the bottom of the pile, and to be avoided at all costs, was a pretty awful school for the 'left-over's' and it had that stigma about which everybody knew and to which nobody would want to own up as being one of the pupils. Fortunately for me, the said Miss Baker had continued to weave her magic spell even on to me as to Aunt Ethel earlier and accordingly I actually passed the exam!

One particular Grammar school was chosen by my family because it was known to be 'good,' had a long history, was in Bow and was also the school that Bill, Ethel's husband, had attended in the 1930s – surely not another learning establishment for me where an old teacher would have family memories! Anyway, that was the family choice and so off I went to the interview which I only recall with a rather dim haze, or, in other words, maintaining my usual dimness. The head teacher at the interview I remember wore a black-gown over his suit, the gown swaying in the breeze when he walked, rather like 'bat-man.'

I was, at the same time, both impressed and over-awed by the surroundings of pannelled hallways, a rather magnificent stone and marble main entrance hall, with a war memorial for former pupils.

Crowning all was a huge shield with the names of all former head teachers going back so many years, too many years in my young mind to have been possible. Overall, it was quite unlike anything that I had ever experienced of a premises to actually be called 'a school.'

Two days after the interview, a letter arrived at home 'inviting' me as a pupil – did that mean I had a choice – most probably not – and so everything was settled for my further education to begin later that year in September.

Before all that there was a rush of preparation and activity as befits such an important step in life – new   clothes and the formal school uniform to be bought – blazer and cap, etc. needed to be purchased from the school's 'selected outfitter,' which meant a journey to the outer reaches of North East London, which could have been Mongolia to me, such a new and 'foreign' area that it was. The saving grace was that the trip entailed a train journey on the main line from Liverpool Street which, in itself, put a seal of approval on the adventure.

Nan and father were on hand to choose from the long list of purchases although the choice was quite strict – specific shade of grey trousers, white shirts, and a cap big enough to fit at the required angle, a scarf only for use from November to March irrespective of any cold weather at other times of the Autumn or Spring. This, then was to be the tone of my soon to be new educational establishment and I couldn't help wondering whether the Dickens similarity was not once again becoming part of my life!

With all preparations done, there was time for some relaxation and the final days at the old primary school to enjoy – yes, it really was possible to 'enjoy' those days without any more real lessons, quite a lot of fun and being sufficiently unaware of what the new school would behold. I was fortunate too that three of my immediate friends at the primary school were to come with me to the new school. It must have been an essence of the brilliancy of my class – and my efforts upon it – that nobody ended up at the local secondary school 'pits'; more likely, though, all thanks to the redoubtable Miss Baker!

The end of the primary school years, teacher good-byes and for Miss Baker her eventual retirement timed to coincide with my own leaving – how's that for a coincidence! Ahead then immediately six whole weeks of freedom before education career part two!

A return holiday to Folkestone was arranged for August which, as always, was really wonderful. I stayed for two weeks with Nan and Grandpop with father coming at weekends, and we were back at our favourite and well-chosen 'private hotel.' No doubt these visits must have caused some difficult memories for Nan and Grandpop as they remembered the earlier visits with my mother but whilst I had occasional thoughts, I was fortunate to have the lesser developed emotions of an 11 year old to soften the blow.

The Folkestone holiday followed the usual and extremely happy and well-ordered pattern but for that year, and as an additional treat prior to my soon to begin secondary school career, a special extra was excitingly included. We had a day trip to France and therefore my very first footsteps outside of these shores and on to foreign soil – and with my own personal passport too. Also, this was the first time that Nan had been out of the country but, of course, Grandpop was a seasoned traveller!

The special day began with an earlier breakfast than usual which, no doubt, rather disrupted the orderliness of the 'private hotel,' before we set off for the harbour with very much the feeling of being seasoned explorers.

Now we were ourselves amongst the passengers joining the ship, a sight I had seen from the quayside so many times in the past. Once on board, there was time for a quick inspection around the ship – 'Canterbury,' one of the then British Railways cross-channel ferries, already by that time quite well worn and with a very staid and elderly looking black and yellow straight funnel. Naturally, as with our 'famous' Margate trips, we were on deck ready for departure and Grandpop, with his usual Navy knowledge, fully described the sailing operation:

'Pulling on the port line now, Boy – and look there' he said pointing to the end of the harbour wall 'that's the Blue Peter flag flying to show our departure'– and so we were off!

Folkestone harbour wall soon receded to starboard and it wasn't long though before the Channel swell caught the ship:

'Oops' said Nan, who had some misgivings about an 'ocean voyage.'

'I'm not over keen on the 'water' 'she said to which Grandpop replied:

'You've been up the Thames, mate,' without perhaps realising the difference, seasoned sailor that he was!

The White Cliffs along the coast between Folkestone and Dover were slowly receding and when looking to the other side we could see the Folkestone Leas and the very 'private hotel' where we were staying

'The gong will be going for breakfast now,' Nan said 'but I don't think that I would fancy anything to eat for the moment' she continued, an obvious reflection on her inner feelings about the sea voyage!

We had gone for about an hour, around mid-Channel, when Nan said:

'How much longer, Pop?'

'Oh, only about three more hours,' Grandpop replied, laughing at Nan's face and grimace.

'Just joking, mate – only about another hour at the most and, look, over there,' he said pointing to the distant left side of the bow;

'That's the French coast!'

France – and my first sight of distant shores, a foreign land. Full ranges of stereotype images rushed through my head in, a horrible and true 'little Englander' fashion of berets and Breton jumpers – croissants, baguettes and the ideal of garlic sellers on bicycles would have been alien to me at that time.

The approaching quay and the first excitement knowing me was the train at the harbourside station, waiting to take those passengers bound for Paris and beyond – yes, 'beyond' in my mind to include the Orient Express and Istanbul, my imagination running wild!

We had arrived! – joining the other passengers we poured off the ship down the gangway and into the customs hall with me proudly and excitedly clutching my gleaming new passport, Nan pretty overawed as well. Our feet only touched actual French soil for a few moments before we boarded a bus for our day excursion – not yet being seasoned enough travellers to actually go it alone for too long.

We saw the sights of Boulogne, the bustling fish harbour, the central marketplace, the shop-lined streets and excited bustle and finally to the old town with the delightful City walls and lookout towers and to view the magnificent, although somewhat war damaged, Cathedral of Notre Dame, the whole tour a real forerunner of what would be known in later years in the travel business as 'the City Tour!' On, next, out of the town and along the coast.

'There's our ship over there' – as if we owned it!

As we drove along the coast and as we had already then been out of England for all of four hours, there was an urge to look to see if we could see our White Cliffs across the Channel, for reassurance obviously, but the slight haze meant only a dim, distant outline – oh well, nothing left for it other than to remain foreign for the day!

Next on the day's agenda was a stop in the small seaside town of Wimereux, very beautifully set with some fine and grand villas, town houses with colourful shutters in the fine streets leading to the sea or along the bustling main centre street. Our destination was to a restaurant in the main street into which we descended for my first experience of a 'foreign' meal which, in deference to us day trippers and to make us feel 'at home,' was roast beef! It's a bit like chips on the Costa's in today's world but anyway, I felt abroad – at least the traffic drove on the opposite side of the road.

The return to Boulogne was via the surrounding countryside, all very rolling and pretty, rather reminiscent of Kent. This whole area of France, the Pas de Calais remains rather untouched even today and makes for a fine exploration destination yet now with the added benefit of the nearby hypermarkets for good value purchases, the beautiful cheeses, wine and spirits, and bread to make your mouth water; take a detailed look too in Boulogne – all very charming and still with a fine enough French feel to make you feel abroad for the day.

On the way back that day, a stop was made to see the Colonne de la Grande Armée, commemorating Napoleon's Boulogne Camp 1803/1805.

'Have we come all this way just to see Nelson's column?' said Nan 'Anyway, where's Nelson?'

This was much to the amusement of the surrounding passengers and a sure sign not to consider European Union entry still for many years to come! Oh well, we cannot help being the English abroad!

After our 'grand tour' we had about two hours then on our own in Boulogne, just to walk and look about but not daring to enter any shops for fear of language problems, this being well before the time of the now regular French invasion by the British intent on bargain purchases. In fact, it was not so long after the mid-1950s that the invasion was in reverse – boat loads of French people coming to Folkestone and the south coast to swarm in the supermarkets here – 'Le cut white bread' – they must have been mad and would have been better to stay at home with all the delicious bakeries available in France!

The heat of the August afternoon and with all the walking around, and tradition forced upon us, the need for tea (!) – so we descended into our chosen cafe to be honoured with our custom.

'P-O-T-OF-T-E-A,' Grandpop ordered loudly, repeating even more loudly and forming the letter 'T' with his hands. Whatever, it worked and we had tea served with a plate of the most delicious cakes and pastries imaginable, enough then to begin an everlasting love affair with France – the way to a boy's heart…

Rather tired but with very happy memories, we returned to the coach and back finally through the soon becoming rather well-known streets and along the quayside to the harbour and the waiting ship, this time 'Maid of Orlean's.'

'Hurry on board before all the passengers arrive from the Paris boat train,' the guide suggested and he was right – with the arrival of the said boat train the ship was swarmed with people.

We were alright, though, on the open deck in the sunny evening ready to see the departure, then the receding French coastline and to enjoy the return crossing to Folkestone.

What a tired and excited boy finally returned to the 'private hotel' that night, not to say how tired Nan and Grandpop must have been looking after me bouncing around with non-stop chat all day.

After the holiday, and back again in Bow, there were still two weeks before the start of the new school, time enough to meet up with friends and for me to relate to them, with a sense of an adventurer, tales of my exploits in foreign parts. Everything is, of course, relative and today, in the early 21st century, day trips to France are nothing more than jumping on a bus. But that visit in 1956 was long before the idea of mass package holiday foreign travel and I don't think it was in anyway over the top to have had the feelings of having taken part in a real adventure. Neither too did the feelings diminish when we made repeat trips during our annual Folkestone holiday over the coming years, becoming very seasoned and experienced Francophile travellers as our day trips went further afield by about 40 km to Le Touquet!

Having then been suitably refreshed with the holidays and all the new experiences, I suppose that I then felt about as ready as I would ever be to continue with the next stage of the education process and the new school in September 1956.

Chapter 6

Time For The Grammar School

There was an immediate positive advantage for me as a result of the first day at a completely new school and that was the day's start was set for 10.30am as opposed for the regular time of 9.00am – so for the year of 1956 my summer holiday was a whole 90 minutes longer – sheer bliss. So, if that couldn't put me in a good mood for the future, then what could? In reality though, every extra minute was necessary with all the fuss necessary to get ready in the new school uniform and so be ready to enter the new world in pristine style.

Whenever a major event occurred in my young life, and what could be more significant than such a day as this, a 'proper' breakfast would always be Nan's solution to prepare for such a highly important happening. So I sat down in the kitchen for a plate of porridge with cream, then followed with bacon, sausage, mushrooms and tomatoes, fried bread and potatoes, a little scrambled egg:

'Not too much egg, thanks, Nan' – bearing in mind my thoughts about eggs that didn't come straight out of a tin, wartime 'baby' that I was!

And if that wasn't all enough, to finish there were lashings of toast and marmalade and plenty of tea. Of course, in our household tea would always be the beverage in those days. Coffee would only be reserved for the 'elevenses' break, that eloquent name for the mid-morning time with coffee and biscuits.

However, the breakfast was a real set-up, the only negative point being that there were then so many sticky fingers and greasy mouth spots that it was almost necessary for a full and thorough wash all over again before being able to make entry to the outside world.

Thus I was prepared and ready for the new adventures of life – set up and raring to go! Many best wishes and warm feelings from Nan and Grandpop, even regards from father as he headed out to work. As I left, I had a good feeling and felt rather resplendent in my new school uniform of blazer, grey trousers (still the short variety at that stage), school tie and cap with badge so that I was instantly recognisable to all around – as if anybody bothered to look, but I walked tall.

Everything was different right from the start. To begin with, I used to walk eastwards along Bow Road to my old primary school – now, significantly, I turned to the opposite direction right on leaving home;

'Go West, Young Man' – and that was me then, going westwards along Bow Road and in the ultimate direction that was to the City and West End of London, so very significant then in my young mind, as always was the idea of the east of Bow compared to the West of the London bright lights. The walk was though only 15 minutes in that direction and the postal address was still 'E3' = Bow. I was a 'big boy' by then and, of course, went by myself, thinking that all passers-by and, indeed, the whole world, was interested in and monitoring my progress – reality was that nobody was in the slightest bit interested!

Because the grammar school in fact recruited its pupils from a wide area including westwards towards the City and eastwards to the far-flung reaches of suburban Essex, the numbers of pupils actually attending from the immediate surrounding area of Bow was therefore rather few. During my walk on that first morning I saw no other obvious-looking 'victims' until crossing to join the final road leading up to the school where many were walking having first come to the Underground station at Mile End. The few friends joining me from my first school all lived in the Bromley-by-Bow area and so being over the limit which, I think, was one and a half miles or 30 minute's walk from the school, were allowed a bus or underground pass for the school journey.

The last few yards to the school meant walking along a rather fine square, Tredegar Square, of what had once been very grand Victorian houses, three and four storey's high with imposing front gardens and wrought iron fences and gates. Then, the houses were very much run down and needing some attention and most were turned into flats rather than individual homes.

Our small contingent of friends all met up at the school gates, for once not having very much to say to each other and perhaps not exactly recognising ourselves in our spotless and brand-new school clothes. We had a quick check all around that ties were straight, caps at the right angle, shoes clean and laces tight and this was it – the first entry into the higher scholastic world.

An older boy, one obviously luckily nearer to the end of his school career and in a very much disheveled state of well worn uniform, spotted us:

'Hey, you lot – new boys?' – we nodded – 'Then go round to the side street and the main entrance. This area's not for you!'

So, dutifully we did just that, went around to the main entrance. That original interview and that very first day, the one with the delayed start, were the only times that I had the dubious honour of entering school by the impressive entrance hall – the one with the stone and marble floor, panelled walls and grim war memorial. Ahead of us, to greet us, I thought, stood one of those austere school-masterly looking figures – another 'bat-man' in black gown.

'Name?'

'Pardon,' I replied in confusion and not a specially good start, probably receiving a dull note relative to my brain from the very start!

'Name?' – oh, I got it that time, although I was wondering why the others had let me take the lead upon entrance!

Fortunately? No, I think not, unfortunately would seem then to me to have been a better choice of word! So, my name was on the list and therefore I was duly admitted. Nothing other then to be left all alone for just a few seconds which seemed absolutely never-ending whilst my friends queued behind me went through the same ritual until all of a minute had passed and we went through together to the 'big hall.' And what a big hall – galleried with rows of benches and walls lined with some pictures, shields and more of those lists of past headmasters going back perhaps over 300 years, or infinity in my mind. Forward was the stage mounted by the Head's chair as a centrepiece to the main hall; off around all sides of the hall, both upstairs and downstairs, were various classrooms – the 'seats of learning.' Two mighty skylights and domes were set high in the roof. And that wasn't all, soon I and my friends would find still more classrooms – the special rooms for arts, geography, music room, the library, a separate science block and gymnasium – I would need all of my potential seven years there to find my way around!

Everything was so much more grand and different from the comfortable small and homely feel of the primary school.

'Gosh!' – was the general and over-awed comment amongst me and my friends. We all sat completely dumb-struck, not really taking it in, as the minutes ticked by to the appointed hour of 10.30. More and more boys arrived, all united in general bewilderment, until in all we were a total of 90 new entrants, absolutely 'wet behind the ears,' all ideally ready to be set into three classes of 30 pupils each as the 'new' and with the sophisticated title of 1A, 1B or 1C. Each of us were allocated accordingly and by surname I was sent to 1B; all my friends, by virtue of their surname, were in either 1A or 1C. It suddenly dawned on me that I was alone!

'I want to go home,' were my thoughts in a nutshell!

Still very little was said or spoken as we sat in our three appointed groups and this was probably the only time in a school career that all boys were so quiet! I was truly now part of the secondary education system.

This was a school with a strictly 'boys only' policy which had never changed throughout its history. There was a 'sister' school for girls some half a mile away but with strictly no connection or contact. Here then was a male-dominated education system and yet again I was experiencing a bastion of the old at a period in time when values were beginning to change to the new. Boys only for its like minded range of subjects and values has some advantages but, in retrospect, does not prepare you mentally nor emotionally for later life – unless one has leanings to become a monk – and this was a major failing of 20th century education inherited from the past. Having said that, and again in retrospect, this failing was compensated by the range of subjects, disciplines and values which were exercised.

The school bell, a governing factor to immediate school life both at 10.30 on that first day and throughout the next seven years, rang out and robot like, everybody, me included, sheep-like went to our allocated pens – sorry – classrooms.

That wretched bell which, as I say, for seven years would govern my life and to which I and others reacted with total dependency. The bell – for the day's start, for the end and beginning of individual lessons, when you would move senselessly from one allocated classroom to the next, totally unaware of all around you but just intent on not being late. The bell – to signify break time and the mid-morning bottle of milk (surely not from 'That Dairy' in Bow Road – who would ever have attracted their attention!). The bell to announce lunch-time and 75 minutes to announce the beginning of the afternoon session. The bell, the best ring of the day – finally to signify the end of the school day and release from the institution of learning and a return to the outside world and home. Could it really be the same bell that did all the same things but for which each sound held vastly different significances?

Quietly then, perhaps, for one of the only few times in my school life, I went with my new colleagues – all similarly and momentarily quiet and subdued – into the allocated classrooms. It was a much bigger room than that which I had been used to at primary school, therefore significantly showing that I was on the way up. Once in the room, there was a 'free-for-all' rush to select a desk but it didn't matter so much for me because I didn't know anybody anyway. In finally selecting a desk, it was just to remember what we had discussed amongst my old friends – don't sit at the front, that was too close under the teacher's eye; don't sit at the back because any self-respecting teacher would always pick on the back row for answers which also was the easiest place to sleep. No, the middle of the class was the place to be and neither up by the wall or next to the window, no – the middle of the room in every sense. I claimed my territory – the very middle of the middle row, you know, like being born in Bow – being at the very centre!

It would be most polite to say that the desks were 'historical' – they must have been new for the time when the school was founded, remembering that long list of past headmasters! To say also that the desks were well worn would be an understatement; to say that they were well engraved was spot-on, bearing the carvings of past pupils who had already experienced all that which I was about to experience.

Briefly I had time to look around and become acquainted with the new classroom. Immediately, I was delighted to note that I had rather a good view of the passing London to Norfolk railway line. This proved to be most beneficial over my school time, when I was able to switch off from droning teachers and check if the 10.30 from Liverpool Street to Norwich was on time!

Enter the teacher – sorry, 'form-master,' yet another 'bat-man' in a black gown. He didn't have to say

'Quiet' – we were! – Nobody was making a sound, let alone a noise and we were all too pre-occupied with our new and somewhat austere surroundings.

'I want to go home'

There was that recurring theme in my mind again!

Introductions followed, both from 'bat-man' and from the individual boys who had all been 'invited' to stand up and introduce themselves. My turn, legs like jelly, dry-mouthed, to mention my name 'Sir.'

'Sit'

That's one way of having some idea of what it must be like to be a dog!

So it went on for 30 times until everybody had introduced themselves. Then followed a breakdown of school rules:

'No running between classes, no talking in class, no eating in class, chewing sweets never tolerated, punctuality at all times' (except of course at the time of the last bell of the day, I should have noted).

The list of do's and don'ts went on and on as I and the others tried to keep up with the writing of the instructions.

Next, the timetable was dictated by the 'bat-man' – and what a timetable. No longer 'sums' as in primary school, but 'Maths'; then dedicated periods of geography, history, English and so many strange (to me!) subjects like science, physics and chemistry – all so much a new world and a beacon of education. When that list was finished, then came the details of the weekly homework arrangements and a schedule of the nightly tasks. All this was enough to have absorbed for one morning and then it was time for the customary freedom of lunchtime. I rushed home on that first day, as I would continue to do daily for a short while until I decided that having friends at school, it was better to stay on at school for lunch.

School lunches – now there's a topic for discussion!

Apart from the fact that first it was necessary to queue in all weathers in the school playground (the dining hall was in a detached building away from the main school); next was the mad rush upstairs to the dining hail itself when the bell rang (there's that bell again), then to pay the money to the very ferocious Head 'bat-man's' secretary, one shilling!, all before finally getting to the counter. On display was always a huge pot, indeed, caldron, of mashed potatoes – you couldn't call them 'creamed' as the potatoes would never have seen butter and milk! – trays of very watery vegetables and meat or stew of some sort, nothing particularly appetising. And if you didn't want something?

'Did you bring a note, Sonny?' – was the message barked by the supervisor!

Still, there was always the pudding to look forward to – and custard, or rather water with one grain of custard powder in it! Anyway, it was good to stay on at school over the lunch-time with friends and there was always a host of school clubs and activities in the time between the culinary delights of lunch and the first lesson of the afternoon.

The early secondary school days were established with a pattern which would continue as the virtual norm for seven years. Happily, to the small group of friends coming from the primary school were added several new ones until you could almost say that a 'class set' was established – several of us were to remain firm friends not only through the school years but beyond too.

Interestingly, everybody at the school came from different backgrounds. No longer was I in a class of fellow East-Londoners, as in primary school. Here, in the grammar school, boys came from the same area as my family aunts – suburban Essex – many commuting the many miles each day to and from school. In my young mind I did envy that some of my fellow pupils actually had to travel by train to and from school and occasionally I would go home via the Underground – for all of one station – just to feel part of these travel arrangements and to identify with this superior feeling. These thoughts were so one-sided because it never did occur to me that I had the advantage being back home and starting my homework within 15 minutes of leaving school, whereas these other school-fellows had over an hour's journey before they got home. Conversely, I never considered that, on a cold and foggy winter morning, I could have that extra time tucked up warmly in bed! – an obvious benefit of Bow, which I then failed to appreciate.

Whilst maybe not immediately, I do realise now that in later years of school I did suffer disturbing feelings because others in my class lived in much nicer places than me; had closer links to the countryside and a better actual home life standard and very lovely homes which became increasingly apparent when making home visits to my friends. By reflecting now though,

I should have realised the numerous plus points of my own surroundings, my involvement with and enjoyment of, all things London – the theatre, outings and my own varied activities that more than compensated for the short fallings of Bow as a place.

What benefits then of school? Well, it certainly wasn't the heavy workload of the regular evening homework which, even on the best of days, was probably at least a couple of hours and much longer than that in the later years. At the time, I could not see how the two words – 'benefits' and 'school' could possibly be linked together in the same sentence! Overall, I must confess to saying that I absolutely disliked school. Frankly, I was not an especially good learner apart from being reasonable at a few chosen subjects. I was hopeless at most sports and games and suffered enormously on many wet and muddy sports fields or pointless runs through Hainault Forest, in Essex, where the school playing fields were situated. On top of al that, I felt most of the teachers had misplaced bullying tendencies and on many occasions I and my circle of friends were the victims of bullying from the older boys in the school, and upon which those in authority turned a blind eye. Generally, it was a sufferance rather than any degree of pleasure that would best summarise my school years, at least until the last years when I did enjoy it better, probably because I then realised that the end was in sight!

If in any way I can now appreciate anything about school from the teaching and learning aspect, it is because I can reflect from a long distance and realise the values instilled and learnt and erase the bad experiences, putting those down to life's path.

Forget then the cold and wet games days – remember instead the thrill on the morning of such days when the Games Master came to the class:

'Snow on the ground' or 'Fog today' or 'Ground waterlogged,' leading on then to the tremendous message:

'No games, today, boys!'

with the result that we would stay on in school in the afternoon and could do our homework before then getting home an hour early!

Forget too the 'mock' exams twice a year and the fright of the results, so publically announced:

'You!' said 'bat-man' pointing directly and severely at me 'Physics – your total mark 1 out of 100 – I could never believe that such a pitiful result could be possible in all my years of teaching – pathetic boy!'

Gosh, I thought, I must have mis-spelt my name let alone not got the Bunsen burner to light!

Remember instead the geography result:

'94 percent – well done!'

Forget the three times per year school reports sent home to father with the oft repeated phrase:

'Must try harder!' – did that mean, I wondered, must try harder to escape!

And on the subject of school reports – why did the aunts always 'insist' on seeing them? – They must all have enjoyed seeing me squirm like a garden worm!

Remember instead the comments for history:

'Ploughs ahead and understands the topics far in advance of the rest of the class!'

Forget the remarks about the maths exam:

'He has a minus capability!' – which, I suppose, was some pathetic attempt at a joke.

Instead, remember the positive comments about efforts in English literature:

'A natural ability to appreciate.'

Forget too the frightening experience at the end of the first full year at the grammar school when we had all taken our end of year exams in which I ended up at nineteenth position in class (the class total was thirty, I say to seek gratification!). Only then for the Headmaster – the Chief 'bat-man' to announce to the whole class that I should be sent from the school to the dreaded secondary school for having come '29th in the class position. That stupid and short-sighted 'bat-man' had mis-read the results list – and what did that tell of 'bat-man's' capabilities? Anyway, it caused me absolute internal mayhem wondering how I would be able to tell those at home and I physically lived in unconfined fear for days on end. I was too timid to point out the mistake, nor to take the matter up with my form-master, I just wallowed in self-pity and this completely diminished the wonderful thoughts of the upcoming summer holidays that year.

The hell and gloom was only finally lifted when the full exam results were posted on the notice board, and my nineteenth position was confirmed and the two unfortunate soles at the 29th and 30th positions merely had it noted by their names that, in the new school year, they were to concentrate on their weakest subject.

I think that I can be forgiven for harbouring some negative thoughts of my school experiences and for the fact that a certain degree of manipulation is necessary for positive thinking. But as I have noticed so many times in life, I was glad to have had the opportunity of experiencing the old system at a time before things changed for ever. Best was the specialisation, the established traditions and sense of occasion, just in fact to be able to say in later life:

'I was there, I experienced that,' I think is tremendously valuable.

There, as I think you'll know by now, certainly plenty of things to forget and the benefit of passing time to aid the reflection process!

The awful gym lessons and the tyrannical and absolutely severe ex-Army Sergeant Major:

'No excuses – I'll cane you if you don't vault the horse!'

'Yes, Sir – Sarge,' etc.

That dreaded gym-horse – I wish that I had come back to school in the deep of night to let it out to pasture!

Or the art lessons,

'Laughing in my face – get out and stand in the corridor' the art Master – who wouldn't laugh at some of his very strange drawings!

Then what about the most chilling school sound of all – the swish of the cane hitting some unfortunate posterior, which, thankfully, was only mine on one occasion in my school career, and which I thoroughly deserved, I might add.

Enough, now, of all these negatives and turn into a more positive mode, because as I have tried to record, not simply insist, there were plenty of positive experiences if not immediately apparent.

The whole host of school activities not connected with the immediate syllabus of learning, were indeed very varied and special. The music department was very active and immediately my interest in music and the theatre, thankfully already instilled in me from my early childhood by Nan and Grandpop, was further enhanced and developed as a result. The enthusiasm of the music teacher was infectious, especially so when considering the school was for boys only and in East London at that. The permanent membership of the after-hours music club was usually around 100 boys, that is to say nearly 20% of the whole school had an interest.

Apart from the class and after-school activities, I was lucky to be able to join in my later school career, many visits to concerts and the opera, furthering still more and widening my scope of these activities. That alone is enough to be grateful for the school experience although try telling me that at the time!

In parallel with the music department, one of the team of English teachers, a very pleasant and affable non 'bat-man' like character from New Zealand, specialised in Drama. His sheer enthusiasm too developed and widened my theatre interests. Consider frequent visits by young teenagers in the late 50s to theatres like the Old Vic or, in the summer-time, to the Open Air Theatre in Regent's Park to enjoy – yes, I really do mean – enjoy – a variety of Shakespeare plays. Simply, because the teacher took the trouble to discuss and explain the plot prior to the theatre visit, then spent the interval on questions and answers, then followed up the visit with a thorough review, all to develop the sound interest and understanding. The haziness and false mystique of the classics was therefore opened up for me and my school fellows and a natural appreciation developed as a result.

Together, the drama and music teachers would put into production three or four performances each school year – classical plays including our own 'interpretation' of performances we had seen in the theatre. Later we would include some Gilbert and Sullivan before raising the stakes still further to include Handel. It would not be for me to comment on the standard or quality of the production or performances, because I was biased and too involved, but I suppose they were acceptable even though the accompanying 'orchestra' were always pretty basic.

These performances were, naturally, always inflicted upon the luckiest families who all dutifully attended – for me that meant that even sometimes I managed to get my father to come along with Nan and Grandpop and that frequently meant that Brenda and Dick would come too – so that would mean that for my family alone we would contribute to the 'house full' notices. Whether the family, or in fact the audience in general, actually enjoyed the performance is another matter – it was for them more to wait and watch for their individual siblings and to applaud specifically:

'Oh, you were so good, son.'

Such was the general interval comment from various members of the audience, but not my father!

'It was – ah – good, love,' Nan and Grandpop would say politely if it was a classics play, but more enthusiastically

'Oh, we really liked that,' when there was any music element which reflected their own real taste in the theatre.

If the family were sitting too near the front, I found that difficult when being on the stage so, as in my class philosophy. I always tried to ensure that they all sat in the middle of the hall. If I could see them, I would always notice father sitting severely in pseudo-pretence actually enjoying it or knowing what was going on! The inflictions and torments of school productions! – but enjoyable for those involved.

Apart from being able to enjoy surreptitious train spotting from behind an upheld maths book in class, a very active railway club was a great thrill of the school years with fellow 'anoraks' coming together once a week for talks, lectures, film shows and the opportunity of exchanging everybody's cherished list of engine numbers. I became even more enthusiastic about railways because of this club and the enthusiasm spread over to many weekends, spending hours on wind and rain swept platforms with notepad in hand, religiously noting all the passing locomotive numbers. A harmless enough activity I suppose, but selfishly dull and boring to look back on nevertheless. Endless, mostly useless, facts and statistics were recorded, notes compared and loyalties challenged between friends:

'London Midland Black Fives, are the best!'

'No they're not – Western Castles.'

'You are talking rubbish – what about Southern Schools?' And so the endless discussion went on about the various Railway Region's engines. If I and others had directed such enthusiasm and thoughts to school curriculum subjects and lessons, then I would have done better than 1% in the physics exam!

Alongside this activity was another growing interest developed by the Camera Club. So, not only now could I bore everybody with a list of engine numbers, but I could also complement the boredom with endless photographs too! That was what exactly happened too, very selfishly.

Then, if all this wasn't enough, I and some friends, as we became even more 'leading lights' of the Railway Club began to organise Saturday trips to various engine sheds and railway works – a total and blind involvement completely oblivious to all else. So, dear reader, let's say enough of all this before you put the book down in disgust.

Forgive me if I give the impression that through all my school years, the most notable and positive result and memories come from the pleasure and hobby fulfillments as opposed to the academic result – but in reality this is true in any case.

'You're pleasure bent' would be how Nan would put it!

However, I was not if I may be permitted to say so, a complete scholastic failure but any positive result was most selective and – if I may give myself the indulgence and permission to use the word – 'brilliance' manifested itself only in a few handful of subjects, such as geography, history and English lIterature.

Without doubt, the reason why geography was 'it' was simply because the subject dealt with knowledge of places I associated with holidays, trips and general pleasure activities – no doubt the early steamer trips to Margate began the interest! Yes, really!

Another notable factor and plus point was that geography involved active field trips away from the school for the day, that was high incentive enough in itself. But going on a school field trip meant going on a train – you've probably now guessed the rest!

One of the geography teachers was absolutely and enthusiastically mad which, of course, amongst impressionable boys was in itself catching. I hope though that I never picked up his over-enthusiasm shown on one such field trip to Kent when he excitedly picked up a piece of rubble from the ground:

'Boys – look here – this piece of rock proves the extent of the ice-age drift.'

'Well, Sir, not really,' was the concerted reply, 'It fell off that tipper lorry moving up the road there.'

'Ah well, that's not the point,' was the defence, accompanied to giggles and much smirks all round.

There were many other similar 'studies,' all an almost similar hilarious content such as a 'thesis' on new town development. Here, a day was spent at Harlow, then a new town in North Essex, some 30 miles from London where the main activity was to record bus and car movements within the principal shopping centre. And 'Sir' – well he was happily pontificating about how, in new towns, the car had to replace walking as the only means to do the shopping:

'The day of the small shop is numbered,' he predicted, rather accurately as it turned out 'people in the new towns must drive to a main centre,' he continued, as we were instructed to continue with our records of car movements.

Scintillating stuff, but then this was 1960 and 'Sir's' pontifications have proved to be spot on to today's traffic problems so obviously he was not too much of an absent-minded professor after all!

The obvious reason why history was my other chosen specialty subject was as a result of my upbringing and interest in becoming steadily acquainted with London sights, national heritage and traditions from an early age. Rather that than admitting to the fact that Victoriana, through my home and school environment plus even my own family upbringing, had always featured so largely in my life.

History to me was an already established interest, more like a hobby than a school subject of endless facts and battle dates. Certainly, to add to the enjoyment at school was also that the history teacher could, unfortunately, not pronounce his letter 'R' which was an absolute delight to me and the class:

'Open your Histowwy books, Boys!'

'What do you know about the Battle of Twafalgawve' – and so it went on in endless hoots for the seven years of my 'gwammawve school caweewa!'

* * * *

Throughout the school career, Bow and the same house in Bow Road remained 'home.' It was still my base, still the centre of my family life with the happy and enduring comfortable set up with Nan and Grandpop at its centre and father passing through on his usual non-committal basis. Everything continued to work well and all were happy.

Nan and Grandpop, although by 1960 already in their early 70s, continued with all the caretaking duties, although naturally things were somewhat easier for them by then. Nevertheless, it is so admirable that they continued to work so hard overall and, fortunately, for both them and me, they were keeping in good health. Life surely though was hard for them and there was never any spare money; even father with his regular work seemed incapable of adding to the coffers, probably spending everything he had earned on his evenings out and dinner entertaining. Still, it was his life, after all, but it would have been good for the family if there had been more finances in the home. On top of all that, Grandpop's regular weekly football coupon still failed to bring any tangible results other than perhaps a very occasional couple of pounds prize.

Still the dream of moving away from Bow to 'somewhere better' was set and established in the mind, certainly by Nan and Grandpop although father, for all his pretensions of 'properness,' never did seem to care or pay any attention to such issues. The desire to move was perhaps even more so as, by 1960, the style and standards, the best things about the old London East End and Bow in particular, were beginning to change.

Even on the level of noise alone, the passing main Bow Road had so much more traffic than in the immediate post war years – there was a constant hum at most hours of the day and through much of the night as well. Sunday morning was sheer and absolute bliss! With more general activity came more dirt: rubbish and paper was for ever blowing around the windows and this was serious for our downstairs basement home. The drains would quickly become blocked and then, with heavy rain, water would soon build up in the guttering and in front of the basement windows. The result on several occasions after especially heavy storms was that flooding would occur with water coming in through the windows to our rooms themselves. What heartfelt moments these were with Nan and Grandpop, and me if I was at home from school, rushing to mop up and move treasured possessions to safety. It was truly wretched and the dampness invaded the house for ages, with a consequent continued musty smell. It must have been most unhealthy but somehow we were all fortunately immune, probably as a result of years of being used to it.

There were changes too in the immediate area environment as many of the familiar streets were cleared of the traditional terraced houses to be left bare with rubble for months on end. Finally, if anything was done it was only to build the wretched, hideous and uniform blocks of Flats. The old Bow was being replaced by something alien to me and whilst I do not enthuse that Bow could ever have truly be said to have been 'wonderful,' or even in any way half perfect, what was happening in the late 1950s/early 60s was an absolute and complete mess. The policy then was to simply replace the older, traditional houses which, whilst not perfect, could easily have been renovated to make them decent family homes with reasonable facilities, and by so doing retain the essential sense of community.

What happened in their place? – Ugly and austere apartment blocks, in which nobody wanted to live and which in not many years would be the future recipe for wild and lawless estates, ghettos and no-go areas. A thorough disgrace and an absolute opportunity lost.

Not only were the old homes razed to the ground, but so too were many of our favourite shops in Devon's Road and whilst, at least in the few remaining years that we continued to live in Bow, some shops continued to trade, the area was never again able to provide the range and variety which had been the charm in my early years.

As many times before, all of this begs me to question the real meaning of the word 'progress.' Why, I wonder, do we always seem to have the real ability of getting it wrong? Is it because we do not think through the issue, take note of what has happened in the past, perhaps even to see how something is being done in other countries or maybe it is because we in this country so frequently seem to have the inability of admitting we are wrong? With that in mind, how on earth is it ever possible to get anything right, I wonder. As they would say in school:

'What is Progress – discuss!'

Our family, in our 'detached home' were, however, somewhat immune from these immediate building changes. Our home as the 'local business centre' did not change and neither did the nearest buildings to us, no matter how much the outside world was in a state of change. The offices remained exactly the same, people too largely the same – in fact an enclave against change if not exactly a time warp. Home continued to be a very extremely safe and secure place to return to, equally as much then as was the case in my early days.

Our desire as a family to move on, though, remained a firm dream but it would still only be a 'dream,' and no more than that, for some time yet.

Father's life went on in much the same way too – off daily on the underground to his civil service job still at Lambeth – spending some evenings out and obviously meeting up with some woman friends from work but never would anything 'come of it.' He obviously felt very comfortable in his ways and his freedom was too sacred to him to consider any dramatic changes in his lifestyle. Whatever, though, it was a very 'airy-fairy' lifestyle, very unfulfilling and with very little positively to show as an achievement.

Even by then coming up to my middle teens, my home life continued in much the same way as in the early years. Still very much a loner, a family-boy who still together we enjoyed our theatre visits, the regular trips and visits to the local sights and attractions, which for me meant even more enjoyment and value when coupled with my school learning's. Family outings and holidays continued as a fine link to the past treasured moments but refreshed with modern and new awareness.

With my friends, I was able to enjoy all these valued trips in a different light to complement the overall pleasures. Saturday mornings were the chosen friends' gathering time – perhaps to London places, the occasional railway station, all right, to be honest more than the 'occasional' station, very many, in fact. All that, plus museums, exhibitions – the lot in fact. Yet here again, and so many times over in life, I had so many reasons to be grateful for the awareness and enjoyment of these sights and heritages that I had been given in my early years.

On a different scale, almost the sublime to the ridiculous, there was the occasional Saturday Morning Cinema Club, a riotous affair as you can imagine with a cinema full of hundreds of screaming kids. The programme never ran to completion without frequent stops, the house lights switched on and appeals from the manager for calm. Oh, give me a railway station with a mass of hissing steam engines any day!

The grammar school era was most notable to me in that it finally, after a couple of years, broke for me the painful Sunday tradition of forever having to visit the Aunts and Uncles at Buckhurst Hill, at least on an every week basis. The 'excuse' of homework and lessons preparation meant that visits were restricted to no more than once or twice per month so that the other Sundays could be spent at home with nicer Sunday activities. This change in routine was most beneficial and was most positive in respect that when I did visit the relatives, I did so with a far better frame of mind and heart – even enough to actually in a small degree enjoy. No doubt too, because also some of my school fellow pupils including one or two of my friends came from the area, visits to suburban Essex were now more positive.

Imagine too that one or two friends were even invited to visit aunt and uncle as well – as if by a real regal command! It most certainly meant that these places were not so hostile in feeling to me any more and I could begin to identify happily with these Essex locations almost as much as with my home. After all, my colleagues at school spoke about it every day and I too therefore felt a close affinity. There is another validity to my change in heart too – the changes taking place in Bow and our family feelings, especially Nan and Grandpop, of hoping to move away to somewhere better, all contributed to see these areas in a more positive and fairer light.

How could I not have appreciated these suburbs? I saw the tree-lined streets, neat gardens, smart houses with welcoming lights, gleaming new cars, the tidy high streets with the variety of small shops then becoming extinct in Bow; no inner City dereliction, dirt and noise. How negative Bow was becoming in comparison and I admit my sights were then widening no longer to feel blindly comfortable with my inner-City environment. This was an immediate process of change I then began to experience in life – or was it simply called 'growing-up?'

Chapter 7

Towards New-found Times

Until my early teens, I had very little regular contact with father's younger sister, Ethel, the one living with Bill at Wanstead. Simply, very much like father's side of the family, they were unable to identify with children and apart from very short visits whilst at Buckhurst Hill, our paths very rarely crossed. However, things began to change from the time I began at grammar school and there was an immediate rapport with Bill who had attended the very same school some 25 years before me. Father and I were duly invited 'Chez Wanstead' one Sunday and then a few weeks' later Nan and Grandpop came too – a remarkable first for them to have an 'official visit' to anybody on father's side. Naturally, this gesture immediately gave me positive feelings towards Ethel and Bill and so civil pleasantries gradually developed. The fact too that they always had dogs made some similarities between my own home and Ethel's, not to mention the fact that unlike Brenda, Ethel was an enthusiastic cook which, as always, was a sure key to success in my mind!

So it was that during my school holidays in the late 1950s and in fact right up to the end of school in 1963, that a tradition was established and I would go every Thursday to Wanstead to spend the day with my Aunt Ethel and to a routine carried out with a set and precise efficiency. All right, I know what I have said about those earlier dreaded Sunday routines in my younger childhood and here I am advocating another relative visit routine, but this was different – it was my idea! – And, in any case, it was only weekly in the holiday times and I enjoyed it – excuse enough!!

The beginning was to be sure to arrive at their house by 08.30 (sharp!), by taking the bus or underground from Bow. Perhaps it was this early morning effort which added to the excitement and sense of occasion and got the adrenalin going – after all, it was the school holidays! And the reason for the early arrival – Ethel ran a National Savings collection round which meant that my being there offered valuable (questionable!) assistance as she went from house to house selling the savings stamps and certificates.

The whole round would take about three hours during which time, calling at many doors, I would see very many different styles and houses – one or two at the top end of the street were extremely palatial and grand and the very last call was very much in that category, even though their business offered was nothing special:

'Four shilling today, please!'

'Oh, thank you ever so much,' said my aunt in deference, before referring to me.

'Four shillings worth of stamps – be careful with the change and so, transaction complete, it was on to the next house.

I don't suppose today, some 40 years later, that too many people would feel for walking the streets with bags full of valuable savings certificates, stamps and loose money and banknotes, and doing so in happy safety! That surely is a negative difference between now and those past times.

Job completed and having returned to the house, it was then time for true accountancy – totalling up the sales, counting the cash and generally reconciling the book-keeping, all in all a real taste of business development! Surprisingly, when considering my maths ability at school, I was fortunately rather accurate but then the simple ability to add up a row of figures was never really my problem – it was always the complications like algebra that left me in the permanent wilderness. So to finalise the administration, it would then be off to the high street and the local post office to 'bank' the money and to collect more certificates and stamps ready for the following week.

With all reconciled and safely put away, the day would move on, happily, to the lunch event. Ethel always made a huge and varied main meal for the lunch, which I tucked into with relish and always topped up with seconds to make for the real highlight of the day. What did I say about the key to my heart?

The kitchen theme would then continue to run throughout the afternoon too, as there would be chutneys, jams, marmalades cakes or pies to be made since Bill was a food enthusiast too – maybe that was something the school had successfully taught both of us! You didn't leave heaped with academic awards but with ravenous stomachs probably as a result of having endured those appalling school lunches over the years!

I liked Wanstead as an area, thinking it had all the best feels of the suburbs, had plenty of open spaces and parks, a fine high street with vivid local shops, tidy restaurants and cafes and a fine bread and cake shop. It was closer to London than Buckhurst Hill and I suppose the fact that it even had the East London post code somehow made me feel more comfortable there too; even the regular bus link to Bow seemed in my mind to bring the places together. Here also was the clear point in my mind that this was the sort of area to aim for when we were finally able to make our move from Bow.

Whatever the results of Grandpop's football pools, I had my own dreams and goals to aim for, all of us.

Uncle Bill would return home from his work in the London Royal Docks – Oh alright – from his desk job in a Ship Repair company. He had to be home punctually by 6pm otherwise Ethel would panic endlessly. Although they had a car by that time as well, Bill would never drive to work 'in town – the only time he would drive urbanely was at weekends when there was little traffic – he preferred to take the bus to and from work and to read the paper *en route*. Bill's apathy to drive in town therefore meant that, at the end of my day's visit, there was no point in my expecting any excitement of a car journey – it was back home on the bus for me, 'fares please!'

However, and to be very fair, the developing family relationships for me with Ethel and Bill did mean that on many occasions there were car outings and often too with Nan and Grandpop coming as well, which was very much a delight. Those drives were a memorable experience because Bill, ever cautious, always drove as if somebody was walking in front with a red flag – very slowly, very deliberate and with frequent stops to 'cool the engine.' Trips would therefore be seemingly endless and even a day to the south coast would mean a start from home at around 6am 'in case' and even with that we would not reach our final destination until mid-morning!

The reward though would be a magnificent picnic – or as it was such a long day, several magnificent picnics with both Nan and Ethel supplying numerous items of goodies, Pride of place went to Nan's home- made veal, ham and egg pie which with Ethel's chutney to accompany it, would always call for 'thirds' not just 'seconds.' To this, Bill would provide the beverage having set up and established a very old, and indeed quaint, primus stove which would take at least half-an-hour to achieve a 'brew-up,' assuming the wind was in the right direction!

No matter how many picnics through the day, there would always be room for fish and chips on the way home in the evening – well we had to stop in any case to allow the engine to have 'a breather!'

These trips together over those many years were many and varied – Folkestone, naturally as a family favourite, but also to the South Coast generally – Brighton and Eastbourne, with Beachy Head and the South Downs. To change direction, it would then be to the Essex coast of Point Clear, Clacton, Walton-on-the-Naze and Frinton (but no fish and chips there – I rather think that even today no fish and chip shops are allowed in that town, it being perfectly genteel!). Some drives further afield, really pushing Bill to the limit, would involve meanders through the East Anglian countryside and Grandpop was always interested in the Stour Valley area on the Essex/Suffolk border and the scene of many of John Constable's paintings such as 'Flatford Mill.'

All these drives were very much on minor roads even from the start in Wanstead; long before motorways, and the M25 was then not even a dream in anybody's imagination. In 10 miles, such as around Abridge in Essex, you were then almost deep in the countryside and the urban comparison in just a few miles was total. I would say that, overall, life was all the better for that then and I do wonder how far we will all have to go soon from the City areas to be able to see a natural blade of grass or farm animals!

Of course it really was so that for me the epitomy of these outings was very much based on the food delights and there was no doubt that food and my appreciation of it was a running theme beginning from my earliest years at home. Perhaps it is correct to say that this almost became an obsession by the 1960s time very much because of Nan's and Ethel's supreme efforts in all gastronomical delights.

Even school played its part.

A food appreciation club was set up and run by the very pleasant New Zealander English teacher (now you'll know why I refer to him always as 'pleasant!') – this club vied for my attention as much as the railway club! There was no cooking as such, that would simply have not been considered correct for a Boys only school in 1960. The idea was to take a recipe, to study in theory and discuss. I suppose that doesn't sound too exciting now but the highlight was that, twice a term, the group would go out together for a meal based on the recipe, and the theme was usually an ethnic one.

Considering that the school in Bow was very near to the original China Town area of Limehouse, a little south of us in the area by the River Thames in Poplar, we had the heaven-sent opportunity immediately on our own doorstep. Our enthusiastic group descended on Chinatown, feeling very cosmopolitan and knowledgeable, although very conspicuous in the strange surroundings. We would then, with much guidance from the teacher, negotiate and enjoy a full Chinese meal.

Chopsticks – no, not really, that was not part of it at the time and we would all ask for spoons and forks. Whatever, though, we all took great excitement from the exotic and different foods, everybody choosing a different course so that, by sharing we had tastes of around 30 different bites. It was great fun and it was all the more so adventurous and different and at a time when there was hardly a Chinese 'take-a-way' in sight!

* * * *

In comparison to the overall growing up years of a young life, to spend seven of those years at the very same school represents a rather large chunk of time, this especially so during a period of ongoing developments in my world beyond the school gates. The changes immediately in Bow were matched by the massive building programme in London as the old war time bomb site areas were replaced by tall and bright new buildings breathing revitalised life into the City.

The Cityscape was constantly changing and I, as a very frequent and aware visitor, appreciated these developments. London was looking considerably cleaner and smarter all the time as a result. What a pity that it is not possible to say the same thing today as it appears we once again return to a place of filth and neglect.

Of course, in the early 1960s, less coal usage had the direct result of producing fewer of those horrible London smog's from which Bow, being in the east, especially suffered from. Similarly, the buildings themselves looked cleaner and the overall ambience was further enlightened by some of the new buildings. To me the high rise offices appeared exciting and I then didn't fully realise or appreciate the fact that they would together in time begin to partially hide such treasures as St Paul's Cathedral. Then these new buildings just seemed to be a signal of a confident and positive future.

I marvelled too at the increased and bustling commercial activities enhanced by school studies and awareness and the realisation that, at the end of school time, then less than three years away that I would need to consider my own entry to the world of business. That, probably, more than anything was enough for me to concentrate the mind to make best efforts at school whilst there was a chance – providing, of course, that it didn't involve physics!

After my less than satisfactory school career to date, I did finally rise to the educational occasion with some degree of working effort during the final three school years 1960/1963. Perhaps those continuing school reports – 'Must do better'; 'Can do it if he tries – were all finally beginning to do the trick. It was all helped too by the fact that the school syllabus was very much based on the specialiation of chosen subjects in the final years. Out from my school routine went those awful science subjects and too I concentrated just on basic Maths – or let's call it in fact just 'sums' – in order to get the necessary basic exam pass. In abundance in their place came longer periods for geography, history, English and literature and so the school lessons time became so much more enjoyable. I was actually getting enthusiastic!

Even 'chief bat-man would say 'Hello' to me, although he probably thought to himself

'Isn't that the Boy I sent away in 1957?'

It suited me the way that it was, whatever the merits or otherwise of such a restricted system. I was more than happy to spend the time just doing my chosen subjects, free from the vageries of those wretched sciences – let them all go up in flames from the proverbial Bunsen burner, and the whole science block of classes as well. The only great loss was no more to be able to attend the classes of that glorious Yorkshire man teacher with such a wonderful way of pronouncing his 'aitches.'

With a great deal of swatting and, yes, really constant and dedicated homework and revising for me, I, in 1961, entered the period leading up to the GCE 'O'-level examinations. There was nothing else for it than to work at it – exams were, frankly, very difficult for me because my mind invariably went blank – i.e. blanker than usual, on entering the exam room, obviously overawed, or simply scared, in fact rather petrified – by the sense of the occasion.

It would seem that I always had the ability to commit to memory the most irrelevant information – you know, such things as engine numbers or train timetables, for example! – but the really important and vital information just simply did not stay within my 'personal computer' – probably I must have had a 'chip' missing! However, by reading, then re-reading, making endless notes and memory jots, some information would then finally stick.

But then how to overcome the nerves of the exam room. That was very difficult and the only answer I found was to concentrate on something nice – food (!), a trip or visit to somewhere special, the theatre – in fact anything like that and this really proved to be a cure.

My GCE 'O'-level exam came in June 1961 so it immediately meant that I could think about the coming summer holiday period to concentrate the mind (but, at the same time, to forget that late August would be the time for the wretched letter to arrive with the results – oh well, that's another day I thought, why to worry about it now).

With encouragement from all the family, when the day of the first exam came, I took further comfort once again from the normality of all around me as I made my way to school. This gave me the necessary confidence just as it had done in exactly the same way those 11 years before when making my way to the primary school for the first time.

The traffic bustled along Bow Road, just as a normal day as it was for everybody else, cars and their drivers going about their normal routine, the numerous buses packed tight taking all the passengers to work, lorries and vans intent upon their deliveries. Other passers by completely oblivious to the importance that the day was for me and the effect that it would have on my life. In fact, not just on a short period of life, I thought, but nothing short of a most significant and supreme relevance on the whole future life. With such thoughts, the enormity of the day upon which I was embarking then overwhelmed my thoughts and completely obliterated my earlier sense of confidence, so much so that soon I became quite shaky just at the mere prospect of what actually lay ahead.

Negative thoughts were, however, soon put aside and in their place once more a feeling of well-being coming from the comfort of the friendly Newsagent':

'Morning,' with cheery wave.

As I continued my walk, the familiar buses passed making their journey westwards to the City and West End and my favourite places. These were the surroundings to comfort me and help the steps to school on that day.

Getting nearer still to school, I then met up with many of my friends as they arrived on their journeys from homes in those far-flung Essex reaches. We met; we talked – about hobbies, happenings, even the last night's television – talked about anything in fact except the day ahead. As usual, it was escapism until the very last moment.

On arriving at the school it was very easy to know that it was an exam day – chief 'bat-man' and all the other 'bat-men' were actually smiling – or, more likely it was a form of smirking as they thought about what was in store for the little horrors that very day! There wasn't much time to think of impending events as the bell – yes, that life organising bell, rang out – always there to control and govern occasions. The bell's shrill, the appointed hour and there was nothing for it other than to enter the exam room which in any case was the familiar school library – perhaps the intention was that all those reference books lining the walls would be there for our use in the exam! Some hope for that with 'bat-man's' evil eye on the situation.

Fortunately, for me anyway, the library was situated at the side of the school that had no view of the railway line. Otherwise I would no doubt have been tempted to keep looking out and then to become pre-occupied as to why the 09.00 from Norwich was running late, never mind the exam. You see what I meant about my being able to remember completely useless information, useless that is unless I had been a Station Master (and I don't think we have those officials anymore either!)

The exam started – papers handed out, face down (the papers, not the pupils!) of course to make sure nobody had any advantage of seeing the questions ahead of anybody – then the signal to turn the pages over and we were off – just like race horses at the start. My first look at the paper – oh good, a place where I could write my name so I could get that right and that must be worth one point, only 99 to go!

All exams followed the same pattern as they probably do exactly the same over the years to the present time but you see, since the school years, I have made every effort to avoid them! Initially I tried to make sense of, and to understand the questions or, as I should say, to work out how I could adapt my prepared parrot fashion answers to fit the question. How could I write about the White Cliffs of Dover when the question was about flooded river plains?

So it went on, scribbling away, ticking off the answers, hearing the clock tick and actually missing the familiar bell, which for once, had been switched off so as not to disturb our labours. But the bell was not off for good, it would ring sometime to signal the end of the exam but for that moment, silence, so get on with the job in hand. Several times some of us would have looked up to check on each other's progress, accompanied with wry smiles when 'bat-man' wasn't looking.

And what was 'bat-man's' day? – a complete doddle it would seem, just sitting in the front, occasionally parading up and down the rows of desks, but mainly enjoying three hours of bliss with his newspaper and crossword. His only obvious care in the world was what was the clue to '7-across!' No doubt that gave him as much trouble as I was having with the exam question about rift valleys – in any case it was nice to have a feeling of affinity in adversity!

The bell. It was over. 'bat-man' came to life, it would be cruel to say – woke up, he then had something to do – collect the papers – or 'manuscripts' as he eloquently called them. We could get up and go and there was much discussion and reminiscing as we left the room.

'How did you get on?'

'That was a choker of a question – difficult to know what they wanted.'

'I hadn't revised that question because it came up last year!'

'What are you all worried about – it was a walk-over – easy' – there was always one in every class, absolutely covered by the East-End expression – 'Know-all!'

Oh well, it was done and with that the papers had been collected and would then soon be on their way to some far-flung area of the country to be marked and assessed by complete strangers without any knowledge of the victims. Home then for the afternoon as it was rare for there to be more than one main exam per day; probably because 'bat-man' would have completely nodded off if he had been faced with two sessions per day, let alone the pupils. To have a rare opportunity for an afternoon at home in school term-time was luxury and almost made the whole exam period worthwhile. Nan kindly prepared me a special tea with all my favourite home- made cakes and buns.

'How was it, love?'

'Oh fine – alright really' would be my all-encompassing reply to cover whatever eventuality.

'Oh, that's good then,' said Nan, reassuringly, whilst making more tea and accompanied by Grandpop's nodding encouragements. Even father would ask about the day when he arrived home from work which was a sure thing to record the event as being something special and not the norm in life!

Thus was set the pattern for the complete 2/3-week period of the exams after which, it being almost the end of the summer term, came a truly marvellous breaking-up atmosphere of organised school trips and outings. Whilst the extra summer sports were, as always, not precisely to my liking, it was good to be in the sunshine and open air and away from the stuffy classroom atmosphere. What were good though were a number of cross—country hikes with a geographical flavour, for instance, around the South Downs or across the New Forest. So special too were the summer evening visits to the Open Air Theatre in Regent's Park, always a delight.

So the days meandered to the very end of term. Making plans to meet up with my immediate circle of friends for various trips and outings; the good-byes too many for seven weeks and, for a small handful that had decided to leave at 16 years whatever the exam outcome, virtually a final goodbye. Of course, it did occur to me that, if the exam results were particularly poor for me, even beyond the hope of a re-take, than I too might have been leaving school for the last time. As much as I wanted to be out of school, I did though realise that, to make later life anything worthwhile, it would be necessary to have the two sixth-form years.

At the start of the summer holiday 1961, it never did occur to me nor did I think about the fact that exam results would need to be faced up to within a matter of 4/5 weeks – that was an eternity away and did not have to be considered. First was the annual family holiday at Folkestone, my much cherished and valued tradition. Afterwards, there were also some days out or long weekends to various places in the South such as the Isle of Wight and Bournemouth. With my friends, we together made some railway excursions to various depots and engine sheds (please do not groan – I won't go into deep details) – all very much hobby opportunities and young male's bonding.

Remembering this was the very early 1960s and our 'boys-only' school background meant that not only in style but in reality too we were light-years behind those of a similar age group today. I and my contemporaries were truly 'children of a different age' and probably very much the last of such a generation. Today's lifestyle is utterly remote from that time and by comparison we were very childish and unworldly. The upbringing and school background meant totally no such issues in life at that stage of girl friends – this for my age group at that time was something well ahead of us…

August simply flew by and with it came the dawning realisation that results day with all its implications would not be too far away. Along with this thought came the significance of it all – the sharp fact that if the results were not satisfactory then chief 'bat-man' would achieve his ambition first voiced some five years previously of removing me from the school – 'better late than never,' I bet was in his mind!

Nobody at home ever talked about what would happen if the exam results were bad – although knowing the history of my school career, all must have harboured such thoughts. Perhaps Grandpop was all the time preparing to take me on as his caretaking apprentice; after all I had knowledge from my very youngest years about the duties involved and thus a most impressive CV! Or, I could have become an engine driver!!

No, the summer holiday period allowed me to gather my thoughts and confirm to myself that I really wanted to return to school for the sixth year. How's that for an anomaly – no, not me wanting to return to school (although that was strange enough), but rather calling it 'sixth year' when it lasted two years! Come on, I know that I was never very good at maths but surely chief 'bat-man' and his brigade could not have been so stupid.

By almost the end of August, and remembering that in those 'glorious days' the Bank Holiday was still in its rightful and proper position of taking place at the beginning of the month (where it should again be now, with an additional Bank Holiday in the Autumn – still, I digress) – there was still no word of the result. Each morning with the arrival of the postman, the situation became growingly intolerable. Worries were even more increased when friends began to call to discuss their own results.

Many thoughts flashed through my mind – were the results so bad that they hadn't even bothered to waste paper and postage to inform me – was I so much in disgrace? The old maxim 'no news is good news' simply did not apply in this case at all.

School was still on holiday so presumably chief 'bat-man' was still dipping his toes in the sea in some place exotic – other than Southend that is! What to do? Nan and Grandpop suggested:

'Go round to the school – somebody must know.'

'Let's wait and see,' said father in his usual not getting involved mode, and also because he probably wanted to live in glorious pretence for some moments longer.

Anyway, I took Nan and Grandpop's advice and went to the school which, on approach, seemed ominously quiet and so different from the usual noise and 'seat of learning' atmosphere. However, having rung the bell at the main gate, a caretaker did appear to say that he thought the secretary was 'somewhere around,' so helpfully put.

'What do you want, anyway?' he added, to which I described my plight.

After some moments, he returned and, telling me to follow him, escorted me through the deserted premises to the secretary's office. I never quite knew what to make of the secretary, she was probably very long suffering after working with chief 'bat-man' for so long, but, gosh, she really was the epitomy of a 'battle-axe' that barked and shed fire from the mouth even more than the Head himself.

'Well, they have all been posted out at least a week ago' was her first, 'helpful' reply. 'I know they went because <u>I did it myself</u>,' she continued in indignation.

'Have you checked the mail at home?' . . . Really!

'Please, miss, do you not have a copy somewhere?,' I said rather bravely, I thought.

'Well – Yes – I suppose I have somewhere, but it really is most annoying because I've done it once and I am very busy you know. In any case they will all be filed away by now' she continued nonchalantly.

'Have you ever thought of opening the files?' – No, I didn't say that, I was too intimidated and growing increasingly frightened about the whole situation, but that's what I thought – this is my life at stake and for that moment it was in her hands!

'Please, miss, please can you perhaps ... (cough and clearing of the throat)... 'perhaps check . . . please?' I said, whilst shuffling from one foot to another.

'Oh, very well,' she said 'I'm very busy you know with the school term starting next week and there's mountains to do. Mr (that's chief 'bat-man') will be in the school before that and things must be ready!'

'Thank-you, miss,' was my garbled reply.

Sweaty hands and perspiring forehead overcame me as 'miss went through the various filing cabinets and seemed to take an eternity going through various papers. There and then I should have noted, for later life, how 'miss' and her filing system, indeed overall office management, would have been in need of a business consultancy makeover!

'Name?' she said and with my reply she then ran her finger up and down the various lists.

'It's not here'

'But it must be'

'Well, it isn't – and I've checked all the sixth form!'

'I'm not in the sixth form,' I mumbled in confused reply. Did I look that age, I thought and at that moment I should have said that I wanted to be in the wretched sixth form if I ever found out my equally wretched exam results!

'Oh, you are a lower boy then are you?' (and that's a fine expression and probably best described me at that moment as I felt even more wishing to sink into the floor). 'I've just wasted my time (to say nothing about what she had done to me nor my time!). 'Wait – I'll have to go to find another file.'

This whole interview and interrogation had really got off on an entirely wrong foot and there was nothing to it other that to wait still some more interminable minutes whilst another set of files and papers were checked.

'Ah, here we are' – then, if nothing else, was surely the cue for weak knees!

'Passes in six main subjects – nothing special though' she reassuringly commented. 'Oh, one minute, yes, history and geography seem a trifle better – and – oh, yes literature too, those three subjects are all As and B's.' she finalised the research. If she thought that As and Bs were a 'trifle better' then I dreaded to think what sort of result would be necessary to receive her accolade of a reward.

'So, it's alright then?,' was my feeble reply.

'It's not for me to say – but I suppose that you haven't actually failed,' she said, never obviously being one for compliments!

'Can I have a copy of the results, please?,' was my simple request knowing that I must have something to take home as evidence.'

'What! – that means I will have to type up a note!'

'Well, I need to show my family.'

'Oh, very well – but you should really check the post and you cannot expect me to waste my time.'

What about my time … More especially so at this potentially earth-shattering moment of life!

So that was it – finally a set of acceptable results, nothing too brilliant except in my 'pet' subjects, but I hoped that it was enough to gain entry to the sixth year, although that would involve a meeting with the dreaded chief 'bat-man' to confirm.

Back home it was nice to have the friendly 'Congratulations' remarks from Nan and Grandpop, then to wait for the homecoming – father's return from work and his quiet study of the result without any other comment than:

'We'll have to see what the Head says.'

Father had always considered himself on the science side of matters and could therefore never relate to the fact that I was brain-dim in those subjects – or simply, just brain-dim in the round I suppose!

The loss of the letter which we should have received with the exam results was finally revealed in the coming few days when – you'll remember my comment that one of the offices upstairs was occupied by the evocatively called 'district surveyor' – that said gentleman returned to work from his holidays and opened his mail which had been locked away for safe keeping. Too safe! Included in the mail was – you've guessed – the exam results letter which had been put into the wrong box by the postman presumably because it looked 'official' and the postman could not have considered that we should be the recipients of official mail! Anyway, the diversion adds spice to the narrative!!

Amazingly, chief 'bat-man' accepted me into sixth form at the interview, bravely covering up his feelings that he had once again failed to have me removed from 'his school.' So I was assured of two further years of school (which, remarkably, was what I wanted) and I therefore was able to remove my job application as assistant caretaker to Grandpop and knuckle down to the sixth form instead!

Chapter 8

The Sixth

I, together with my group of friends, must have been all so very academically gifted and overall intelligent, that my immediate circle, that had by then been together through it all for some years, took example from each other. Therefore, we all stayed on and were accepted together into the sixth 'year.' It was so then that as a group we had come into the school together and were then about to embark together on the final two grammar school years.

Fortunately, both for me and all my friends, that 'sixth' year was indeed fun and a far better overall experience than had been the case of all the previous school years. Of course this was said with the benefit of maturity and that the lessons – or rather lectures – were only in my chosen subjects of geography, history and literature, the three subjects which I was studying for the GCE 'A'-level exams, all taking place over two years and which then heralded the end of my school career. What a magic sound there was to those words – 'the end of my school career' – if that wasn't enough to make me keep going and to make supreme efforts then I don't know what else could have possibly done the trick instead!

It was good too that the grammar school was enlightened enough to include a couple of general life interest sessions each week on matters completely outside the curriculum such as current affairs, debates and politics, papers and the media. Newspapers always created heated discussions; most of my age group up until then had been used to a diet of semi-populars like *The Express* and *The Mail* (although, because of my late mother's connection, we used to have the *Telegraph* at home) but now we were at school being introduced to the likes of *The Times* and, the then, *Manchester Guardian*. The analysis of the different ways to report and the stories featured was enlightening even though the subject may sound incredibly dull!

The whole issue of current affairs was thrown very much into the centre ring at that time by virtue of the fact of the Cuban Missile Crisis and the implications certainly concentrated our minds. At that time, we were beyond the time of army conscription but this crisis brought the whole possibility back into consideration. There were general sighs of relief when the crisis was averted. I do not think that any of us ever gave any thought to a military life and after the discipline of the school years I am sure we could have endured the army too. After all, all of our parents had done just that, so why not us?

We were not, any of us, teenage tearaways as such and in many respects, I suppose, really most subdued apart from harmless enough schoolboy-style pranks. If there had been a 'call-up' to the military we would have had to have gone and surely we would have the spirit too of our background. No, it was though just a simple relief to know that a potential crisis was over and the mind was free to concentrate on less weighty issues.

To lighten the load, the discussions on music, theatre and the arts carried on in the sixth year and, as always, were most absorbing and further developed my enthusiasm. Certainly, all these special subjects were of tremendous value and probably more than anything else at school gave valued benefit for all of later life.

The prefect system was very much in force at the school and amazingly, given my normal stand-off relationship with chief 'bat-man,' I was chosen to be one of the prefects for the two sixth form years. Oh what fun to have the delights of organising the queue at school lunch-time or in making sure that no boys were in class during the mid-day breaks etc. As if anybody would have wanted to be in class anyway when they did not have to be! Still, I suppose that there were benefits from their sense of responsibility and it was a so-called positive point at the school that prefects were not allowed to inflict any corporal punishment on the luckless pupils other than to 'give a hundred lines' or report the case to the form-master.

If all of the time at school had been as good as the last two years were, then no doubt I would have had a more positive view of the whole exercise! In the spring of 1962, it was announced that the geography group could go on a school study trip to Norway. Apart from my thoroughly happy day trips to France, the trip would be my first real opportunity for overseas travel. With the prospective news I rushed home with the forms and information and, of course, to see not only if I could go but also whether my Family could afford the cost.

First, I excitedly spoke to Nan and Grandpop as soon as I got home, even before sitting down to the traditional afternoon tea and cakes that alone underlines the sheer importance and magnitude of the event!

'There's this planned trip to Norway, here are the details and everybody (my already exaggeration!) will be going from my class and I must, simply must go too,' I excitedly shouted. It was, of course, incredibly selfish of me to present this issue in such a way and a lot to expect of my Nan and Grandpop to be able to totally support the cost.

'We must see what we can do, also talk to your father about it,' Nan and Grandpop said. 'We can see you're excited and no wonder; it's a wonderful opportunity for you. Don't worry, love, we will do our best.'

When father came home, the whole issue was presented to him, first by me but most notably ably supported by Nan and Grandpop.

'We'll see,' was all father said. What more could I have expected, his 'we'll see' was his stock phrase when presented with anything requiring a decision.

Nan and Grandpop could see my disappointment and realised how important the trip was for me. On top of that there were only a couple of days before the answer had to be given at the school, so time was extremely short. I went to my room to get on with homework, although barely being able to concentrate on the issues at hand. In the background, I hear agitated discussions coming from the living room and later that evening noticed that father was in one of his very special sulking and not talking to anybody moods. A bad sign indeed.

During the next day at school, I tried not to think of the issue but it did not make it any easier when I knew that several of my colleagues had already got the go-ahead from their own families. I just kept quiet about the issue but, nevertheless, found it very difficult to concentrate on the lessons on hand.

That evening, Nan and Grandpop told me that they had checked their savings, done some financial sums and felt that they could just about scrape enough together for the trip. That was absolutely marvellous of them and so typical of them to put my needs in front of all else. But what did it say once again about my own father?

Father was equally as unmoved or bothered when he came home and I told him of Nan and Grandpop's kindness. In fact that was the key for another prolonged period of his moodiness and not talking and so the subject was not again discussed. Whatever, thanks to my Nan and Grandpop, I was going on the trip and so could tell the school the very next day.

Fortunately, then, all was set and I could begin, with all the others, to look forward and to plan for the up-coming trip. In itself, the whole journey was to be a milestone in life at that point too. It was to be the very first time to actually be away from home for any length of time, on my own and away from the family. I suppose that, by then, being nearly 17 years of age it does sound rather strange to be talking about being away from home for the first time! It had simply not been anything that I had done before and I was not alone in this fresh experience – all of our group of ten were 'home boys' and therefore in exactly the same position!

Lovingly, Nan helped me pack my bags and I know she was upset even though the total trip was only to be ten days. I felt sad too, especially so when my true parents, Nan and Grandpop, were then well into their 70s. The fact that they were still both working, and thankfully in very good health, didn't take away the real situation that they were both getting older and had a very tough life still. I did feel very thankful to them and responsible for them. Once the excitement of actually going away had subsided, I must admit that I then felt more than a degree of sadness at having to leave them for ten days.

'Bye, love, we'll be alright and looking forward to your coming home' said Nan.

'I'll write, but you and Grandpop look after yourselves.'

'We will love, see you soon.'

I left home rather quickly then with very mixed thoughts – of course, excited for the trip but still very much with a lump in the throat and much loving and homely feelings to Nan and Grandpop. I always realised that I owed absolutely everything to both Nan and Grandpop and a time of going away made such feelings that much more poignant.

Our group met together at the school and set off with the one geography teacher (not a 'bat-man' any more without his gown!) who had the hapless task of leading the trip with ten teenage boys – but times were different then?!

Naturally, the first stage of the trip was lovingly mundane – on the familiar Underground to Central London and the mainline Railway Station at King's Cross. Here, right away, I was in my element as we boarded not just an express train, but indeed a 'boat-train' for Newcastle and very much having the need to restrain myself from checking the engine numbers.

Being very much a southern boy and having then been no further north than Buckinghamshire on those relative visits, even the train trip north opened new horizons for me. Places flashed by – yes, trains actually travelled fast in those days! And places which had previously just been names on an atlas were then there in reality – Peterborough, Doncaster, York, Durham and finally Newcastle – all for real and no longer just a figment of imagination.

Then it was just like 'doing a Folkestone' – the train went directly to the harbour at North Shields on the River Tyne and the station right by the side of the ship. Excitedly we boarded 'Leda,' one of the Bergen Line's passenger/cargo ships then serving the route, carrying our bags and packages and clutching our tickets – we were travelling 'in style' and had two sets of cabins that were really like small dormitories with six bunks in each. From the noise and perpetual smell of oil, we must have been located right next to the engine room!

How exciting when all the announcements were first given in Norwegian, naturally it being a Norwegian ship, but one of my colleagues, you know there's always a 'wag,' observed that the Norwegian passengers would have an advantage over us should an 'abandon ship' call be given. Charming!

As always for me on a sea voyage, whether off to France or going on the steamer down the Thames, we were all on deck for the departure and I probably voiced my experience about such matters – you know being a typical know-all bore! Slowly the ship turned in the Tyne and headed for the sea and we were soon beyond the breakwater and turning to the north-east *en route* for Norway. Then, fortunately for the accompanying teacher, most of us were quiet as we watched the coastline at Tynemouth and Whitley Bay slip away behind us, and significantly therefore England and our homes too.

Sombre thoughts though didn't last long, the North Sea roll made certain of that which only added to the sense of excitement and fun. Nevertheless, we all headed to the ship's café and for the first of our budgeted meals, carefully controlling the amount that our families had given us to spend on the trip. Everything then was so exciting and new, nothing more so than the first night sleeping at sea – but there wasn't much sleep. Boy's constant chatter, the drone of the engines, made sure of that and the permanent rolling motion was – just perhaps – causing some less good feelings by that time – but let's move on!

Landfall the next day was Stavanger and, as this was well before the day of roll-on/roll-off ferries, the consequent time in port was a few hours giving our group time to go ashore and to look around the town. Norway had been invaded!

Back on board and the afternoon was work related as we all sat notebooks in hand, as 'Sir' lectured to us about the fjord-indented coastline as we sailed northwards towards Bergen. Still, it was far better than the classroom as the hanging valleys and glaciers of geography speak were coming alive right before our very eyes! Even at that time in spring, the appreciable difference in the light evenings was already evident as we approached Bergen and port in the mid-evening in bright sunlight. Norway duly allowed us all entry to their country and we all trooped off to the hostel booked for our overnight – this time we all slept!

A day in Bergen on the following day and a study session at the fish harbour – most enlightening! In the evening a lecture at the hostel – no nights on the town and obviously for us at that time there was no meaning for such a phrase, such was the true degree of naivety 40 years ago!

The expedition continued the following morning by our returning to the harbour, this time to board a coastal steamer – there, my favourite 'steamer' word with memories of my Thames trips. We had a journey lasting most of the day from Bergen, first north along the coast before then sailing up the mighty Sogne Fjord, a place surely designed for geography teachers to go absolutely wild with enthusiasm on both geography and geological features.

Facts were shouted so fast that my hands were so sore with writing by the time that we finally arrived in the late afternoon at our destination – the fjord-side village of Balestrand. Off the ship once again and we made our way to the hostel and our home for the next five days.

Forgeting all the aspects of work and note-taking, it really was a beautiful spot – so clean, calm (even despite the arrival of our group!); the wonderful colourful wooden houses, the gentle village life, the steep mountains falling down to the fjord side, the bustling boat activity of the fjord itself with the frequent ferries just like buses in Bow Road, the distant glacier of Josteldal, in fact everything could not have been more different from Bow!

Our days in Balestrand were divided between field trips, lectures and note taking with hardly any time for much else except, of course, the importance of completing the promised letters and cards to be posted home. I remember too how wonderful it was to receive letters from home as well and re-assuring to learn that all was well.

The Norwegian food was enjoyed by us all even though it came as somewhat of a revelation to us London boys to experience and see that there were ways of eating fish other than frying it and serving it in newspaper with chips! Smoked – what was that? Let alone the variety of herring in sauces. And what about cheese and herring at breakfast time? – that was really something that took a lot of getting used to!

Of course, it was great fun and it was even more remarkable that 'Sir' seemed to be almost normal and human when away from school and, most importantly, not wearing his 'bat-man' gear. The brain teamed with thoughts of what it would have been like had 'chief bat-man' had been there as well – oh, better not, all Trolls together!

Certainly, the days were extremely well filled and the overall trip rather well planned. Never did we ever have to double up on our tracks, always seeing something new, always learning and always absorbing at all times. Time absolutely flew by and it was in a flash finally the day to leave Balestrand. I believe that we had at all times been too busy to cause any disturbance to the good folk of the village, so probably they had not even noticed especially our coming and going.

Naturally, we left by fjord ferry but this time by a different route across the Sogne Fjord and then along the neighbouring Aurlandfjord to Flam. Here another fjord side village and yet another opportunity to study the location relative to the surrounding area. Here the main difference, and endearing to me, was the fact that the village not only had a boat connection but a train as well – heaven! – and we had to travel on the train, my first ever experience of travel on a foreign train!

The magnificent journey of under an hour up the valley to the main-line junction at Myrdal surely earns its title of one of the great railway journeys of the world. Fabulous scenery of mountains and waterfalls as the train leaves the fjord side and twists and turns up the valley and into the mountains themselves; then curves through numerous tunnels to quickly emerge into the most spectacular scenery and, very obligingly, stops at intervals to allow passengers to take photos. That must be where our own railways today in the 21st century have taken their cue of frequent stops – except the passengers have forgotten to bring their cameras!!

So to Myrdal and the big train – on the main Oslo to Bergen line and itself another spectacular experience. Our route back took us on through the mountains and through the pretty towns of Voss and Dale and so back to Bergen. We had then one more night to stay on Norwegian soil, back at our familiar hostel used on the outward trip. 'Sir' thought that we should spend the evening finishing our notes and writing up reports etc., just in case the North Sea should not be too friendly on the following night. He must have been an excellent predictor prophet because the sea was bad – very bad – gale force winds as we made our way home from Bergen to Newcastle, this time aboard the good ship 'Venus.'

At first, the rolling and heavy seas just seemed to add to the sense of the adventure and I often thought about how Grandpop had told me of his time in the Navy when on one occasion the seas were so rough in the South China Seas that, even with engines fully going, their ship had hardly moved an inch in 24 hours. On such a basis, I began to think that we could take about a month to get back to Newcastle.

Would the food last out on board for such a time? Oh, don't talk about food!

Not surprisingly, the cafe and restaurants on board were very quiet but 'Sir' insisted that it would be best for us all if we tried at least to have something to eat.

'It's good for you, boys,' he said. Sadist!

The herring looked positively revolting as did all the various dressings and sauces. I, like many of the others, managed a bread roll and some soup.

'That's very good,' 'Sir' enthused, and 'it's good, solid fare to settle the stomach.' Did nothing take away his enthusiasm or was it simply he thoroughly enjoyed seeing his pupils subdued?

So the journey continued, bouncing around the mighty ocean rather like a cork – and a green one at that! Eventually, once we arrived at Newcastle, amazingly less than 30 minutes late which says much for Scandinavian seamanship, even the railway platform seemed to be rolling. It was certainly a rather subdued group of boys spending the journey back to London on the train and nobody seemed especially bothered to go to the café counter, let alone have any real food.

It was a fabulous trip, so full of happenings and things and places to see and even though it was the first time away from home and families for any length of time, there was too much to absorb, too many new experiences to have become homesick – sea sick on the way home perhaps but no other bad feelings. And to top it all, we actually had learnt something – the geography had been all around us and before our own eyes.

Whatever the feelings of the trip, it was lovely to be back home, to see Nan and Grandpop well, and then to bore them, father and all the family, with endless tales of the mighty expedition. By that time I really believed that father had a sense of guilt about his behaviour when I had first asked about the trip, plus, I suppose, a sense of further guilt that it was only money from Nan and Grandpop that had made the whole trip possible for me. Surely his 'friendliness' wasn't because he had missed me – now that would be a stupid thought!

Once again being back at school, there was a more mature sense following the trip – I had grown up enormously as too had my friends and we had a far more beneficial relationship with 'Sir,' even so that perhaps I should no longer refer again to that particular teacher as a 'bat-man' – he was human after all!

* * * *

Spring moved on into summer which that time was a much easier interim period as there were no real exam results to worry about, just some revision notes. But the summer did bring a very significant event – of course, there was to be the usual and still wonderful holiday in Folkestone but in that year I was also to have a week away with a couple of my friends – a first alone without any elders of any kind, although given our then style and attitude we were just younger in years versions of 'little old men!'

Immediately school finished in mid-July, the three of us were ready for the off – our big escape, in fact, although not really so because none of us had any negative feelings about our home lives and truly valued our surroundings. Simply, though, our appetite for travel had been whetted by our recent Norway trip plus my own upbringing at all times had included so many trips as part of the usual way of home life. Now, it was just a case of spreading the wings and adding to the variety of experiences.

Now it was north again for us – this time to the north-west and to the Lake District and for a week in a guest house near Keswick. I always had a certain penchant for these strange sort of small 'private hotel' types of establishments and so I was now inflicting the experience on my poor unsuspecting friends, with no idea what they were letting themselves in for!

Once again, we travelled by train and this time the excitement of a completely different route north than our spring journey to Newcastle. Then I saw places of such hallowed railway significance as Crewe, although just from the train window as I resisted the temptation of actually getting out there! I suppose that I would have dearly liked to have spent the whole holiday there and had I gone about it much longer, then no doubt my friends would have wished just that!

The journey continued on further through Wigan and Preston and to the hills of the southern Lakes before finally the quaint branch line from Penrith to Keswick. Once there, being upcoming and budding men of the world, feeling very important and somewhat grand, we took a taxi to the said guest house, situated right by the shore of Lake Derwentwater.

A summer holiday school task had 'lovingly' been set and our small group of three had decided our paper would be about the Lake District. Frankly, though, we did very little academically during the break other than keeping the occasional notes which we would write up later at home with much copying and exchanging of each other's work. No, this trip was very much our version of the Victorian Grand Tour (there I go again – never being able to resist reference to the Victorian influence!).

Albeit ours was just a tour on the English style. We did the touristy things – rowing on the lake, lengthy hikes and rambles around Borrowdale and generally enjoying the countryside and fresh air away from school and London. Of course, we 'studiously' compared the geographical features which we saw in the Lake District with our recent Norway trip (or was it like the old music hall song – 'oh yes we did; oh no you didn't!). This was the early 60s and we behaved in a very 'proper' and respectful way.

We could not resist a most 'daring' pursuit of a visit to a pub. Very sheepishly though, all looking so very terribly embarrassed.

'You go and order'

'No, you, I'll find a table.' What an excuse, the whole place seemed to be empty.

In the end, there was a perfect solution, we sat outside and since there was a serving hatch to the bar, we didn't actually have to go inside at all. Honour was saved, we just ordered ginger beer and could honestly be truthful that we had not broken the law nor behaved improperly!

Discos or night-life – well there simply wasn't anything on offer anyway and, even if there had been, I very much doubt if we would have understood that aspect of life anyway.

Really, the Lake District was then, and as it still is, a most magnificent natural country area so well deserved of its status of National Park and so much different from our home ground of London and South-East England. It was a true revelation to us that here in our own country was the glorious scenery of mountains which, in many ways, was so similar to that we had marvelled just a few months earlier in Norway. Even the sparkling lakes were a good substitute to the Norwegian fjords. A big plus point for us about the Lake District when comparing to Norway was that there were fish and chips for sale in abundance!! (even though we couldn't get a taste for that northern delicacy 'mushy peas').

Back to London again as becoming experienced travellers, we all had enjoyed the experiences of being on our first holiday away on our own as upcoming 'Young Gentlemen!'

A degree of sophistication perhaps, but not too sophisticated to enjoy, as ever, the family holiday in Folkestone, although 1962 would in fact be the last year for that. Always it was good to have valued the traditions and links with the past, that is both historically and my own past, and so have always thoroughly enjoyed doing and participating in the time-honoured events.

The Romney, Hythe and Dymchurch railway was a great a thrill to me in 1962 as it was on the occasion of my first visit over ten years beforehand; then, even after my own recent eye-opening travels I still thrilled at the day trip to France that year just as much as before, putting equal values of delight to all these events and happenings. In these growing years too I equally valued the time with the family, and by this I mean especially Nan and Grandpop, as I did the time with my friends.

Similarly, I continued somehow still to value my home life and the familiar Bow surroundings. Naturally, it was nothing special in reality, in fact entirely basic, especially so when comparing to the homes and surroundings of my friends, and indeed the aunts and uncles in the leafy streets of suburban Essex. Of course, it was because of familiarity, the sense of comfort and being rather too against the thought of change. That was through the experience of childhood years but life would not allow such a pattern to continue for long.

I do admit to the twinges of discontent which were then beginning to slightly nag brought about by life's new experiences and also by the feeling that, as Nan and Grandpop had in those pre-war years enjoyed short years at Leigh-on-Sea, they should once again have the opportunity for a better life. This was especially so when considering that in 1962 they were both still working hard at their caretaking duties. They so deserved better and I, in growing up, felt responsible too.

Father wouldn't and probably couldn't do anything about the situation – probably never even crossed his mind. So often I felt that he surely would have wanted better but 'better' for him was to be just in the mind, to pretend but do nothing.

By chance, I met during that summer time, a work colleague of my fathers and was completely taken aback when he said to me:

'You are very fortunate that your father has taken the trouble to make sure you have a good housekeeper at home to look after you. It costs him so much you know and the poor man never has any money he can spend on himself. Such a supreme sacrifice, you should be so grateful,' he continued in what was a very demoralising and accusing fashion.

I was absolutely flabbergasted! I was lost for words!

'Um, yes, um, good-bye,' was all that I could possibly say. Stupidly, I never even spoke to my father about the incident, I was too afraid of his reaction. Often, though, I wondered if his colleague had told him what he said! Luckily, I had the presence of mind also not to tell anybody at home about the conversation, it would have been too hurtful.

This event, more than ever, made me determined that I would leave school after the 'A'-levels, then in a year's time, to immediately start work with the aim of making a move possible at the earliest opportunity.

Not only that, but equally the growing awareness of things better elsewhere was also the cause of these beginning twinges of location discontent. Important too were the awful changes taking place in Bow which had by then multiplied even more. Soon it hardly resembled the area of my young years many of Nan and Grandpop's friends had moved away. The best values and traditions had changed to be replaced always by something far less good – whether that was local services, shops or the homes and buildings themselves – all then subject and victim of overall decline.

My mind was set but first had to be the final year of school with all efforts to achieve a positive exam result. So, remembering the old school report maxim:

'Must try harder!'

* * * *

The very last school year was not too much of a hardship for me as I continued to enjoy the study of my chosen subjects. On top of that was the expanding involvements and interests in the theatre, arts and music generally really made those final 12 months of the school career extremely worthwhile and made up for the agony and heartache of all the earlier years. I wasn't alone in these thoughts as all my friends had very similar feelings, all together as an united bunch.

Very naturally, the final year of the sixth form was also the time for a transition period between school life and the outside world, a thought that I particularly enjoyed. Even chief 'bat-man' began almost to treat me as a young adult and not as a school idiot. I wouldn't say he was human because that really was beyond his school capacity, but it was in a different spirit.

He would lead, for example, a school critics circle reviewing new films, television and theatrical productions, plus a general review of the arts world. Together, we would compare our collective thoughts with how the newspapers and media covered events, why and how the views differed. All very adult and mature stuff!

How nice it was too not any longer to be one of the newer boys in the school and having to suffer afresh all the difficulties and strangeness of those younger years.

It was good too not to be a victim of the school bullying anymore, a fate that not only befell me but many others when new to the school. Very terribly too, nobody seemed to have wanted to do anything about it.

'Grow up, boy – it's all part of the school tradition, it'll be the making of you.' This teacher's comment just about summed up the attitude but it was a horrible thing to endure. Why, I wonder, if it was so much part of the 'school tradition,' didn't I and my friends, when we were older, act in the same way to the younger boys. No, not because of being 'goodie-goodies,' but simply because we ourselves had suffered and didn't see any fun in doing it to others.

That last school year brought even more significant changes to my aspirations and thoughts of life importance. Girls? No, not yet! – and in that line I, and fellows like me, were very much the victim of the 'boys-only' school system. No, it was a waning interest in railways to be replaced by driving and cars. At last the chance to dispose of all those stored books of engine numbers and to clear away the boxes of stored model railway sets, by then gradually collecting dust. Of course, with sense, it would have been good to keep them but I wasn't to know that, in future years, there would be an enormous value put upon such models and I could have been wealthy!

Cars, then, were the new 'it' and so the desperation to learn to drive and to acquire my first 'set of wheels' to achieve for my 18th birthday coming in the next January, 1963. At that time, though, it had to be nothing more than a dream despite my dropping numerous hints. After all, there had been a couple of good trips and it was perfectly understanding that the money for driving lessons was simply not there. The uncles with cars were naturally too protective of their precious vehicles to allow me in the driving seat to learn and, in any case, I don't really think that they had the ability of instruction. No, for that moment the car had to remain a dream but it was difficult when many of my classmates had already begun their own driving lessons. This all added to my determination to leave school in the coming July to find work and thus earn money. University, even if by a miracle I had gained sufficiently high pass marks in the exams, was never considered an option by me but that is a matter I should have dealt with in a more adult way.

The various determinations did the trick and I really did study for the final exams. No longer was I bothered to check from the window whether the 10.30 from Liverpool Street was on time – thankfully! Instead, though, perhaps there was an occasional stare at some passing car with consequent dreams flashing through the mind. Earth shatteringly, I didn't even bother to attend the school railway club so much either and even donated my considerable collection of old railway magazines to them to ensue that my name would live on there for ever! Railways had lost my championship in favour of the car; let's accept therefore that the main reason for the decline in the railways in this country over the years has purely been because of the loss of my enthusiasm and guidance!

January 1963 – my 18th birthday – an occasion memorable enough in itself and which was marked by my first ever proper visit to a pub. 'Proper' – yes, that is to the actual inside of a pub and forgetting that altogether slightly embarrassing and awkward visit during that Lakeland holiday where we sat in the garden anyway! Of course the first proper visit just had to be with Nan and Grandpop to one of their favourite 'watering holes' in Bow Road.

'Well, love, what would you like? It's on me.' Nan said.

'Port and lemon, please,' was my reply. I honestly did not have a clue what to have and I naturally didn't want to have ginger beer that time, so I merely copied what I had heard that Nan enjoyed!

'You do the order then, boy' said Grandpop, and so:

'Two port and lemons, and one rum please,' I announced to the amused barman, the rum being for Grandpop in true Navy tradition.

After the pub, it was next door to the café for lunch. That café was still then a Bow tradition which, like the pub, had survived the then current epidemic of the extensive bulldozing and demolition work in Bow. The café served lunches to the corporate populations of the offices like those in our very home. Their menu could be termed as 'good, solid fare' and included popular items like steak and kidney pudding or traditional roasts, all followed by rather good fruit pies or steamed puddings such as my long-term favourite – 'Spotted Dick,' for 'afters.' Any order given would always be accompanied by the commanding question:

'With or without?' – referring to custard, of course!

On the Saturday following my birthday, we had a family theatre visit and being then a mature adult it was not the pantomime any more. Gilbert and Sullivan Operas were then the highlight of my theatre experiences, a growing enthusiasm coming as a result of Nan and Grandpop forever singing or humming various pieces over the years – even father was known to join in, strange as that may seem, but true nevertheless.

So off we all went to see the D'Oyly Carte Opera Company and a performance of 'The Gondoliers.' I remember being thoroughly captivated once again by the theatre and in the sheer enjoyment and pleasure of the Gilbert and Sullivan experience. The delightful music, witty story line and all in such a topsy-turvy make -believe world which, for me, is what I wanted the theatre to be about.

No matter how much I enjoyed outings and involvements with my friends, and the consequence of growing independence, I always valued the family outings and indeed all the times together. I never had any sense of embarrassment or feeling for distance when being out with the family – far from it – just simply enjoying all the time together, savouring every moment and the added experiences in the tapestry of life. I am glad that I did, because it would be too late in later life to regret otherwise.

My friends at school and I used to often think and talk about the very subject of families. In fact we all had a similar feeling, were all very much home boys and all felt entirely comfortable with such an environment.

The Easter of 1963 was to be my last real school holiday as naturally by that summer I would have left the scholastic life for ever. With my two main friends, we decided that we should make a special holiday and having odd jobs, some savings and a successful passing around of the begging bowl to the relatives, we together had enough money to plan a short Easter visit away. The place – Paris – over the Easter weekend. Forget the exam preparations, forget any geographical projects – you know the sort:

'The City today, relative to its geographical surroundings – Discuss!'

No, simply this trip was just to enjoy – and all then being over 18yrs, to sample some local brews!

As we were by no means then seasoned independent travellers, we visited a travel agent then newly opened up in Bow, in fact in the place of a tried and tested former grocer! Simplest, we were advised, was to book a package of travel and hotel, indeed the valiant forerunner of what would later be called a packaged 'City-break.'

With a sense of world experienced travellers, we set off on Good Friday by coach from Victoria in London and through the familiar landscape of Kent to an airport near to the coast known rather romantically as 'Kent's garden airport.' I think that my friend best summed this up by saying:

'Looks more like Kent's cabbage patch to me' referring to the grass and weed-strewn fields and runway (yes that was grass too, no Terminal 5 here!)

With some trepidation, we boarded an ageing DC3, which somehow burst into life and rattled along the grass runway, very much like an old and well-loved lawn mower. Equally miraculously, it finally noisily took off. Very slowly the fields and farms of Romney Marsh disappeared below the wing. I was sorry not to have been sitting on the left-hand side of the plane and would then have had the possibility of seeing Folkestone and that part of the Kent Coast from the air.

The old plane droned on, and managed to cross the Channel, not only by skimming the wave tops but at what seemed to be a reasonable height. After only about 20 minutes we crossed the French coast and after only a few more minutes safely landed at Beauvais in Northern France. There, we had to go through the Customs and all felt very proud to have a chalk cross placed on our bags. From the airport at Beauvais we next took a coach and, with ever wider opening eyes, finally reached Paris. Bow to Paris in eight hours – not bad for 1963.

We piled out from the bus on to the streets of Paris, right in the heart at Place de la Concorde. Passers-by would have been excused for thinking that here was a bunch of young urchins just up from the country; such were the wide eyes and expressions on our faces. Gathering our bags, we then set off, map-reading skills to the fore, to find our hotel.

Our arrangements, or rather the travel agent's arrangements, then quickly fell apart when the hotel claimed no knowledge of us or our bookings, indeed nor of our travel company either! What was different then to now with the security of package holiday arrangements on foreign travel – nothing! There was nothing for it for us other than to go to the tourist office and in 'school-boy' French, added with much waving of arms in the air, to try and get some cheapest possible accommodation, no mean feat for an Easter weekend! The tourist office was helpful and some pretty basic, and certainly cheap, accommodation was duly found.

'Accommodation' – well a room with three beds in a most seedy part of Montmartre and with our savoured budget severely strained by the need to pay for this new accommodation when we thought we had already paid for our hotel arrangements back in England. Consequently, there was no champagne nor bright lights possible for that trip – rather everything on the cheapest possible budget and the baguette, beautiful as they are, had to suffice whether it was for breakfast or petit-dejeuner!

As in many ways, the early experiences in life such as that let down by that travel company in 1963, had a huge influence on me and, in this case, it put me off travel agents for good. I vowed there and then, and kept it up ever since, to only arrange travel by booking the hotel and transport reservations oneself and only directly with the principal! At least then you are in control and have the direct confirmation paper in your own hands.

Our highly strained finances meant that we had to walk everywhere in Paris but our endless hikes meant we saw all the sights both from a far distance and from a direct perspective the closer we got. That was the one advantage of being penniless – missing out on the gorgeous-looking cafes and patisseries, not to say the bistros and the chance for some wine tasting was certainly anything but a bonus point. What a sad little bunch we must have looked, traipsing around endlessly with a constant mouth watering expression. All alone in a foreign land – but enough of remorse, this was Paris and it was spring time and we a small group of young men to enjoy it.

How limited our thoughts then were, once again the victim of a very straight and closed upbringing. We hadn't a clue of the real world. Delights then for us were sights, the famous museums and galleries, the trip on the Seine and even the thrill of taking a train by ourselves to Versailles because it was cheaper than an excursion bus. We stayed in Montmartre but never once set foot along the street to even pass by the Moulin Rouge, let alone to gawp at the pictures. Dull? – rather simply not grown up then nor aware of the world outside our immediate circle. But in our limited confines and doings, we had a good time and set back for home with the mind of seasoned travellers in a relative sort of way but far from reality.

Once we had returned home, we made remonstrations with the travel agency who, in turn, presumably took appropriate action with the tour company. It was, however, many weeks before any tangible result but we did finally get 25% back, although how that was worked out, none of us really knew, but it made a small donation for individual piggy-banks! What a pity 'Watchdog' wasn't around in those days – we may have received more substantial recompense.

On our return to school we enjoyed some degree of hero status as a result of our 'adventures' in Paris – although I suppose those more enlightened and advanced in years than us thought it was a made-up story to cover-up what we really did in Paris and how we spent our money.

Any further thoughts of adventures were soon put aside as the final countdown to the all-important 'A'-level exams began. They were to take place during May and immediately afterwards would then be the pressing need of thinking about how to obtain gainful employment.

The pattern of the exams followed very much as those for the 'O'-levels, two years earlier – equally lengthy studying and swatting, then the day of the individual exam and that special atmosphere in the exam room except that for that time it was much more intense – these were the exams for real whether the individual students to find work or seek an all important University place.

'Time – put your pens down and close your manuscripts' – that was it, 'bat-man's' words to herald the very end of the final exam paper.

Nothing more could then be done – just a sense of relief and oblivious to the fact that there would then be another horrible period of waiting until the results which would be due in late August and it was only then the end of May. I and all my school fellows had to stay on in school through June but would be allowed to finally leave at the end of June for an extended summer holiday prior to jobs or University. But the month of June was not like school at all – there was nothing real to do scholastically, just extensive times spent on current affairs and the arts, some outside visits, even off to the Oval to watch cricket – generally a reasonable life of leisure. We were also allowed time off from school to attend interviews and to generally plan for our future, preparing to become real 'men of the world,' as opposed to just wide-eyed school-boys!

I was for the job market!

But before all that, I had a surprise post-exam gift from Nan and Grandpop – money and arrangements for driving lessons! Naturally, I was so delighted and felt so very humble that my dear grandparents had scrimped and saved the money just for me to be able to do something that I really wanted.

'Look boy, they say you need one driving lesson for each year of your age' said Grandpop 'Here's enough money for 18 lessons so that should do it,' he continued confidently, 'the first lesson is booked for the coming weekend!'

Overwhelmed, I mumbled my grateful thanks.

'So looking forward to our first trip to Southend, love,' said Nan. 'We'll sit back and you'll do the driving!'

In the excitement of the moment, the fact that there was no car at home didn't immediately occur to anybody but, first things first, I was on the way to fulfilling a dear wish to drive. That prospect therefore made me even more determined to find a proper and suitable job to begin as school was finished later the same summer.

Come the following Saturday, then, it was back to being a pupil and learning again – this time, though, the subject was driving and it was in a completely different spirit with which I set off to the driving school in Bow Road to begin my lessons. Memories of the toy dummy driving wheel which I had enjoyed when being out as a child in Uncle Dick's car filled my mind as I approached the school car, a Ford Anglia with that 60s distinctive sloping rear window.

I was immediately told to sit in the driving seat, which seemed to me a somewhat bold step, but the first half-hour was no more than instrument and control instruction. After that I was told that there would be some actual movements! What a sense of excitement as we moved off, me in control, setting off amongst all the traffic of a Saturday busy Bow Road. Quite a bit of jumping, jolting and stalling, I painfully remember, and with sweaty hands tightly grasping the driving wheel, for real this time, and the instructor was in valiant control of the dual pedals and frequent grabs of the hand-brake.

'18 lessons, one for each year of your age' – Grandpop's comments rushed through my mind after the horrors of that first lesson. Perhaps it should be one lesson for each month of life, I thought, that would have appeared to be more appropriate, based on that very first lesson. Once again I was suffering in an exam situation!

The instructor said little at the end of the lesson – perhaps he was too shocked to speak – but I did think that he looked very pale, given that it was already summer-time!

'Have you arranged your next lesson?' he quietly asked.

'Oh, yes, I've booked a series of 18 lessons' I replied, probably with too much enthusiasm.

'Um – well – ok – yes' he mumbled, obviously rather hoping that perhaps one of his colleagues would be fortunate enough to be able to continue the course.

Nan and Grandpop were 'excited' to know how it all went when I got home:

'How did it go, love – did you manage to drive far yet?' Nan asked happily.

'Oh,' I replied 'I managed to pull away from the curb – but it felt very strange!'

'It will do, boy,' said Grandpop 'But it will come,' he continued to re-assure. 'In my day there were no lessons or tests – you simply applied for your licence, got into the car, had a few trips and that was that – nothing to it!'

I really couldn't understand, given my years of travelling in cars, why that very first lesson had been so awful such a nightmare. Surely a case of the teacher/pupil syndrome but, I thought, that would have only occurred in school-type subjects and not in things that I really wanted to do. Perhaps it was just sheer nervousness and it wasn't made any easier by the fact that one of my friends was going to the very same driving school and I was sure that news of my lack of abilities on that very first lesson would soon be common knowledge.

Fortunately, though, all the frights had manifested themselves during that very first lesson and my 'first-night nerves' had considerably calmed by the time for the second lesson which was altogether better. The improvement continued over the following immediate lessons and very soon I was even able to drive in a straight line!

I must though have made an impression on the first instructor because I then began to have a different instructor, in fact three in all until a regular came on to the scene.

'I'll shout, I'll scream, I'll give you absolute hell, but by golly you'll learn to drive with me,' he said, ever so politely. 'I've taught princesses, I've taught diplomats,' he continued.

'What, in East London and in Bow,' I thought to myself, 'some story that.'

'Now, I am going to teach you!' There was no stopping him; he was on his hobby-horse, well and truly! 'I don't know what it is like for one of my pupils to fail the driving test.'

'Well, there's always a first time!' I continued to think to myself.

I know that there was no conscription in my time, but this driving instructor experience surely sufficed as an alternative to army experience! I couldn't help but think of what Grandpop had told me about his time and how I wished I too could have just got into a car, had a little and gentle drive around and then walked into the Post Office and collect a licence. Anything would have been better than this!

At school, we compared notes on our developing driving skills and as to how the lessons were going. Obviously, there was a race on to be the first to pass the test and to get a licence. I listened very much in awe when others told how they found it so easy.

'3-point turns – there's nothing to it, simple, I'm doing it all the time now.'

'Are you?' I said, but rather wishing not to say that I had invented a new 3-point turn – it was called at least a 5-point turn, maybe 6 – in fact prize for whoever could do it in the most number of turns!

There was more talk in school then about driving prowess than about absolutely anything else. Nobody would have thought that we had all recently sat the most important of exams that would not have an enormous effect on the rest of our lives nor that we were all about to embark on fundamental changes as we left school for work or further education.

* * * *

As a 'side issue' to the driving lessons, I needed to concentrate on the process of actually getting a job! There was a careers advisory service, of sorts, at the school undertaken by one of the geography teachers (not the one who took us to Norway), but very much on a 'sideline' basis, like his keeping cuttings of jobs he had seen advertised in the press over the years. Indeed, his records were from so many years that many of the pages had turned yellow with age. More than half of the companies had long ceased to trade so the 'careers service' was not especially helpful.

The fact that the so-called 'careers service' was so unprofessional and so hit and miss, was a grave failure of the system given that in so many other ways the school had maintained reasonable standards. The fact that the school had succeeded in getting me to pass some exams and even to enter the sixth form is testament to some degree of their achievements but in the area of what was to happen next, they failed.

I wanted to try for a job where there was an element of geography, which, after all, was one of the few school subjects that I was actually any good at, and knowledge of the world was involved. It would have been absolutely stupid to even consider anything scientific and the mind would boggle at the thoughts of what would have happened if I had been let loose in some laboratory!

My other governing thought was that I had always felt for being able to work in the City of London ever since from those bus trips as a child and seeing the hustle and bustle there. A sort of romantic ideal, I suppose, but at least it was a start and consequently somewhere to start to look.

Father's role and the style of the government Civil Service didn't somehow appeal. Hardly surprising, given the strange and somewhat stormy relationship between father and son. Anyway, as I was used to throughout life, my father, once again on the career issue, took his usual uninterested and non-committal, stand-off stance.

Grandpop suggested the possibility of the shipping industry, which immediately fired my imagination and recalled the happy memories of those numerous river steamer trips. Whilst that may sound rather silly to make one's mind up about a career, based on childhood outing memories, it did seem plausible. Better that than if I had based thoughts on the days spent on draughty railway platforms! Then, to add to the developing idea, Ethel's husband, my Uncle Bill, worked in a ship repair company in London's Royal Docks, so together with all these elements a possible seed was sown.

With a standard draft letter supplied by the said 'careers master,' I set about my very first letter of a job application:

'I am 18 years of age and have studied… My 'A'-level results will be known in August and I am confident…,' I wrote, feeling very important and very much assured of potential success. Having researched about 20 companies and therefore sent off 20 letters, my next task was then to lay in wait for the postman each morning to that time make sure that there would be no further repeat of the exam results problem – i.e. 'official letters' being put in the 'district surveyor's' mail box!

At least in the early 1960s, all companies responded and so within a comparatively short time 20 letters duly came back and with that a chance for an interview with five of five companies.

June 1963 was therefore very noteworthy and a very busy time for me with the diary full of job interviews all interspaced with the continuing driving lessons which by then, thankfully, were proving to be more positive. To help the upcoming important interview occasions, Nan and Grandpop, with a contribution from father, gathered money to buy me a business suit.

As in my early years then, we all travelled together to Oxford Street in order to make this special and significant purchase. It was a very conservative purchase, in medium grey with a very slight, soft checked pattern and – most importantly, it was three-piece with a very dashing waistcoat. I felt extremely self-conscious when I tried it on and paraded in front of the assembled family!

I don't believe that there was anything strange that, in 1963, an 18 year old should be with his family all together to choose and buy that very first business suit. Because they were different values and different times, it seemed perfectly normal to me and all rather endearing when compared to the much more forceful and early adult society I would experience in later life.

Again, I do say that I have never regretted having the valued experience of such style and times. Old fashioned, maybe but in any other way strange then I do not think so. It was a kind of family togetherness and, whilst we were a small family, it was acting as if we were such a large fraternity.

After years of school uniform, I felt rather strange and a little awkward in a business suit – something which I had aspired to but in reality when the time came it did not feel completely right.

'Little old man, cut-down,' a very pertinent and London East End joking expression, was exactly how I felt. But if it didn't feel right then, I told myself that anything was better than a school cap and blazer and after that I very soon felt comfortable and normal again.

Thus I was set. Then with shining shoes to complement the new clothes and so ready to begin the round of five interviews. Amazingly to me at the time, I found the experience far less daunting than most of the immediate past school experiences. The fact to be treated adult like rather than the former teacher/boy situation that had been by immediate past norm, I found so wonderful, a breath of fresh air. Too, I felt at ease and kept reasonably calm although the reality was that I had little sense of the occasion or of the enormity of the event. I must have looked like the little boy with wide open eyes in the very big world, quite a sight!

Sometimes at an interview I would meet with the department manager if it was one of the smaller companies, but in the larger organisations it would be with the staff manager. That to me was more like the feeling of being back at the school as there was some similarity in the demeanour of a staff manager and a 'bat-man' character, although without the gown. It was fortunate for me that I was doing that round when I did, what I would have felt today if having to face a so called 'HR Manager,' I really dread to think of the consequences!

From the five interviews came three reasonably firm job offers, I say 'reasonably firm' because all were conditional upon 'satisfactory' 'A'-level exam results. I really felt reasonably happy with that result so I suppose that somehow I must have said the right things or, rather, acted so 'dumb-struck' that they all felt rather sorry for me. So for me to decide, it was all down to the 'terms and conditions' – or who offered the most money!

'Money isn't everything,' my family warned, 'What about the prospects for your advancement and for the company's future.'

That did seem a little grandiose for me to consider at that time. At 18, the word 'prospects' to me meant immediate money and I could not set my mind too far to the future to think of things like company worth or pension possibilities. Did I need the *'Financial Times'* or a crystal ball before making a decision, rather than relying on my personal maxim of shortest hours and most money!

Feeling very corporately important and in demand in the work-place, I made a short-list of two of the companies that 'suited my requirements' and attended the second interviews. With a further positive response and consequent further consideration, I finally accepted the position of Clerk in the Freight Department of a major shipping company based in Leadenhall Street in the heart of the City of London. Significantly, the office was situated on the very route that I had travelled so many times in the past on those Bus trips from Bow. It was that sort of re-assurance being in known surroundings that I found to be most comforting, especially so when going to embark on such an important stage of life, and that made me feel very good overall.

And so it was all set – I would therefore start on the very first day following the early August Bank Holiday. In those years it was still the time when we had the August Holiday at the proper time at the beginning of the month.

Great, I thought, my very first day would be a Tuesday and my first working week would only be four days – and I was to be paid for five! The whole idea sounded very good to me, the perfect arrangement for the very first working week and, in my dreams, perhaps the sound ideal for all future working practices – four days work for five days pay. Now that sounded rather a good political gambit!

However, before becoming too completely carried away, I did realise that the only cloud on the horizon was that the 'A'-level results were due and everything was dependent on them. But still, the chance to dream!

There was nothing for it other than to hope they would be in order otherwise my first job in my new working career would not last longer than a month! My thoughts then raced at the idea of being back once again looking for a job so soon at the start of my working life! Surely not, I told myself, if the worst came to the worst there was always that assistant caretaker role to Grandpop in reserve.

* * * *

Immediately then after all the excitement of the interviews in the business world, next ahead of me were the final school days. This glorious period led up to the end of June and after that there was to be the whole month of July for 'rest and reflection' before the world of commerce would open its arms for me. That period gave plenty of time for some more driving lessons, although it would be wrong to say that they were in any way a degree of relaxation.

I had my good days, a very few, but these were more than offset by the very bad days, indeed some still horrendous lesson days.

I was by then really beginning to fear that, for some reason, I would never get the hang of being a driver. With that fear, invariably my performance in the lesson would go from bad to worse – oh dear, it was painful. Sometimes, the lesson would involve collecting the pupil for the next lesson who would sit in the back whilst I finished my turn. That I positively hated and the nervousness made me even worse.

'This will show you how not to do it,' the instructor would say to the next pupil, sitting in the back! If anything was sure to make matters even worse for me, then he could not have made a more apt comment. I could see their smiles and faces in the mirror, which would cause my face to go redder and hands even sweatier!

I could not understand my poor ability, having spent so many former years being out in cars with the uncles, being used to traffic and on top of that being so much aware of all that was involved in driving. One day, though, the lesson did go much better and with a misplaced sense of achievement, I said to the instructor that perhaps I should consider about the driving test.

'It is not a good idea to put in for the driving test, just yet,' was the instructor's reply. I wonder why!

* * * *

The time flew by of the final weeks until soon the final days and then the very final school day itself arrived. I had experienced for seven years a traditional education from a traditional 'boys-only' grammar school. Nothing wrong whatsoever with the system, just that I was simply not the most brilliant pupil and I suffered accordingly. Therefore, I had no mixed thoughts, just a sense of thrill to finally get away. There was very little to miss and the group of friends that had been consistent for so long had all made a pledge for regular and on-going contact as we branched into different fields of life.

Certainly, there would be no loss from not seeing 'chief bat-man' and his team, the regimentation and style of school had long paled and I was confident and full of expectations for the outside corporate world. I had had enough of the school world and simply wanted to be free. There were some good times and I had positive memories of the additional, non-scholastic activities of the school years, an appreciation that I had gained in the arts, theatre and music through the various school societies and involvements.

But, overall, I was happy to be ending the scholastic career and was certainly very pleased not to be going to University. I have often wondered, though, how I would have adapted to the University life had I decided to go (and, more importantly, had I been accepted)! That, I will never know the answer to, but I am certain that I would have benefited from the experience and would no doubt have become a more mature and independent individual as a result.

The very final day we gathered as usual for class registration just as if it was our very first day, all diligently answering our names:

'Present, Sir' – as if the day wasn't anything special at all!

There were no lessons, and we all spent time reading the newspapers, even discussing the day's topics, the cricket results, in fact creating a most unreal atmosphere. This was the very last day of our school lives, we should have at least been running amok or at the very least carving our names on every desk and cupboard that we could get our hands on. But 'No' – we were discussing current affairs and cricket! It was so weird and strange, almost a let-down for the day that all of us had been dreaming of and looking forward to for virtually all of our school lives.

If the morning was strange, then we collectively decided that things must change at lunch-time, enough was enough!

'What shall we do?' I began the debate.

'There's no question,' one of the others replied, 'When they (meaning the teachers) all go to have their lunch, the staff room will be empty – we leave our memories there!'

'No, that's useless, they will know – far better to mix around some of the lockers,' suggested another.

'You are all wrong – what's the point when they will find out,' someone else said. 'Far better that we just all go out and enjoy ourselves, anywhere away from here – what about the Pub?'

Now that was an idea, greeted with universal acclaim. But something still had to be done in the staff room.

Yes – that was it! – some 'quiet' re-arranging of the timetable and class room numbers, which, amazingly, were always only ever pencilled in on the staff notice-board – that would keep everybody busy for some time at the beginning of the afternoon after which we could return somewhat late from our own lunch adventures!

We drew two names from a hat, of course, an old school cap, and the fortunate pair, which luckily didn't include me, went to the staffroom as soon as all teachers had gone to lunch, 'amended' the timetable, came back to join us and off we all went off to the pub in a degree of mad hysterics and foolishness even before we had had a drink!

The pub was, in fact, just opposite the school and from there we had a most wonderful view of 'chief bat-man's' study. Oh, the glory of those moments as the glasses of the finest bitter were lined up and drunk with a reverent salute across the road to the man, his study and the whole institution! It was a pity that we couldn't quite see the staffroom, knowing what mayhem would occur there during the early afternoon as a result of our timetable adjustments!

In a considerable degree of merriment, we finally left the pub at the early afternoon closing time and returned across the road to the school. Our 'efforts' had worked, as there was a degree of mild panic with some teachers running around in confusion, looking for their classes and their pupils! Naturally, suspicion immediately was directed at us and by then, all being under the influence of alcohol, we readily admitted to our ploy. Luckily, it was taken in a degree of good humour which made us all wonder why such frivolity had not been more apparent during our earlier school years. It would have been a better place as a result – for us, anyway.

'Good luck, boys' - a note of almost friendliness by 'chief bat-man,' or was it that our alcoholic breaths had intoxicated him too! More likely, he was as glad as we were that we had all finally come to the parting of the ways.

'Bye, Sir – all the best to you too,' was our general reply before rushing as soon as possible out of the school gates lest the whole thing should be a dream and the dreaded bell and the words 'next lesson' would ring out instead!

That was it – it was all over, the end of that particular era. I said that I and most of us left school without regrets but nevertheless our collective final school action was to register for the 'Old Boys Association,' which sounds very contradictory indeed. A lot of us maintained membership and visits back for many years but it was an entirely different sense to visit the place as an outsider to being an 'in-mate.' Most certainly the case of 'the grass being greener!'

So we went our different ways – all on holiday but some like me to work preparation and some to get ready for University. Having been in one place for seven years, I would have thought that there would be some degree of sadness in saying 'good-bye' to colleagues but in reality that was not so. The mere fact about actually leaving school seemed to over-ride all other thoughts and considerations.

It was then for the holiday month of July and trying not to be too overshadowed by the prospects of the dreaded exam results, so important for all of us whatever our final destiny was then due to be.

I had survived school, or, more importantly given its long history, the school had survived me, which, in itself, is even more remarkable. Perhaps, best to say that we had survived each other but now it was no more a feature of life, it was over, it was a period of life's history.

* * * *

There was to be no holiday for me or the family during that special month of July – no money – I was still a non-earner and a consequent drain on all resources. Everything there was had been spent, unselfishly, on my driving lessons, my trip the previous Easter to Paris, and on the new suit and clothes for my work. But as a kaleidoscope of the preceding years, and with a sense that this was about to be a true new dawn, all the hallowed and pleasurable trips of my childhood and youth were re-enacted and with great enjoyment too.

It was as if the clock had been reversed to the mid-1950s as, together with Nan and Grandpop, we visited Southend and the traditional lunch in the restaurant on the end of the pier. Another day to Folkestone, a day had to be enough as any holiday was financially out of the question – but how we enjoyed the day putting into ten hours what others would have done in ten days! On other days, we enjoyed the river trips or simply just having outings in London itself. It was a magical time and I could not have wished for a better way of spending that interim period between school and work.

Alright, I was then 18 and about to embark on a commercial career but it was truly lovely to relive again those happy moments of childhood. Nor did I feel in anyway childish or silly to travel around with Nan and Grandpop, or even, on occasions, for once, with my father. I didn't even feel bad about visiting the aunts and uncles – I must have been somehow mellowing about that latter fact. Simply, it was my personal 'Grand-Tour' and homage to the past and I revelled in it, even more so when the school clothes had been discarded once and for all. There would never in my life be a time like that one again.

So many changes then about to happen yet, contradictorily some fundamentals remaining more or less the same. Bow and my home were both there, almost the common denominator between these two immediate stages of life, giving a real sense of continuity and belonging.

Even though so many aspects from my childhood times had changed beyond recognition, many other things had changed hardly at all. Some of the small shops in Devon's Road, and its market, albeit reduced, were still there in existence. Bow Road was, of course, so much busier and 'my' trolleys had long gone, but other scenes of childhood were constantly there to remind me. Our house had no changes – still the offices and Nan and Grandpop caretaking, father in the civil service, the aunts and uncles residing 'properly' in suburban Essex – all a semblance of sameness in my own changing situation. Given how my first few years had been so turbulent, by comparison the following ten had been most stable.

But first – still some more driving lessons and that final month of freedom brought at long last the much needed and significant improvement in my skills, enough even for the instructor finally to say:

'What about putting in for the test date, then?'

Gulp – 'What' – 'Ok'- well, – yes, then - I'll do that!'

Three-point turns, hill starts (where were there ever hills in Bow, I don't remember?); emergency stops (of which there were many during the early stages of my learning!). All had to be done now with ever growing awareness and, when I finally received notification of the test date, it was to be on a Saturday (which I wanted – I couldn't have asked for time off work!!) at the end of August, then about six weeks away.

That end of August then had all the potential to be a highly crucial time – the exam results due, getting used to work and 'hopefully' being able to keep the job on the back of those results and finally then the car driving test.

It was just like being back at school all over again!

Chapter 9

The City Calls

To begin with I did not see very much difference between that very first day for work in August 1963 compared to the first day to the grammar school seven years before.

It was just the same hectic preparations at home, the checking of new clothes but first to start the day, the real plus point, was Nan's traditional big cooked breakfast. Masses of sausages, bacon, mushrooms and tomatoes accompanied with good supplies of toast and marmalade.

'Sets you up for the day ahead, love,' Nan said, and she was right even though it took some effort to beat the nerves and to do justice to the meal.

Even so, I was still apprehensive and with that strange, nervous feeling in the pit of the stomach. The only real difference from the school time was that for the working day everything was happening two hours earlier in the morning! But at least it was a Tuesday (the previous day being August Bank Holiday) and so the first week was only to be four days, which, of course, should be the trend anyway

I had decided that it was more fitting and potentially more business-like to travel on the Underground from Bow Road, following in father's footsteps on the District Line, in preference to taking the bus to the City and Leadenhall Street. The tube had a greater sense of potential and upcoming managerial quality than the bus - ambitious snob that I was!

Of course, I didn't travel with father – I'm not so sure even if that would have worked anyway and it would have created a very strange and awkward atmosphere for the first day in any case. In reality though it was not an option, the fact was that he had to leave home earlier and I had a more leisurely start well after 8.30 am for working day. What an immediate luxury, to be talking about starting the working 'day' some-time after the leisurely hour of 'eight-thirty!'

To act correctly from the start and to look the part, I even bought a newspaper at the station, naturally *The Telegraph*, always having an affinity to the paper as mother had worked there. I always felt it comforting, appropriate and a tradition on memorable occasions to have that paper. A psychologist would obviously say that I did this to have a feeling of mother's support with me. It was all nothing more than appropriate show because only having just five stations on the tube barely left time to read the headlines, let alone the leader page. And what about the City pages, stocks and shares – well, all that can be left for later!

In keeping up the family custom of always getting off the Underground one station early to save the fare, I did the very same that day and got off at Aldgate East, rather than travel on to the real City station of Tower Hill. From Aldgate, I enjoyed the walk to Leadenhall Street and the sights and sounds of the journey to accompany me as I began this new life.

In the rather beautiful and warm air of a very bright summer morning, first I passed the 'Tubby Isaacs' jellied eels stall to remind that the street was still in my familiar East End. Even in this day of my new venture, I was still happily connecting with my roots, I confidently told myself. Next came the boundary with the City at Aldgate, the real stepping stone from one old life to the new one. Past thoughts were not altogether lost though, as right there in the City street was a very special Eel and Pie shop of East End fame. All the cooking was going on in the very window where there was already a huge bowl of mashed potatoes to go with the weird-looking pies and the thick, pea-green gravy. Quite a sight for 9 o'clock in the morning and enough to turn an untrained stomach over.

Better to hurry on after that sight – I hadn't fully digested my breakfast even!

How quickly after that point the surroundings changed when passing the City boundary. Immediately then were the impressive office buildings, the banks, the insurance companies and the various companies of the shipping fraternity. I then felt like my very own 'David Copperfield' having finally reached and then to actually be treading the hallowed pavements of the City, my new world in effect.

Very much I felt like the 'New Boy' – very conspicuous, very out of place and a strange, empty and almost frightened feeling. I doubt, though, whether anybody else really noticed me, all were intent on rushing to their own places of work. In any case, why should they notice me, I was then just another face in the already massive crowd.

Masses of people were rushing to and fro, a sea then of bowler hats and crisply rolled umbrellas, neither of which I had. I did, though, have a plastic 'pac-a-mac' in case of rain, and that was hidden neatly out of sight within the folds of the paper! *The Telegraph*, being a broadsheet, therefore had a range of plentiful uses.

By the time I reached the building of the visionary company that had chosen to hire me, my legs were really like jelly and I was bathed in sweat. I went through the enormous swing doors into the pillared hall – surely a re-incarnation of that very hall at school, I mistakenly thought because this one was so very much grander. In any case, here there was no sounds such as the swish of the cane, no faces of petrified and nervous school boys, only my nervous face instead.

'Can I help you, Sir?' a uniformed Commissionaire kindly asked.

I didn't possibly realise that he was speaking to me.

'Can I help you, Sir?' he said again.

'Oh, so sorry,' I replied, 'I am supposed to go to the staff department. I do have an appointment,' I continued to stutter. What must he have thought of me, the Commissionaire by comparison being so much polished and in control, so at ease compared to me, the wide-eyed new boy in the equally new world!

'Sea-going or shore staff, Sir?'

'Oh, shore, please,' I replied, wondering what on earth would happen if I had said 'sea.' Probably I would have been deported there and then to Australia for at least one round trip, not to be seen again at home for months! My mind absolutely ran wild with the thought of what such experiences would bring, me being then such a 'home-boy' by character.

'Take the lift to the second floor, Sir,' he advised.

'Thank-you, Sir,' I answered, by then so thoroughly mixed up between this situation and the similar feeling situation occurring on my first day at school.

I joined the throng queuing for the lift which finally clanked into position and the lift gate was opened by yet another uniformed person. A rather gruff 'Good-Morning' was mumbled at everybody who crammed into the ancient vehicle which then moved up slowly through the musty and drafty lift shaft, all clearly visible thought the mesh of the lift gate. Nobody wanted to get out at the first floor so we continued at express pace to the second, where I and a few others duly got out.

Then a short walk along a corridor, vaguely familiar from my interview times and then to finally arrive at the staff department. There, I was actually 'welcomed,' which I found a rather nice experience after all those school years. A few forms there then had to be filled in, notably one form highlighting the fact that the permanent condition of my appointment was dependent on the 'satisfactory A-level results.' This sent a cold shiver down my back and the real thoughts of possibly my being 'expelled' within a month of my arrival!

The next ordeal of the day, in a day that for me was already filled with ordeals, was being taken back downstairs to the big hall, another nod from the Commissionaire, then being taken through the imposing swing doors into a cavernous and high galleried room which was the freight department. However, this was obviously too grand a location for my first corporate experience and I was taken on further, very much in 'tow' and utterly appropriate for a shipping company environment, to a side corridor and to some smaller offices. There I was introduced to the department manager, or rather he was in fact one of the company directors which, naturally, added to the sense of occasion of the day. It reminded me of the 'district surveyor' situation of my own home-life office.

Polite introductions then were exchanged and I wasn't entirely sure who seemed more ill at ease – the director, the staff or simply me.

'Good Morning and welcome to the Company' and I, exactly like school, was called simply by my surname. In fact it was so like the school feeling overall but, hopefully, this time I was to be paid for the privilege.

Next, in the day of all days of events, I was taken on a tour of the appointed department by a far lesser personage than the director, and then introduced around the various members of that particular department. It was all a buzz of different faces, of names that I couldn't readily remember, in fact all of a complete haze and total bewilderment. I was finally taken in further tow, to continue the shipping theme, by a chap a few years older than me.

He happily told me that he was himself leaving the company in a couple of weeks and that I was there to take over his job. Why was he leaving, I wondered, what had he learnt about the job, about the company, even about the immediate work-place, that I, as yet, didn't know and perhaps would learn? More thoughts of wondering and foreboding clouded my mind, everything was so strange and I felt very ill at ease.

Well, in any case, with this man leaving soon, I would need at least to settle and concentrate. 'How to run a complete shipping company in two weeks' was the thought that immediately ran through my mind, importantly then beginning to think that I would be in control!

Nine working days to learn it all – if the first day was anything to go by, I would be lucky to have learnt how to find my way to the post room, let alone actually become a 'clerk.' And what a glorious, almost archaic title that was, conjuring up thoughts once again of Victorian times, quill pens and high-backed chairs in smoky, dim and murky offices. No, where I was set to be wasn't quite as bad as that but it certainly did have leanings in that direction.

In a continuing state of trance I went to lunch with some of my new colleagues, proudly clutching my supply of luncheon vouchers and wondering what I could buy for the then three shillings value. In reality though, for once only, I didn't feel in anyway hungry and, as always on such occasions, the simple thought of 'I want to go home' invaded my mind.

Everybody else seemed so assured, all accustomed to the somewhat stilted and unnatural office type talk, very much unreal to me and I felt very out of things.

Even though I had been many times to the City, to be a passing visitor was somewhat different from being actually part of its life. Everything felt so very different. All the masses of people in the streets, all the mayhem and scramble to get served in one of the street cafés and to gobble the lunch in time. Then to negotiate the busy streets back to the building and through the labyrinth of corridors to 'my' office – or rather, the room shared with four others.

The building itself was then around 117 years old and whilst it was certainly very grand from the outside aspect, the imposing entrance and the areas immediately around the main entrance, my allocated space by contrast was rather dull, cramped and almost dingy. To raise the word and similarity again, it was almost 'Victorian.'

There was a high window to the room overlooking the corner of St Mary Axe and Leadenhall Street. That at least was good because there I was able to see the familiar buses passing from and to Bow. In that respect, it was just like my experience with the railway line at school – my look and connection with the outside world!.

The endless corridors around the building were extremely foreboding and gloomy, extremely dimly lit, almost depressing in fact. Masses of different, mainly small, offices led off in varying directions. Very occasionally, people would emerge from these various places but otherwise it seemed to me that once ensconced in the morning and after lunch, then all would hibernate until the time to go home. All in all, a very strange and peculiar atmosphere – perhaps I should have introduced my old school bell to liven up the to-ings and fro-ings!

The filing room, very much my domain during the first weeks, was something really special – creepy, dismal and very much below stairs and lacking any decent illumination other than a single lamp – probably that was just 40 watts too! To accompany and to add to the atmosphere, there was an extremely musty smell too. The fact that I spent so much time there more than anything at least shows that I began my working life very much from the bottom! Whether from that I would ever reach for the top, then only time would tell

My colleagues, apart from the fact that everybody seemed to be called only by their surnames, did all seem reasonably pleasant. Interestingly to me, in view of my 'probation' period pending the dreaded exam results, most of them had been in the company for many years, almost so that they were almost very much part of the company's 'furniture.' Of course, then, it was much more the norm that people would be in one company 'for life' – work that is, not imprisonment. To me, though, during those first days, there was a degree of similarity between those thoughts!

I could not help then wondering whether I would be just a passing visitor if, perish the thought, I would have had to leave with bad exam results. It did lead to a feeling of uncertainty throughout the early weeks at work, merely just to add further to my sense of unease.

* * * *

One extremely positive aspect of City life and work in 1963 was that the hours were most gentlemanly. Of course, the start was at 9.30 and the working day ended most promptly at 5 pm – and I mean most promptly. There was then no ethic of working late and everybody from the directors downwards – and it was 'downwards' to me as a humble clerk – all poured out of the building in droves, spot on time. It was such a rush that the main swing doors were locked by the kindly and very understanding Commissionaires, into a permanent 'open' position to help the very swift and one directional flow!

'Don't be late twice in one day - just in the mornings!' – that was the company saying, almost a company motto and everybody kept to it rigidly.

I'm not saying that everybody went home immediately, although most did. Others though made straight for one of the City's famous pubs for a revitalising 'snifter' before facing the station and the journey home! All that was still a different world to me and one that I was not immediately a part. Being then a 'good boy,' and realising that to be a member of the 'pub-set' meant a City apprenticeship of at least ten years, I was one of those who made immediately for the station.

Retracing exactly my footsteps of the morning, the walk back from the City to the Underground Station at Aldgate, then the tube home, I was then home by 5.30pm thanks to the efficiency of the District Line. In all respects, then, it really was a very gentle kind of schedule and a perfect introduction to the whole idea of working life.

To be home so early to me was just like the school routine again, having the evening meal at around 6 pm before Nan and Grandpop began their evening caretaking work activities. Then, without homework to do, I could even lend assistance, combining the role of City-boy by day with that of caretaker's assistance by night. With that expertise, I could even consider to volunteer to help clean the offices at the City shipping company as a part-time sideline!

On the end of the first day everybody, even, amazingly, father wanted a fully detailed account about all that had happened – what did I do?; what was I expected to do? How were my colleagues? Did I like it?

'Fine' or 'Alright,' was my answer in brief reply.

The fact was that I was simply overwhelmed by my very first day in the corporate world and was completely incapable of giving a factual account of events. It was most fortunate that my very first week at work was just four days and thus a gentle introduction to the new life.

The time flew by in a mainly continuing haze until finally Friday evening was reached. I needed that much cherished weekend at home to gather my thoughts before beginning my second working week and hopefully then to be worthy of the salary that the company was paying me.

Salary – oh, yes – a princely sum of £275 per year plus, of course, the supply of the daily luncheon vouchers. I was in the big time!

So, after a couple of weeks then, the chap I had been hired to replace accordingly left. As such events of somebody actually leaving the company were rather rare, there was something of a party feeling in the office on that day and at lunch-time we all, in turn, went off to the pub as a celebration. Having by then been used to seeing the same colleagues in working mode, there was then the new experience of the same people out of the office. No, perhaps that wasn't so strange, the conversation mainly turned to work issues and if not, was extremely jilted and false.

'Nice day,' 'Busy here today,' 'Are you looking forward to your new job – ah, what is it?' I very much got the impression that everybody put up with each other in the workplace but that was it – work and own lives, social times were completely separate and private issues. That, too, was exactly how it was with me so it did not appear strange.

With the departure of my former colleague, I was duly awarded my own desk and corner of the coat rack to mark the occasion! With my then developing duties I was able to see more of the overall office building as I paper ran from department to department. No, I wasn't quite as lowly as a messenger-boy, but as this was the time long before e-mails or even an extensive internal telephone system, there was thus an evident need for walk-abouts. This, of course, gave a semblance of importance to an actual paper-pusher, a sort of paper-chase executive!

The entrances and the main area of the building were certainly grand, adorned with paintings of the company's ships and various world destinations served. The extremely high ceilings in that part of the building were hung with the most spectacular chandeliers. Liveried Commissionaires bustled to and fro plus a constant stream of other smaller fry like me, big bosses and even some bigger bosses going about their tasks with some occasional acknowledgements, although more normally simply a passing nod. I think that it would be fair to say that there was an overall air of quiet efficiency within the 'corridors of power,' all much more restrained and therefore quieter than my then recent school experiences.

On rare occasions, but very notable for me, I had a duty to take papers to the main board room in readiness for a director's meeting. That room was really impressive with enormous paintings adorning the walls, both of various company ships and past chairmen going back to 1837. As for the centre table – I had never seen one so big nor with such massive chairs surrounding it; I suppose that my eyes must have been wider than the room! So that must have been the place to aim for, I thought. The table at which to sit at some time in the future – assuming that in the first instance those wretched exam results – 'that day' then less than a possible two weeks away – would determine. When would my own picture line the same wall, I hopefully wondered, and should I sit already now for the first portrait?

My own office duties soon became to make sense and I began then to learn the hallowed terms of the shipping industry.

'Bills of Lading ' and or 'freight rates' started to become part of my everyday vocabulary too. Great and heavy books of tariff freight rates to far-flung corners of the world piled up around my desk as I found out that my important duty was updating these mighty tones with rate changes and amendments – by hand! My desk was submerged by these massive volumes which, once again, led to my visions of various characters from Dickens toiling away at their first-time commercial experiences. I laboured away, slowly but hopefully surely, wondering why my erstwhile colleague, just recently left for pastures new, had somehow overlooked several months of the work!

'Good groundwork and training, old chap' the manager cheerily said.

'Um, of course,' was my garbled reply.

The way for me successfully to do the laborious task was to romanticise about the place names in the tariffs. To visualise the world through those books of freight rates – Port Said, Aden, Bombay, Port Swettenham, Singapore, Yokohama, Sydney, Wellington – and so on, letting the mind happily wander the world whilst amending the pages. It was a dream world full of exotic destinations and no more just a printed page of boring and endless freight rates.

'You seem happy enough' said a colleague.

'Um, of course,' I said, which was turning out to be my standard office reply.

'Funny chap,' everybody must have thought, 'Doesn't say much else than 'Um''! Still, they didn't say over much either, so we were all well suited!

There was very little general office talk and therefore little to get to learn about the bunch of people then as my colleagues. Everybody just emerged from somewhere just before 9.30am and with polite – 'Good Mornings' simply got on with the task in hand. Lunch-time for them be the time for other short exchanges of messages then all was quiet until later in the day.

As everybody suddenly appeared in the morning, then they all equally disappeared, but at greater speed, especially at 5pm, all to be gobbled up by the bowels of the earth at various tube and railway stations. It was as if people mortalised just for seven and half hours per day, Monday to Friday, and outside of those hours just disappeared from the face of the earth. Obviously everybody else's basic life was in some way similar to mine – just important to be at home and within each other's private world of reality. Work for them, as me, was probably no more than a means to a financial end rather than any particular delight.

At least the working day for me was a little different. I don't somehow suppose that any of my colleagues then went home to take their turn at office caretaking duties, cleaning and polishing etc. But then, on the other hand, since nobody actually talked in any detail about their own lives, perhaps the others did do exactly the same as me and we were all completely in oblivion of each other's secret lives!

* * * *

Towards the end of August, I became even more agitated about the morning mail, which, fortunately came before I left home for work. I asked Grandpop to tour the offices every morning just in case once again the vital letter could have been misdirected to the wrong letter box. That contingency wasn't however necessary as finally the dreaded envelope arrived one morning, delivered by a rather happy and cheery, whistling postman, just before I was about to set off for work. Was it a good omen, did the postman know something that I didn't?

This was it!

First, I could only stare at the envelope. Was I about to head to work for the last time in that job – would the former school 'chief bat-man's' vision of my dismissal from his school finally become reality in the work-place?

Oh, gosh – how long did it take to open an envelope when fumbling with hot, sweaty and shaking hands. The situation seemed so completely unreal, yet it was all a potential turning point for my life.

A simple piece of paper delivered the news – passes in all the three 'A'-level subjects and pretty good grades for geography too. I was too mesmerised and in a sense of shock to really take it all in!

'You've done it, boy,' Grandpop said, standing next to me by the letter-box.

'What is it?' said Nan, responding to our rumpus.

'Three passes,' I spluttered out.

'Oh great, my love – well done – now off to work and hurry, you'll be late and you don't want to get the sack!' What a thought that would have been – got the exam passes but got to work late and lost the job anyway!

'We'll have a special meal tonight,' Nan called out as I rushed out of the door, underground station bound.

By the time that I reached Leadenhall Street, I was literally walking on air. Getting to the office seemed especially thrilling and shortly after 9.30am I bravely asked if I could see the director.

'What is it about?' said the very protective secretary.

'It's my exam results,' I said.

'Oh – well, he is rather busy but perhaps I could fit you in for a minute or so later in the morning' she said, rather inferring that the matter was of such little importance and could not disturb the corporate day. Of course, in reality, it wasn't important to anybody other than me!

Anyway, I finally saw him before lunch and received his quiet 'well done' and instructions to go immediately to the staff department. The manager there was considerably more vociferous and even offered 'hearty congratulations!'

'Wait a moment, please,' he instructed.

'Right,' he carried on 'so we can now confirm you as permanent staff – and I am pleased to say that your salary is immediately increased by £25 per year to £300 per annum.'

That's great, I thought, the brain quickly acting as a mini-calculator to express the dramatic increase in terms of pounds per month. At work for less than a month and already got a salary increase, I thought. Can't be bad and must keep that up on a monthly basis!

'Now,' the staff manager continued, 'here are the forms for the pension scheme and the other company health cover details.' This was surely a case of giving in one hand and taking away with the other – or rather that what it seemed like to me! All in all, it immediately took back quite a bit of the recently awarded increase! The thoughts of a pension at that early stage of life seemed to me to be in infinity and not worthy of immediate consideration. But then, in another sense, the use of that magic phrase 'permanent staff,' now as reference to me, was truly wonderful to my ears. The enormity of the real significance of those exam results, the worrying about them both consciously and sub-consciously for the immediate past weeks, plus the realisation of what would have happened should I have failed, caused my knees to wobble as I returned back downstairs to my office area and my desk.

For the rest of that day, I hid myself rather conveniently behind my tariff books without doing too much, thinking, dreaming but nevertheless vowing to make it all up and work extra hard the following day. That certainly wasn't the time to actually be found to be slacking at work!

By the time that I got home, the enormity of everything was beginning to sink in. No longer was it 'What if'; 'if' was now not a question, perhaps 'what now' was the more relevant. As always at times of family celebration, Nan had prepared one of her truly memorable special meals. That time we started with a delicious home made vegetable soup, then roast beef, 'Yorkshires,' of course, summer vegetables of runner beans, marrow, new carrots and some oven potatoes. Pudding? – of course, my favourite, summer or winter, 'spotted dick' with lashings of custard. The others would enjoy something more appropriate for the time of year, like summer pudding but I simply could not be weaned off of my steamed puddings even on the warmth of a summer's evening.

All this culinary delight put me in an even more highly positive frame of mind. To top it all, we all decided to go to our favourite local pub as soon as Nan and Grandpop, with my assistance, had finished their evening caretaking chores. Before that, and to show what an obvious good frame of mind that I must have been in, I wrote a letter of thanks to 'chief bat-man' and a couple of the other 'bat-men,' probably out of a sense of relief and gratefulness of never having to see them again in a school-boy/school-master capacity.

Together, we all had a most joyous evening in the pub, some pleasant rounds of drinks and even although full from the big meal, still room for some pies and 'Scotch-eggs.' Even in these circumstances, we were a somewhat private family and made no special comment to others in the pub, even though many had known us for a long time. We talked with the others about work, what it was like, what I did; we talked about the summer doings, also about our immediate home life and the caretaking, but not a word was asked, nor did we say, about the results. It was better that way – you can imagine how difficult it would have been had the exam results been a failure! Overall though it was quite a joyous evening and we were rather a merry bunch deposited on the pavement at around 11pm.

Father was not to be seen, naturally, throughout the evening in the pub, although he had said that he might 'come along.' I knew that non-committal phrase though and didn't expect him! To be fair, though, he had wished me well at home, and, by that stage of my life, there was a more responsible adult-style relationship between us. He still spent the life privately in his way, perhaps mysteriously, but at least my becoming an adult seemed to make it easier for him to relate to me and we by then had some semblance of reasonable conversation.

* * * *

Now that particular exam results and their potential influence on my fledgling working world hurdle were out of the way, my thoughts then had to be turned towards the immediate following Saturday – the day of the Driving Test! On Friday evening, immediately after work and even before having dinner – which in itself was proof enough as to what must have been the seriousness and importance of the occasion! I went straight to have my final driving lesson. That is to say, the final lesson before the test!

'Well, if that's how you'll be tomorrow, then don't bother to turn up,' the instructor said, thus immediately inspiring me with enormous confidence.

He was right, though. That final lesson had been deplorable and I do not remember doing anything right and there was nothing new in that realisation! Simply, there had been too many and major, recent happenings in my life for me to concentrate properly. It was completely inappropriate that I should then be attempting that driving test.

The next day – and the actual test itself.

I had an hour before the test and after meeting up with the instructor, who by then had already decided that there was nothing he could do for me but instead spend a relaxing morning sitting in the car with *'Sporting Life'* close to hand. Anyway, I sort of drove towards the neighbouring place to Bow of Stratford, where the test centre was situated, even managing to park the car reasonably well within the car park.

'Well, you can only do your best,' the instructor said, continuing 'Whatever happens, put it down to experience and then it will be a great deal easier the next time.'

So he had, unsurprisingly, already written me off, but perhaps he was simply just looking forward to the prospects of more lessons with me!

Oh dear! Naturally the instructor was, as always, perceptively right. On the test itself, I even turned left when the examiner said 'right.' The sunny streets of Stratford in East London, on that late August Saturday morning had never seen anything like me on test! 'Three-point turns' – more likely six-point turns plus two curb bumps; 'hill starts' were hill slips, and so on.

'Sorry, but you have not passed on this occasion' said the examiner. 'It may help you,' he continued 'if you consider specifically the points that I have noted on this slip of paper,' at which point I was handed the dreaded rejection and failed advice slip, which, needless to say, was completely covered with 'comments.'

The instructor was waiting, by then having finished his *'Sporting Life'* and probably planned his bets for that afternoon – and I certainly was never considered as one of his bets!

'Well, it's like I said,' the instructor pontificated, 'put it down to experience and see what happens the next time.' With that, we, or rather I, drove back to Bow and, rather amazingly, at that moment when the test was over I drove in a reasonable enough way, although the instructor seemed passed caring, probably he was not used to having a failed pupil to ruin his credibility!

'Well,' I thought, reassuring myself, 'at a salary at £300 per year it would be sometime before I would be buying a car in any case!' However I adhered to the old maxim:

'If at first you don't succeed, then try, try again,' which is what I did.

I put in for another driving test immediately and got a date for early October. Then took a couple of more interim lessons and under the less stressful circumstances, passed on the second attempt.

'Goodbye,' then to my 'friendly' driving instructor, then free to terrorise some other poor victim!

* * * *

Back at work on the following Monday following the car test failure, there was no need to worry about any colleagues asking how it had gone. In keeping with what was the obvious code of practice, I hadn't told anybody and kept the unwritten office rule that private matters were not discussed.

An immediate antidote to my potential misery was that it was pay-day week – the magical day being on the 28th of every month. 28th August 1963 then a 'red-letter day' for me - my very first receipt of the confidential pay envelope! To me then it was all so unreal, just a simple slip of paper to say how much had been paid into an agreed bank account – no hard cash to fondle or handle – It was necessary to rush along to the appointed Bank in St Mary Axe at lunch-time and begin financial transactions.

How I treasured the fruits of the very first 'pay packet,' or, more correctly, paper advice of a bank deposit. I was finally 'a salaried person' – my pocket was 'hot' – it felt very good. It somehow didn't matter – and probably did not occur at the time – that the next payday was then a month away and that some degree of budgeting was therefore necessary even at the tender age of 18.

So what did I do with my first month's wages – firstly a bit of a spree on very many small things by then deemed necessary and possibly a lot of non essentials. The first major purchase though was a season ticket for the Underground for my daily travels – how good it felt when presenting my 'pass' for the first time. By virtue of the fact that I then began immediately to save from having to buy a daily ticket, I had become a budgeting person by the back door anyway.

I must admit, however, that at this immediate time, I didn't pay too much attention to my Aunty Ethel who always had an eye on the main chance, and tried to recruit me to become one of her National Savings customers! For old times' sake though I did join her scheme in September and, as even further proof of my growing financial awareness, I also asked at the appointed bank in St Mary Axe:

'May I have details of opening a monthly savings account, please as well as a regular account?'

'Yes, certainly, Sir – the regular account with cheque book is straight forward enough. About the savings though, do you want a direct deposit savings account or do you want to make voluntary deposits?' the Banker asked.

'I think that I prefer direct deposit transfer,' I said with the true authority of an already established long-term City worker. Also knowing full well that, if I decided upon a voluntary account, then the deposits would be very occasional, extremely few and far in between.

That was it then – easy – already for the monthly salary there were established outgoings and that was even before any money had been set aside for pleasurable pursuits! The car thought was still a distant dream but, nevertheless, still something very important to aim for – soon!

With the first pay day, the confirmation of my permanent position, I grew in confidence daily as I went to and from work and perhaps, even at least in my mind, I was then becoming a mini 'City-gent.' No, I didn't have a bowler hat nor even a rolled umbrella (the plastic pac-a-mac still sufficed!). My only true contribution to a 'City-gent' image was the rolled *'The Daily Telegraph'* and my wearing dark suit, white shirt and reasonably sombre tie but, notably, not yet at that time a tie of the 'old school variety!' It was all, after all, very much in keeping with the agreed 'City uniform.'

I thought that I fitted in with the crowd after the first month – indeed, very much settled in.

The confidence of those exam results, the further confidence of having received my first pay and then the realisation of actually being able to do the office job without undue problems, even though the job was fairly undemanding, all though added up to making me feel rather comfortable with my life then.

Life to experience in the City of London in the 1960s was the opportunity of experiencing a style and a way of life of a very tried and tested institution. A way of life of traditional values which had not then yet been subjected to very much change. I found it quaint at work to be called only by my surname, as if a reality jumping from the pages of old novels or history books. I dread to think of the eruptions in the office had anybody called a colleague by their Christian name, let alone the manager, not to say one of the directors or the company chairman! The atmosphere wasn't altogether severe though and everybody seemed to benefit collectively from the sense of respectability.

There was quiet order in the office too. It was not through any degree of subservience, simply that everybody got on with their duties, their own way of life, no interference, just perfect order, keeping themselves to themselves. Of course, work wasn't 'fun'; there wasn't even 'fun' in the workplace. But then I and probably not the others either, were not there in the office for 'fun.' We were there to earn our money, to live. 'Fun' was something then to be had outside of the office, in each person's private world and that was something kept totally separate. That suited me very well and I had no regrets about that. It was simply the 1960s experience of working life.

I suppose that it was this well-organised division between the workplace and the home life that was responsible for the strict adherence to being on time to leave for home promptly at 5pm! That was not all either. I liked, and we all benefited from, the less workaholic attitude about the office and work generally also at that time. That wasn't to say that work was in any way neglected nor inefficient, no, not at all. In fact it was real and constructive work.

I soon learned from the others and happily did so myself, to work diligently and effectively but very much keeping into the times of the allotted office hours. I liked and appreciated the fact that all the work was done without any endless round of useless, time-consuming corporate meetings which, by contrast, seem to be so prevalent in the working world of today. Less waffle and more constructive work would seem to sum up the corporate philosophy then – and I believe it worked. Not only were the companies more successful, but so too were the staff more happy and less stressed.

We all had the right amount of working time in comparison with our more than precious personal and home time that in itself made for a degree of office life satisfaction. I felt very relieved that I had joined a company and started in a business with a reciprocal feeling of contentment all around. Oh happy days, and paid for them as well!

To me, a tremendous novelty in those early working years, coming as it did in stark contrast to school, was the hallowed City tradition of the occasional, or rather, not so occasional, long lunch 'hour,' in fact almost a City culture. Although this was confined initially to people in managerial or salesman roles, there was equality and it did on several occasions 'filter down the ranks' to everybody else's benefit. Then, and only, then would the restrained and private facade so normal in the office be broken.

'How's the family?'

'Do you find the schooling good in your area? We do have a problem with secondary schools and are thinking of moving to within the catchments of the local grammar school.'

With that, my ears pricked up – should I volunteer information about the 'bat-man' establishment!

What about the life for you in Bow, then?' somebody asked, finally turning the spotlight on me. 'I don't know very much about the East End and having lived for so long now in the country (that was Haslemere in Surrey), I can't imagine about the town as home.'

'I've been used to Bow all my life,' I replied, 'but it is nothing special, in fact really very run down and becoming quite horrible,' I continued, truthfully.

'Does your family, or even you, not want to do something about it, then?'

'Oh, yes, we do,' I replied and went on to tell about our family connections to Southend.

'Now, that would be nice, to live by the sea,' my colleague commented and to which, naturally, I nodded complete and utter agreement! Having achieved entry to the working world, I already knew that a home move to some place more desirable than Bow was very high on my personal agenda.

The conversation, or gossip rather, kept on that sort of level, never too inquisitive nor intrusive, but still a long way from the normal level of office talk. I suppose that I appeared rather reserved too and, realising the rather special and almost unique nature of my own home life, I felt reluctant to talk too much about it.

The lack of the so-called sharp edge professionalism in business then was really very endearing. I liked the example set by a company salesman who each day would position himself prominently in a favourite City pub early at lunchtime, there to remain firmly until closing time. Business clients would know who and where to meet and would thus stream in and out of the chosen hostelry arranging sales deals accordingly along the way. All done without the need of strenuous travelling or sales call necessary - just friendly banter and a business exchange. So gentlemanly, so very proper!

The pub was then so much the City institution and the very hub of 1960s business networking. There was really no other competition, not having then to compete with a number of other eateries such as coffee and sandwich bars. There was surely nothing as good as the then pub's offerings of good, chunky fresh bread, great wedges of cheese and mountains of pickle, perhaps accompanied by a decent tankard of ale. A modern 'plastic sandwich' is simply an insult in comparison. The City pub was a hallowed and much-respected tradition and places were all a buzz – and the workplace in the afternoon was all the better for it! The thought of a hurried sandwich or snack at your desk in the office was simply not *de rigueur* – it was simply not done!

There was another positive result from the then lack of coffee shops with their ubiquitous plastic cups of boiling, indeed, scalding, coloured and flavourless water masquerading as coffee. That was the wonderful 'tea-lady' who would bring coffee mid-morning and tea in the afternoon direct to our desks.

'Morning, all' was the cheerful call, accompanied by the clatter of cups, twice per day, precisely to put an immediate time to that part of the routine.

Cheerful banter followed, and woe betides anybody who asked for extra milk:

'Cor, you going to get tanked up at lunchtime, luv, and want to line the stomach!'

It was most likely true too!

The immediate atmosphere of the City life and the grandeur and traditions of my surroundings were something I felt very privileged then to be a part. Apart from the need to have lunch and with a quick hostelry visit, there was still plenty of time during the valuable whole hour at lunch-time to take some City walks and to admire the surroundings. In fact, that for me represented a fine opportunity to see again and become more acquainted with the well known sights of my childhood years, but then through a different aspect.

The early 1960s were still naturally the time before too many high-rise office buildings had changed the traditional City landscape of which I felt then to be very much at the centre. The Lloyds Building was just across the road from where I worked, just a short walk along St Mary Axe and for a quick check on my bank account on the way!

Yes, all was well, I was still solvent – just – oh dear, how many days to the next pay-day?

Continuing on from St Mary Axe and I would be in Houndsditch and that remarkable, pass-card for entry only store. Luckily, 'my' company supplied staff with such a pass and the old Houndsditch Warehouse became quite a focus for a wide range of purchases, virtually from a pair of socks right up to all manner of electrical and household equipment. It was easy to know exactly who had been there in their lunch-hour, simply by seeing various parcels of all shapes and sizes stacked under desks in the afternoon.

'Been at the Houndsditch then – any particular good offers today? – Really, I must go to-morrow.' If anything would break down the reserve of the office, then the Houndsditch certainly did the trick!

A little further on from Hounsditch and you would next come to Bishopsgate, with Liverpool Street beyond. The return to the office would then be by way of Threadneedle Street, the Bank of England and the Royal Exchange. Leadenhall Market, just across the other side of Leadenhall Street was, and indeed still is, a gem of a place. I would gaze mouth-wateringly at the fine poultry, game and butchers shops, the specialist cheese shops and fish mongers, all set beneath the magnificent grand roof of the market area.

Slightly further afield, but on a fine day within the capability of a brisk walk when foregoing the inevitable visit to the pub, was Tower Bridge and my wonderful childhood memories of the steamer trips to the sea. That walk would then lead me to the Tower of London, around to the area of Tower Hill and, especially nice in the summer-time, the lunch-time brass-band concerts which were regularly held there. Finally, of course, there was my 'old friend' of London Bridge to visit, but I was then far too 'mature' to render the song! I suppose had I done so, then all would have assumed that I had spent too much of the lunch-time adding profits to the publican – or forgotten to take extra milk from the tea-lady in the morning!

The 'Good Old Days' can always appear to have been so much better, filled with happy and the most positive thoughts, perhaps almost too pleasurable to be the real world. Perhaps that may have been so at that period of life, but in reality I do not really believe that to be the case. I was revelling in the way of the life and my experiences, fortunately too at the time when there were no real cares or disappointments. Naturally, for me, the sense of freedom from the years of school had a very positive effect and added to my overall good feelings – plus some coins in the pocket!

* * * *

I had found my right working niche then in the shipping world. The work and atmosphere really thrilled me, even if I was a relatively lowly office clerk with initially fairly basic duties. Obviously, my interest in geography and developing interest in the world and the thought of travel were main reasons. I continued to live in my little dream world with the romance to me of distant destinations and place names even if, at that stage, they were purely names on Bills of Lading and other such commercial documents.

Whatever though, I was indeed a shore based, make-believe sailor. To add to my state of imagination, the only thing missing to me during those first working months was that I had not been on, nor even seen for real, one of the company's ships!

After an initial three months or so, and in the Autumn of my first business year of 1963, I was somehow 'promoted' to more responsible duties although still with the title of 'clerk.' No doubt I would need to work for at least 20 years before finally being rid of that title. But what's in a title, it is the reality of the actual job that matters most - and now my own duties were expanding!

Firstly, it was necessary most days to make visits to other shipping company's offices in the immediate area. This I naturally enjoyed, given my enthusiasm for walks in the City and seeing the sights, I could now walk the City Streets in work-time and be paid for it as well! Whilst these other companies I visited were often business competitors, there was never any 'them and us' negative feeling – really all colleagues in the shipping fraternity and same line of business.

'How is it with your company today – is the next sailing to Singapore full and do you think that there may be anything to divert to ours (sailing) the following week?'

This was typical of the exchanges and upon which I had been instructed to co-operate.

'We've still got some space, but refrigerated is full' was my thoroughly informed and valued business response.

'Get the Docks to start diverting freezer to us then.' The deal was on its way and I reported accordingly when I got back to my office. All set then – signed, sealed, delivered and the City Streets walk all duly worthwhile!

Then, secondly, on to the next stage of my spectacular career advancement! I became one of the team having to take the freight papers to the ship itself on sailing day – wow! I got to see a ship. Travelling by the Underground back down to East London, and a bus to the Docks, or even sometimes starting off from home first thing in the morning, the job would take a very large part out of the day – and it was never a tradition to 'hurry!' Usually, my destination was to the King George V Dock, one of the then Royal Group of Docks, places once again all so familiar to me from my earlier river steamer cruises. That just goes to show how worthwhile that childhood time was spent!

The more senior, long-serving, staff would get the plum jobs of Southampton, which really was an 'away-day' and even I, once or twice, got the chance of a Tilbury visit which was almost, and could easily be made into, a full day. Still, it was a fine chance to be out and to be a ship-spotter, as opposed to an earlier train-spotter!

In the Docks, the company would maybe have two or three ships berthed at any one time but normally the whole Dock would be full of ships trading from all around the world to such evocative places in the continents of Asia, Australia, Africa and the Americas. Mainly the ships were busy freighters but about once a month my duties would take me to one of the passenger/cargo ships trading to the Far East (that is Malaysia and Japan rather than Stratford and Leytonstone in 'far' East London)!

Then it was special to be shown around, to walk the highest deck and to see the familiar London sights from ten stories up, to see the command bridge itself, then the cabins, the spacious and extremely luxurious public rooms, the lounges and even to marvel at the thought of a cinema right there on board. I could so easily dream and have thoughts of long sea voyages, of far-flung countries and distant destinations.

The highlight of that day, undoubtedly, was the chance of having lunch on board – some soup and a fish course to start, perhaps a huge and spicy curry for main course and a very exotic and creamy pudding to finish. That was 'work' and being paid for it too!

Normally my freight paper dealings were with a fairly junior second or third officer, the 'ranking' system being very much a prevalence in the Merchant Navy; a Captain would not be seen talking to the likes of me. Many of these Junior Officers would not have been so much older than me but had a so much wider life's view at that time than I could possibly then have had. Worldly-wise and very life experienced indeed, with a host of seamen's adventures and tales to match.

Often, during those visits. I thought of my own first day at work and the question upon arrival:

'Sea or shore staff?'

Should I think about sea?

'Probably not,' I thought being too much of a home person and in a rather too comfortable life to contemplate such a major change. Importantly, too, I felt too much of a responsibility towards Nan and Grandpop's welfare and future to make such a drastic change in life. Rather then, and better for my temperament, to settle to fantasising on my day visits to the Docks and leave it at that.

There always appeared to be such a hive of activity at the Docks even though there was a justifiable reputation for endless strikes and industrial actions, this being in the hey-day of Jack Dash, the local docker's union leader. Perhaps then it just 'looked' busy, but nevertheless there was always a scene of crane after crane raising and lifting load after load to and from the ship's holds, endless streams of lorries delivering and collecting cargo – in fact endless noise and mayhem. I could never understand how all the paperwork, fairly flimsy at that, and freight details were ever reconciled from the seeming mass of happenings – but somehow they were!

Before finally making my way back to the City, or perhaps simply to lengthen the day just long enough for it then to be home time and I could go directly home instead, I often took the opportunity of calling in on my Uncle Bill, at his office at the Docks. That wasn't entirely a skive, because we would talk business – the shipping world for a moment and then update about the latest cars for considerably longer moments.

The commercial bustle was exhilarating and the chance to get to know and to experience the various ships of the company's fleet was then a thrill for me. But I remained true to my thoughts, never 'Down to the Sea and Ships' for me as such – I felt contented to remain firmly shore-based staff.

* * * *

My gaining and subsequent growing confidence in the business world, coupled with my ability to earn the regular monthly salary, soon turned my thoughts during the first Autumn of work to the possibility of buying a car – getting a 'set of wheels' in fact!

I didn't believe that my St Mary Axe bank was then quite ready for the prospect of lending to me on the scale of my wishes – likely at around £150 – or almost half a year's salary so I thought that I best leave them to get on with their far more important corporate business deals! In truth though, I was then too scared to ask and, in any case, I found banks as institutions generally to be very austere and frightening places – very much not then for me.

Therefore, I touted thoughts around the family and managed to 'kindly persuade' my aunt and uncle, Ethel and Bill, of the viability of such a deal. Obviously, my foresight of actually having opened a Savings Account with her, plus my carefully planned visits to Uncle at work in the Docks, all very much paid off! They agreed and lent me enough to cover most of the purchase and small savings from my monthly salary were just enough to cover the remainder with some left over for payment of the road tax, insurance cover (horrendous as a first time driver) and the first tank of petrol.

But what to buy – that was the main question to keep me busy over the ensuing weekends, not to say during the odd day-dreaming moments behind the tariff-books at work.

'Best to go somewhere you can trust,' Bill advised. 'I know a place in Wanstead – they are pretty good and give a guarantee too,' he continued.

'Right then, I'll come along on Saturday,' I said and the beginning of a deal was in sight.

There wasn't anything in my price range that first Saturday to visit but I left details and was made to feel confident of a positive result. In fact, later the following week I got a phone call from Bill, a personal phone call in the office, then something of a rare event. I arranged to go later that evening straight from work, liked what I saw, had a test drive and the deal was done. I was then the proud owner of a grey Standard Pennant, then seven years old, a sort of Morris-Minor style car, very solid, very dignified as befits an up and coming City person! The garage had to service it so I arranged to go on the following Saturday to pick it up.

I was on cloud nine that day as I went by bus with Grandpop to Wanstead to collect my new car. It was, fortunately, all ready and waiting, gleaming in the forecourt; to top the sense of excitement, it started first time and I managed to move off without stalling! Next, off to negotiate the immediate Saturday morning busy streets of suburban Wanstead.

The actual drive home to Bow was most meticulously planned to travel along a back-way route through side streets wherever possible to avoid too much traffic! The plan worked, I never had to pass a bus, negotiate and major traffic hold-ups, just a simple and rather clear ride home.

That very same Saturday afternoon, I took Nan and Grandpop on our first car outing together, a very wonderful and very proud moment for me. I was certain it was the same for them as well, as I felt that I was finally in a position to be able to give something proper back to them after their having done so much, indeed all, for me over all the years. We drove to the Epping Forest area and generally toured around some picturesque Essex villages

- or, in other words, anywhere with very little traffic! I wasn't quite as bad as needing to have somebody walk in front of the car with a red flag, but I was cautious! So too was I very mindful of all the comments made by the instructor during those months of learning plus the many bad gaffs I had so often committed. That day I wanted to be perfect and very fortunately it was and we duly arrived home safely in the late afternoon after a happy first driving experience in the new car.

Living as we did on the main road in Bow was no place to leave my treasured possession even though the place was not nearly then so potentially crime ridden. Grandpop had suggested and had kindly arranged for me to have a 'lock-up' at a row of garages along the road. That place was therefore the home of my immediate 'pride and joy,' safely under lock and key.

I must say though that I never liked the garage – there were always a lot of vans and lorries parked there as well and it was always difficult to negotiate the lines of vehicles and to get the car in and out safely – especially so for me then with my very limited driving skills! An inordinate amount of twists and turns of the wheel were needed simply to enter or leave the garage and after that was the need to have to cross the main road before getting on the way. On top of all that, the lock-up garages had a petrol filling station in the forecourt which, in itself, added considerably to the amount of traffic. All this meant that, after a few times, I became a reasonably competent driver but I still found the actual garage a nightmare.

Now, I had a new Sunday ritual which was then, naturally, car cleaning and polishing, generally tinkering around. Always I was sure to start the car by turning the starter handle after locating the contraption through the hole in the front bonnet to the engine block. What an effort, dirty hands and grease spots everywhere and all just to 'save' the battery!

Car trips themselves were mainly at weekends, even then kept locally not really because of my lack of prowess as a driver but rather because of the cost of petrol. For all that, though, it was still great fun for me, plus I saw a lot of East London streets! After some months though, and with the benefits of the extra monthly salaries adding up, I gradually became more adventurous, even to negotiate Blackwall Tunnel to the realms of South London. Soon, I was ready to spread the wings even further and drives to the places of my childhood, especially Southend and Folkestone, became part of my regular itineraries. With the car, I had notched up a first positive achievement!

* * * *

The effect of my having joined the Shipping Company must have indeed been somewhat significant for them as they announced to all staff in November 1963, only some three months after my arrival, that the whole company would be moving from Leadenhall Street to allow the site to be re-developed. The temporary address – would you believe only about a half-mile away, but eastwards, out of the City, and with an 'E 1' postcode – surely a case of the East London boy returning to his roots!

So I had just arrived in the nick of time to have been able to have experienced the true City life and it felt rather sad to move, even though not so actually far away. One plus point for me personally though was that I was closer to Aldgate East Underground station so that my daily commute times were even further reduced. Working life was, as a result becoming even more relaxed than ever.

At that time of life, having lived all the time in one home in Bow, I had never even had the experience of moving house, let alone the prospect of being part of an entire office move, altogether even more daunting!

'All boxed files on the right to go!'

'Files with yellow labels for storage!'

'We're all getting new desks,' somebody said.

'That will mean packing everything up,' others continued to comment as giant tea-chests lined the corridors. That period of clearing up and packing caused more consternation and idle talk within the confines of the office than ever before. Altogether though that was hardly surprising, I had only been there for three months whilst many others in the office had been there for very many years. Their routines and comfortable office traditions were being broken! Many could not accept that the office was not to be any longer in the actual City, it was for them an end of an era and they were saddened by thoughts.

Finally, with everything safely indexed, we all went home our various ways on one Friday evening only to return to the new address in East London, but on the fringes of the City, on the following Monday morning. Then, as if by magic, everything was safely in place. File boxes and crates were stacked beside the new storage cupboards; personal boxes by the side of new desks. In fact everything was – and please excuse the phrase – 'ship-shape!' – and ready for the first of the telephone rings and the new day's business soon after 9.30.

Without doubt the new building – or, rather the new building to our company – was probably dating from the 1930s by outward style and was nowhere near as grand as was the old base. However, most of us were re-assured that that it would be a temporary base perhaps for three or four years whilst the old site was razed to the ground and redeveloped by the then popular, if un-inspiring, tower block.

Work was the same – location wasn't! In fact on one side of the building where my office was located was Middlesex Street – better known as the famous East London Sunday Market, Petticoat Lane! Looking to the west though and it was the familiar City skyline and scenes of my usual lunchtime walks and haunts, also still the destination of my City business rounds.

However, one benefit of the company move to the new local business community was the enormously positive effect on the profitability of the local pubs and an immense jump in their mid-day weekly trade! It really was a dream location and a potential goldmine for the Publican, a situation that a few months before they could not even have considered even in their wildest dreams. On Sunday they had all the trade of the lively Petticoat Lane Market and in the week they had us!

The coming off my first Christmas as an employed person was another milestone and one which I found immensely exciting. There were some extended lunches (!) both in the new found Middlesex Street pubs and in the time-hallowed City haunts. Double celebrations, in fact, which tended occasionally to carry on into the evenings too. As I have said, a number of colleagues often had the habit for a 'quick snifter' after work and before taking the train home – at Christmas time this invariably became rather longer than a 'quick one.' I liked the whole atmosphere and always as a 'Christmas person' I so appreciated to see all the business offices decorated and the huge Christmas Trees both inside and outside the building so well decorated and illuminated. I remember too the traditional Carol Service and the plentiful supplies of mince pies and mulled wine, with – more mulled wine, everybody getting very much into the Christmas Spirit!

Of all the pre-Christmas traditions at work, the most important was the annual salary review which always took place a few days before the holiday. Known as the 'march-past' because the review was always given by one of the Group Board Directors who, to be fair, hadn't a clue about the person they were actually interviewing so a Commissionaire would need to announce the name of the individual as they entered the room.

All the morning, various fellow staff members trooped in and out of the office, only being briefly in their own personal interview and then coming out, often rather red faced, but not saying very much about the experience. It was impossible for anybody else to get any advance sense of what sort of pay increases were being offered, everybody was too private and others too much in respect of privacy to ask.

Being a lowly 'clerk,' I had to wait some time, in fact it was well into the afternoon, long after the lunch-time, when finally, I was called in and duly announced by the Commissionaire.

'Well done, lad – you'll get and additional £30 per year on your salary. A step in the right direction. Ah! Happy Christmas to you!'

And that was that. Interview over, no more questions to be asked nor answered until same time, same place next year. Perfect industrial relations early 1960s style! Still, I had a salary increase after only having been working for four months, even if it meant I still only got £330 per annum.

The interviews and pay reviews time rather signalled the end of the working year and everybody then got in readiness for Christmas. Me too – it felt fine then to finally start the short, three-day holiday and for me, my very first holiday as a salaried person.

Back in the normality of my home and to the family Christmas routines handed down through all my known years, it was impossible then for me to know or to realise that I wasn't really still at school. The only two immediate changes to my life to make me aware about my own personal changes in circumstances, was the happy jingle sound of some money in my pocket and – along the road some 500 yards away – was my little car tucked-up safely in its garage.

As Christmas life-style hadn't changed, neither too had my normal way of home life which even in the first years of work was totally similar to the preceding years. I was still very much a home boy, somewhat naive and rather young in many respects for my age – by no means world-wise nor in anyway life experienced. Here, I reflected so often in comparing myself to those young ship's officers who I met so often on my company ship visits, their different attitudes and wide life outlook to me. Having said that, though, I was then quite happy and totally content with my life. My upbringing and background had thus moulded me and I felt, by choice, responsible and a natural concern for my Nan and Grandpop. This did make my life different and therefore me, as a consequence, a different person.

It never actively occurred to me nor was I ready to consider then any sort of 'boy/girl' relationship of any depth. This was total emotional immaturity and merely underlines my being a little boy in a big man's business world, perfectly able to cope in work issues but quite out of touch and with a grave inability on relationship issues. There had been changes, though, and naturally the workplace was a thoroughly different place from the boys-only atmosphere of school so I met naturally with girl work colleagues and there were some very distant friendships, very much on an official working basis, as a result.

In so many ways, my life was somewhat restricted and I do consider that I missed a lot generally accepted as being normal in life, absolutely admitting to being emotionally immature as a result. However, my own circumstances make it completely clear to me that I would not have wanted it to be in any other way. To have left home and to have started an own fully independent life at that time would have caused me grave misgivings and thoughts of having severely let down Nan and Grandpop. I felt that, as they both approached their late 70s I had to be there for them and from my very first day at work I had the aim to ensure that we could all finally move from Bow, as their wish had always been, to 'somewhere better.'

* * * *

October 1964 marked a momentous occasion in our family life, a thoroughly happy and marvellous event – Nan and Grandpop's Golden Wedding Anniversary. It was a time of warm feelings and true family glow, a time to celebrate and reflect upon my grandparent's lives as they had together faced up to and had overcome the life's traumas, their own business and home loss in the 1930s, then the war years and the hard work of the Bow years, the loss of their only child and still to be doing the daily caretaking duties when then in their 70s. Such marvellous people, honest, hard-working and sincere, they both so truly deserved to be the centre of attention and celebrations for all that they had achieved and more especially so on their big anniversary day.

The actual day was a Saturday so a real big party was planned for home and reminiscent of the many childhood parties I had enjoyed over the years and which had given me so much pleasure. Now, though, it was my turn to lead the arrangements, I had by then had very many years' experience of special party preparations, so also my turn to say 'Thank-you.'

Set, then, to the well-trusted format, arrangements happily got under way with a great sense of approaching occasion. Masses of food began to be prepared at home in the preceding days and naturally Nan was very much involved herself in that, I merely taking on a general helping and especially washing up role when I got home from work in the evenings. There was then naturally the customary patronage of Lyons Corner House and their delicatessen for the final and extra special range of 'goodies.' Here, though, was the one most significant difference this time in that I went in my car to collect the various items, foregoing the usual bus arrangements. Instead, I drove to the very West End, importantly parking close by to the shop and proudly returning home with a boot laden with the most appetising selection of savoury and sweet, delicious foods.

Neither Nan or Grandpop had any large own family then left, but this was more than made up by an assortment of different nephews and nieces who came to the 'do,' plus many friends from Bow who they had known for most of their many years in the area. Even some relatives actually came from father's side, in an unprecedented show of solidarity within the family, which was a true thunderbolt result given their normal relationship. Unsurprisingly, they did not stay for too long, rather though making an almost regal and fleeting appearance but it was 'the thought that counts,' as the seasoned old expression tells!

Flowers were delivered all day with, it seemed, the doorbell constantly ringing. Grandpop sent Nan two dozen red roses with the endearing message:

'Thanks for everything, Mate.'

Nan had the day before a special hair appointment and as a result looked amazingly lovely, especially when she wore her new golden dress which she had bought from her favourite Oxford Street store, D.H. Evans.

Desks were once again borrowed from the upstairs offices, just as they had been for my own childhood parties, to give extra tables in our basement rooms. Beds were also cleared away and taken upstairs in return. Everywhere in the house, the reception rooms, the hall and the staircase were cheerfully decorated with streamers and all the flowers carefully displayed in the variety of beautiful glass vases that Nan had collected over the years, some, indeed, having come from her own mother's time. To add to the party atmosphere, and just like Christmas, the room decorations were completed with balloons, paper chains and fairy lights. Pride of place though, and the real centrepiece, was the main table heavenly laden by masses of food and a most beautiful flower arrangement.

It was Bow, it was East London, but for that night the place was a Palace and the atmosphere was made to be the most magical as a result.

Naturally, it was a great homespun party and evening, a chance for family reminiscences, celebration, general happiness and very much laughter. It was very much our own world with the curtains drawn against the outside life, a chance for our own life's creations and thoughts to be wherever we most wanted to be. Above all, it was a chance to celebrate and be happy for Nan and Grandpop on their very special day.

With the flow of more food and drink, the increased merriment soon led to significantly loud renderings of favourite and traditional East End Music-Hall songs. 'My Old Man Followed the Van' so many times by midnight that 'he' must have by then been thoroughly used to his journey! It was as if the clock had been put back the 50 years to 1914 and the wedding reception rather than the Golden Anniversary, even some old hats and clothes accessories had been got out of boxes to give the authentic atmosphere to the evening. All went on until the early hours, merriment and well-being was created and, since we had no neighbours, we didn't have to worry about causing disturbance, which was just as well!

As finally people began to leave, their own journeys home were made the more easy by the big 'doggy-bag' boxes each was given, so much food having been prepared that it would have been impossible to be able to eat it all ourselves. In any case, even in the cold cellar, and still without the aid and advantages of refrigerators, food would have soon gone 'off.' By Nan and Grandpop's generation, it was totally abhorrent for the idea of letting good food 'go to waste' and it gave then a good sense of feeling to be able to give the luxuries to their friends and family, in any case.

The troop of happy crowds then slowly dispersed along the very dark and very quiet Bow Road, some walking all the way home, then quite safely even in the dead of the night, others continuing the party evening spirit by taking a taxi home to the various reaches of North and East London. And ourselves, we continued the good feelings and part spirit too by simply leaving all the washing up and clearing away until another time, perhaps in the hope that a 'good fairy' would magically appear to do the proper thing! In itself, that was a highly significant event and was probably the one and only time in their lives that my grandparents had left the mess to be cleared another day.

That 'another day' was certainly not to be the next day either. Despite the late night, we all managed, and with clear heads too, to be up in time the next morning for what was to be my treat to Nan and Grandpop – a Sunday outing – and that had to be to one place only – to Southend naturally.

On a fine Autumn morning, we drove the well-trusted route through East London into suburban Essex and along the 'famous' Arterial Road and finally into Southend, along the seafront and to park with a sea view close to the Pier. Not a picnic for us that special day, even if we would have had sufficient food left over even after the 'doggy-bags' to feed most of Southend! That special day we took the train along the pier to have lunch in the Restaurant at the end of the pier, at a reserved table to ensure we had the very best sea views.

'I feel like a Queen,' said Nan, happily.

'Well, if you are a Queen, mate, then I must be a King,' Grandpop replied with equal joy.

After lunch we returned to the town, enjoyed a promenade walk and to round off the very happy and traditional day, had a plate of prawns and cockles at Leigh before the journey home. The car behaved itself and we duly got back home by the early evening, by then somewhat exited and just a little tired after the two days of celebrations.

The fairy's magic wand had to stop waving sometime, though, and the first thing to do immediately that Sunday evening was to get the desks and chairs returned to the offices upstairs, in readiness for the coming Monday morning. However, the general chaos and cleaning in our home rooms lasted still for a few days, much to Nan and Grandpop's disgust as they didn't feel right unless everything was spic and span! But, for once, though, it didn't matter. The time was a very special and noteworthy anniversary perfectly allowing the usual mould to be broken.

Chapter 10

Towards New Horizons

The early working years and the subsequent deposit of coins in my pocket meant that as an up-and- coming monied person, I could develop my love of the theatre and music with visits to the theatre and concerts directly after work in the week, always being sure to be out of the office on the dot of 5pm! The excursion was especially good on Monday evenings when the prices were at their cheapest, incentive enough. If the show was particularly popular, the 'trick' which I soon learnt was to go quickly to the theatre in the lunch hour and 'buy' a ticket which was in fact for a camp-stool on the pavement, with name label, thus reserving a place in the queue for the evening performance. When returning to the theatre some five hours later, both the label and stool were still safely in position, that I could be sure, such was the honesty of the times.

Immediately after work, then, there was more than enough time for a quick snack, or, more appropriately, a big plate of fish and chips in any one of numerous establishments on and off Charing Cross Road. Suitably fed then and ready for the performance – in one of the back rows of the 'Gods' all for, in old money, 'five shillings.' It was all a sense of doing and an adventure and I suppose that life's easier now by simply going to the kiosk in Leicester Square for the half-price ticket availability, even though 'half-price' now is at a somewhat different level!

After a couple of years at work, there was money too even for holidays! A colleague in the company had a couple of cottages in deepest Suffolk, a beautiful rural location close to a small village called Huntingfield, near Halesworth and not too far from the coast at Southwold. East Anglia had always been a family favourite location and Ethel and Bill had already been spending their holidays in Norfolk for years and I had made visits to them there. So it was agreed – we, Nan, Grandpop and I, would go for a two week holiday during the Summer of 1965 when I had the benefit of almost two years work and salary to match.

Our destination was Huntingfield which was some 110 miles from Bow and I felt confident that the car and the driver could just about make that! Throwing my geographical skills completely to the wind, and acting as if I was at least 50 years older, I contacted the AA, the is the motoring organisation rather than the drinks rehabilitation people, importantly, for a route suggestion. I can hardly believe that I could have been so unenterprising when considering my own enthusiasm for maps and things. In fact when I got the directions, I didn't like then and returned to my own plan anyway!

The holiday therefore began with the usual escape route from Bow through suburban Essex, after which there was a most pleasant drive through many of the lanes and by ways of the best of rural Essex and Suffolk. This was my first real holiday for some years, since the family holidays at school time and the couple of holidays during the very last year at school. For all of that, it felt extra special, plus the real and added excitement for me of actually going somewhere different in my own car. I must say too that it also felt immensely good to be giving a well-deserved break for my grandparents and a sort of belated Golden Wedding present too.

From the very start, it was a good holiday; the cottage was idyllic and completely filled everyone's ideal dream of a true country cottage with wooden beams, sloping ceilings (and floors) and a big, welcoming 'Aga' in the kitchen. The peace of the countryside, the clean air, all contrasted so very much to the increasingly noisier and dirty Bow.

We soon settled into the country life routine, the friendly people, regular visits to the village shop – and naturally to the pub too! I would enjoy endless rambles in the countryside, becoming at one with nature and seeking the inner-self – or, in other words, day-dreaming! I wasn't in the least bit lonely nor did I in anyway feel to be missing out from like minded and same age company. I wandered the fields and byways feeling absolutely at ease with life, pleased then to be on holiday and pleased for once to be away from the hustle of the City even though London was so close to my heart.

The fresh air, the nature and the complete unspoilt country surroundings had a profound effect on me. I saw Bow for what it was becoming and, with that, the realisation that life would have soon to move away from Bow if there was to be any sense or purpose at all. One day, when visiting the nearest town of Halesworth, I saw a job advertisement in a local Bank and was most sorely tempted to apply. First, though, I took another long country walk and really considered the situation with very many quiet discussions with my inner self.

What was my problem with the place to live?

Was there a problem with my working life?

Did I have a problem with living at home; did I want more from life?

What changes, if any, did I want to achieve?

Would the answers to the questions be solved by a possible move of home and working life to, for the then example, a bank in a small East Anglian town that is always assuming that I would even get the job.

Some sitting and relaxing in the afternoon sun in a luscious field of ripening corn began to fill in some answers to the many questions then rushing through my head.

The country life was an ideal, very nice on my part to be experienced, but I really considered that it would be impossible for me to live in such a location all the time, especially to be so far away from London and the City attractions and entertainments that I valued. Fine - that was one problem sorted, so no point even to going to that bank the next day.

So, the actual working life and style was eliminated as the potential problem, in fact it was the realisation that I suppose I always knew and that was that London for work and its attractions suited me very well – it was the place to live that was therefore the core problem.

It was Bow in the firing line! But then this was something always in the back of my mind. It wasn't new. I realised that my own family had, even in the 1930s, made the move away, only to have to return in their changes circumstances. I made the final resolve there and then, in a Suffolk cornfield, that it was my responsibility to make sure that finally we could all move away from Bow. A home in a location away from the East End and near enough for working in London and to be able to enjoy the City's delights with ease. With my mind so made up, I returned from that country walk with renewed enthusiasm and charged up with plans to make the immediate life so much better for all of us – including father if he wanted to be one of the number. That afternoon, I must have had some degree of sunstroke! – nevertheless, I felt so confident of my plans.

Back to the holiday spirit, we all enjoyed the car trips in the beautiful East Anglian countryside and made also a trip to neighbouring Norfolk and a visit to Ethel and Bill at their own holiday home near the North Norfolk coast All very unspoilt and natural countryside which, with my new found inner spirit and will, I enjoyed the rural beauty for what it had to offer, fully knowing that my own destiny was not for that particular sort of permanent life.

To add to my dreams of the rural ideal for at least the holiday time, this was very much furthered this time by visits to the idyllic and traditional seaside town of Southwold, on the Suffolk coast Another place that sits as a time warp would be very hard to find, it was so completely untouched and unspoilt. The seafront itself was fronted by rows of very colourful beach huts, all very Victorian. Behind the beach huts, a line of grassy green cliffs topped by a brilliant white lighthouse surrounded by very tidy town houses.

I felt very much as if I had, by some miracle, been dropped into an imaginary stage setting, so unreal did I find the experience of the town, a sort of East Anglian 'Brigadoon'; the fine and beautifully renovated pier only added to the theatrical overall feel of the place. How magnificent and so totally charming, I felt, and if that wasn't all enough, the town even had its own Brewery to support and supply the very fine local pubs and restaurants. Where that this town was close to London, so ran my imagination, thinking ahead to the eventual task of finding a place to live. I could then think of no more perfect combination of a home in a seaside town like that, if only it where within easy distance of London.

'Wake up,' I told myself. If it was closer to London, then it would be so small and idyllic as a place! With those sobering thoughts, the bracing North Sea air very much re-delivered me to a more real world!

To add even more to the reality, within a few days the holiday was over and we returned once more to Bow and to normal life. My thoughts, though, were firm and readily in place from that Suffolk cornfield!

* * * *

Father had not come on the holiday, although he came for the middle weekend. He was still living at home with us all and still worked in the Civil Service. Interestingly though, he had moved within the Civil Service to a clerical position at the Tower of London. During his very first weeks there, he somehow had met a lady tourist from Canada. I can imagine that must have been when he was going to and fro and had simply seemed someone looking rather lost Probably he would have given the impression that he was at the very least the Governor of the Tower! Anyway, letters began to be exchanged and some rather warm friendship somehow developed, I suppose relative to father's normal and very restrained emotional ways

So it happened that, later in the year of our Suffolk holiday, the late summer in fact, after only a very few months of constant letter exchanges and just one or two brief phone calls, father went off on a holiday to Canada, to Montreal, to stay with his new-found lady friend.

I drove him to Heathrow and I found the whole idea of a flight to Canada most exciting and somehow wished to go as well, especially so, speaking corporately dully, that North America generally was one of the few places in the world that I didn't deal with at work.

It was such a strange experience I felt on that journey to Heathrow. Here I was taking my father to the airport to go on holiday, in fact to be going off on a date! The roles, by normality, should have been completely reversed. In reality, that would not have even been possible, father didn't drive! Nevertheless, it was certainly odd, and perhaps for the very first time in my life, I felt rather sorry for my father. He usually did everything so very slowly and always without commitment. Had any previous association looked like getting 'serious,' he would have backed off immediately. Now, somehow, he had got himself into this situation and it seemed the nearer that we got to Heathrow, the more nervous and subdued he became – and he was not the most talkative person even at the best of times. Now, it was positively the hardest work!

At the airport, he became even more disorientated, completely flustered and quite incapable about what to do.

'What's your flight number so we can find where to check-in?' I asked.

'I don't really, know, I've forgotten,' father replied.

'Well, you have got your ticket, haven't you,' I asked, somewhat in alarm.

'Don't be stupid,' father said, in more of his usual spirit, obviously alarmed that I should be actually offering to help him and showing some compassion!

'Let me have the ticket then, and I'll find out where we have to go to check-in,' I said.

He then fumbled for what seemed to be an eternity before finally finding the ticket, after which we headed off to the British Overseas Airways check-in desk. Father was then back to his fumbling and nervous frame of mind, enough to make me ask him if he wanted me to come with him as a minder!

'Don't be foolish,' he replied, more than loud enough for everybody in the vicinity to hear – he was once again his typical self, quite humourless and so dismissive of any well-meaning help or kindness. The check-in formalities were very soon completed and with that we said our very formal 'good-byes,' by that I do mean formal with a cursory and swift shaking of hands! With that, he disappeared through the customs channel.

He had annoyed me during those final check-in stages at the airport, when I had really wanted to help him, when he seemed so at unease with the situation. Somehow, though, I did feel very sorry for him once he had wandered off alone through the departure gate. At that point he had seemed totally vulnerable and completely lost I am sure that he really could not believe the situation that he had let himself in for and, for all his bombasity, he probably simply felt very unsure of himself, even possibly not actually wanting to go at all.

Father was away for only two weeks in Canada, during which time we received just one card and no telephone calls, perhaps not surprisingly given the then cost of such communications. When he returned after his holiday, and I naturally collected him at the airport, but there was little news.

'Did you have a great holiday?'

'Yes, I don't know about 'great,' that's not a word I associate with, it's so meaningless. But it was rather interesting – a very nice country you know.' That was it; father was back to himself, in command of the situation, unable once again to put a sentence together without making some sarcastic comment. This was a true Jekyll/Hyde situation when compared to how he was on the day of his departure!

'And how about . . .'

'Oh, she's very well - sends her wishes.'

'What's the house like where she lives, and how do people live in Canada?' I continued to ask in an effort to make conversation and to really find out what had been going on. Once again, this was a true reversal of roles between father and son when trying to find our about a date!

'Pleasant enough house, the family also have a country chalet in the hills out of the city,' father answered.

My ears pricked up 'That sounds rather nice,' I replied.

'Rather rustic for my idea of life,' father replied, rather disparagingly, especially so when considering our own family's poor home life-style.

'When are you planning to go again, or is Elaine coming here soon?' my questioning continued.

'Oh, I don't know,' father said, 'Anyway there's nothing more to say about the visit, I'm rather tired after the flight and just want to get back to Bow now.'

Well, I thought, if your only thought is that you want to get back to Bow, then the visit must have been considerably less than a success!

And that was that – father closed down the news channel and we could all, that is Nan, Grandpop and me, only guess about the outcome.

Certainly, letters still continued to be exchanged and the following Christmas time there was indeed a visit by Elaine to London. Nan kindly suggested to father that she should stay with us and we would give her a traditional family Christmas. Father positively went deathly white at the thought and immediately said a most defiant 'No!' Probably, knowing my father, he would have spun some story line about where he actually lived thus making any home visit quite beyond possibility.

Elaine came a few days before Christmas and even though I offered to take father to the airport to meet her, also to make the car available to drive them around, he said his usual and defiant 'No.' That always meant the subject was closed without room for discussion! Elaine duly stayed in some small hotel near Russell Square. Father didn't spend Christmas at home naturally and I really have no idea how the Christmas itself actually went for him; even though he came home alone every night, he enforced his own news embargo! One evening, between Christmas and New Year though, I was invited to meet Elaine and father for the evening, dinner and a show.

I very much liked Elaine, found her to be a very bubbly and open personality. In yet another reversal of roles, I found myself being heavily questioned by Elaine about father's life, about my life, what we did and where we lived. Oh, the stories I heard from her that night about how father had told her we lived in a big house in the centre of London.

If so, I thought, why was Elaine staying in a hotel? I soon had the answer to that which was, indeed, a bombshell!

'Bob' Elaine said to me. 'Bob' – whose 'Bob' – silly me, father was using an imaginary name! Elaine continued 'Bob says that it was so unfortunate that I couldn't stay with you in your fine London home.'

'But, you . . .' I was just saying when I caught sight of my father's thunderous expression!

'Bob explained to me that he had so kindly given your housekeeper the Christmas off, so there wouldn't have been anybody to clean the house nor even to prepare the food and he's so wonderful, your father, he didn't want me to have to do the chores!'

I was speechless! Housekeeper, big house, nobody to look after us, prepare the food. What had father been saying, what stories had he been telling.

'Bob tells me,' Elaine continued 'that you have been staying with a friend over the Christmas.'

'Yes, I have,' I spluttered and felt very much like saying that I had been staying with friends, my very best friends, my Nan and Grandpop, the same people who did everything to look after 'Bob' as well!

What, though, was the point. I was too disgusted to be bothered and was most thankful when it was time for the theatre and a chance to enjoy the escapism of the show for three hours and not have to be part of this make-believe world between my father and Elaine. Afterwards I couldn't even be bothered to tackle father about the stories that I had heard and I made my mind up too that I would not tell Nan and Grandpop the story about the housekeeper – that would have simply been too cruel and so completely unjust

Soon after New Year, Elaine returned to Canada and we did not meet up again. That was it and after that visit, apart from a few very occasional letters, further contact soon faded completely. There was no further mention by father nor by me about Elaine and equally the whole episode was over. I do believe that Elaine must have found out for herself that there were some pretty strange surroundings to her 'Bob' which simply did not add up and she retreated safely back to Canada. I don't think anybody could blame her and she had a very lucky escape!

* * * *

In many lives, when thinking of heading forward to new horizons, there is nothing more significant than a 21st Birthday to concentrate the mind, even to reflect and evaluate, take stock, not to say prepare the way ahead. For me, January 1966 was such a time for me. I looked forward to the immediate celebrations, of course, but before doing so I felt really concerned about the very state of my life, toiling with so many thoughts and emotions.

Father's failed relationship with Elaine very much brought into perspective my own failings in emotional attachments. Here was I, at 21, without ever having had a steady girlfriend relationship and, perhaps, worse still never having had even an occasional low-key friendship. Neither did I feel the need or longing for such a relationship. That was odd, it was not right and even though I used to feel that my upbringing and especially the years spent in the boys-only school environment were to blame, by 1966 I had been away from school for three years in the 'bigger' world. In any case, by then very many of my old school friends had secure relationships and one had already become married. The immediate future already then indicated a fairly busy round of attending marriages of old school friends with me as a single always sitting awkwardly at the back of the church and making some excuse about not attending the reception afterwards.

'Why don't you get a girlfriend?' Nan often said, 'We want to see you settled and happy.'

'Oh, I haven't thought about it,' I rather untruthfully replied. 'In any case I am happy at home with you and want to look after you both,' I continued.

'That's not the point,' Nan continued. 'It's not right that you do not think about your own life and in any case, Grandpop and I will be alright. It would make us so happy to see you becoming settled.'

But that was the true point. I really did feel responsible for looking after Nan and Grandpop, nobody else would and I felt secure and happy in that home environment. My ideal for life's improvement was to get a place for us together away from Bow and for Nan and Grandpop to be away finally from the arduous caretaking duties. I felt that to be the immediate direction of my destiny and I had no intention to be deflected or to consider any change to that ideal.

So it was that my 21st birthday was duly celebrated in a traditional style with family and friends at home, me trying to avoid at all times inquisitive questions about my life and future plans! If anything, though, my own happiness once again having such a happy time with the home parties, home life generally plus the continued thoughts and associations with the similar delightful parties from all childhood years, all merely strengthened my own resolve that my personal plans were channelled in the right direction. I had made up my mind and being extremely stubborn in that respect, there would be virtually nothing that would make me change. That was that!

A most pleasant addition to previous major birthday celebrations was that this time I had the added pleasure of some long lunches at work with friends and colleagues. It was so that others got as much fun from these occasions as the 'birthday boy' himself, always enjoying any break away from the usual routine. The City was still then ready for any excuse to celebrate! No matter, though, how big the lunch, there was always the need to provide cakes for each and all to go with the afternoon tea round!

'Cor, luv, is it your birthday?' the 'tea-lady' happily enquired. 'Ere, luv, have some sweets,' she continued, producing from a bag she kept ready on the trolley for such occasions. 'All the best luv' and that very much made the day too.

By the end of the day, I could be excused the feeling of a certain light headedness but also a sense of contentment and happiness at my particular lot. No celebration period would though be complete for me without some theatre. It was more than fortunate that, in my special birthday, year D'Oyly Carte were performing Gilbert and Sullivan Operas in London and there were plentiful opportunities for frequent visits to the theatre. I'm sure that I saw virtually all the repertory that season to become even more enchanted by those priceless pieces of English Operetta.

Perhaps all this just goes to show why my lifestyle was then as it was – I was so perfectly happy and thoroughly contented, so obviously too comfortable to make any major change. On top of everything, with the occasion of my 21st birthday came another promotion at work too – I was no longer a clerk but, instead, a 'freight assistant' – the only way forward was up!

* * * *

Following my '21st', with the secured workplace and the slow gathering of a few extra pennies, plus the fact that Nan and Grandpop were by then well into their mid-70s, then was surely the time to finally plan and to execute the long desired move from Bow. Even father, obviously somewhat reeling from his experience with Elaine, agreed and said he would come if the place was 'proper' – I wonder what he meant!

There was, after all, for all of us only one place to consider moving to and that was the Southend area. Saturdays and Sundays in spring 1966 were absolutely reserved for frequent journeying in the by then faithful car to look around the Essex coastline from Leigh-on-Sea, through Southend itself and on to the mouth of the Thames Estuary at Shoeburyness.

I realised unfortunately that there was no possibility of considering buying a home. Collectively, I very much regretted to admit that we had insufficient savings for a deposit and my own salary was not enough in itself to allow for a mortgage. Father had barely enough put aside to even buy his train fare, a pretty disgusting result after over 25 years of work and his living since 1953 in virtual rent-free surroundings. It was more than obvious that, whilst his friendship with Elaine had been in the knowledge, there had been many other costly similar relationships that we had not known about! Still, that was his life and style and I was determined that I was not going to let that be an obstacle to finally achieving our own particular and very special dream.

Father adopted his usual detached position to resolving any issue and didn't even wish to come with us as we went on our new home search.

'Let me know when you have found something, then I'll come to take a look,' was his highly non-committal comment.

Our task was therefore determined to concentrate on rental possibilities. Fortunately we were very lucky and it transpired that there were quite a lot of very decent and highly delightful such properties available throughout the area. We were almost spoilt for choice.

Overall, it didn't take too many visits before we had found an ideal place as our future home – a detached house in Westcliff-on-Sea, which had just been converted into two flats, the ground floor flat with a garden and an upstairs flat with verandah. A quick discussion and second look around, that time with father as well, and we all decided on the groundfloor flat. Soon we had signed on the dotted line and agreed an entry date for April, about four weeks away. On the way back out of the Southend area, we called on a removal firm and made the necessary arrangements. That was it – all done – we drove back to Bow in an overwhelming sense of disbelief.

Amazingly, even father on the way back seemed quite excited about the prospects of the new home. That was surely a most significant day in life in so many ways. Not only about the new home being secured, but also that father was travelling with us in the car, a rare event in itself. Almost as rare was the fact that he was with us in family spirit and joining in our overall obvious enthusiasm for the move. Unbelievable!

In a remarkably swift time, when thinking about all the years of aspirations and planning, the closing of the Bow years finally came about and with it the realisation of all our longed-for dreams. There was much to do in those four hectic weeks but first Nan and Grandpop happily wrote their 'Notice' from their Caretakers' job. That in itself was quite something, to be writing a letter of 'Notice' at the tender age of 77 years!

After having lived so many years in one place, there was a mass of packing to be done plus endless cleaning up until the very last days before the move. I took the week off work but not father, he simply carried on as normal, probably that first flash of enthusiasm had simply been too overpowering for him. Soon we were all then finally ready for the removal van and our 'red letter' moving day.

After the actual move, and when all the furniture had gone, we had the immediate realisation of just how basic the accommodation had been and, in fact, could not help but realise just how dumpy had been the place that was our home. I had lived there for 21 years, father somewhat longer and Nan and Grandpop for about 30 years – none of us had sad feelings upon leaving. Bow was no longer as it had been in those early years and changes had not been for the better. The happy memories of our home were in our personal belongings and furnishings and they went with us in the move – the shell of our old house had no such qualities.

So it was, with no aching feelings, that the keys were finally handed in; goodbyes said and then quickly away in the car and along the so familiar route of the Southend Arterial Road, this time in a one- way direction, to our new home in Westcliff.

* * * *

The arrival of the removal van and us, at our new home in Westcliff, was virtually simultaneous. Nothing strange in that, when remembering that I had a little car that had to be driven with understanding and sympathy! The slowness of our own journey was most certainly not due to the fact that we were reluctant to leave Bow and the old life. Far from it, in fact, the whole journey – all 40 miles – had been like effectively going to the moon, so great was the contrast between the former home and the new one. We all felt literally on air at the prospect of the new life opportunity and were determined to make the very most of the chance.

No matter we had arrived. Father, true to himself, had decided to follow on by train, making the excuse that the car 'would be too full if we all travelled together' but by late afternoon he joined us during the first stage as the furniture was being moved in. Our complete family unit was once again re-united, this time in our new home.

We had too, as a family, really moved on in more ways than one – historically the new Westcliff home dated from the Edwardian era, Bow was from the Victorian times.

Our groundfloor flat was indeed very fine and especially so when compared to our former old home. Also, it was enormous compared to Bow – three large bedrooms, two with magnificent bay windows and the 3rd with a French door to the garden. Then there were two bathrooms, dining room, kitchen and a magnificent feature lounge, again with a huge bay-window overlooking the garden. Then to top the delight – literally – I could stand on a chair in the front room and just see the sea. That was simply no comparison to Bow and the former trolley-bus wires!

The big, oak front door led to an entrance hall almost to me with a reminder of school – an impressive black and white marble floor and leaded side windows, all really rather nice, in fact very overwhelmingly wonderful for us after the Bow years. And not forgetting the other 'family member' – my car – there was a proper detached garage at the end of the garden for that too!

Even father seemed unaccustomedly thrilled by the move and as for Nan and Grandpop it was for them a dream finally coming true: To be at last free from their caretaking duties which they had stoically done for around 30 years and to be able once again to pick up their Southend life which they had so cruelly lost at the same earlier time. They were not the type or sort of people to actually retire, even in their mid-70s, but it was indeed the time for them not to have to work any more, to be able to enjoy the home and to be happily living once again in the pleasant seaside surroundings.

Our immediate new home area was indeed fine and especially so when compared to our previous home. All of the neighbouring houses were of a similar Edwardian nature, indeed, grandeur would not be too fine a word. Some were still large houses that hadn't been converted whilst others, like ours, were as flats. All had large gardens and the leafy avenues led directly to the main Westcliff shopping street which, in turn, went on to the actual seafront area itself. The station was less than ten minutes' walk, all very convenient for the soon to begin daily commute to London when father and I would re-enact the same journey my mother had done those years earlier. That, more than anything, was surely a case of history repeating itself.

But what then would I make of the Southend area as a place to live? Would it live up to my thoughts and expectations and how would it fit in with my sincere thoughts and aspirations from my afternoon in that Suffolk cornfield? I had, after all, spent so many days' outings to the place that I felt very acquainted there although to visit a place for a day is a very different thing from actually living there. Really, though, there was no cause for concern or dissent, I felt very much at home from the outset. Everything felt right, I was a square peg in a square hole and the family seemed equally at ease.

Southend then as a town was so much like so many English seaside towns, it had seen better times and as a resort it was simply a place for East Londoners to come for a break. How true that was for me and my family, we were East Londoners and now we were there for our break – hopefully a very long break too!

The unfortunate part of the town was especially along the actual Southend seafront itself and the horrible amusement area known as the Kursal, pure razzmatazz junk. However, the neighbouring areas to Southend, of Westcliff and Leigh, were like from a different planet – sedate and well-manicured gardens, flower beds along the cliff top, wooded cliff walks, some fine hotels and restaurants and tree lined streets and wide avenues. Even the sea promenade was home to a number of sailing clubs which in itself gave an overall improved feel to the place.

It gave me such a glorious feeling to be able to walk out of our new home and within a few minutes be on the cliff top with the wide estuary views across to the Kentish Hills or out to the opening aspect of the North Sea. In equally swift time, I could be down by the sea promenade and, even if sometimes, at low tide, the sea was a long way out and all that would be visible was miles of mudflats, there was at least the salty tang in the air to compensate. Should I feel the need to be by the sea at whatever the state of the tide, then the famous pier was as always there and over a mile away at the end of the pier was deep water aplenty!

For yet another aspect of the sea, the old town area of Leigh was extremely interesting with the fishing sheds, the boats and their loads of cockles and seafood and inviting taverns. Certainly overall a diverse and mainly pleasing area to be home and one which already had a special place in my heart from the frequent childhood experiences. And to add to the real 'icing on the cake,' London itself was under an hour away. I really felt that I had the very best of all possible worlds.

Living there did not in any way detract from the pleasurable memories from my very many happy childhood experiences – it added to them.

So began a few days of settling in and once with our favourite items of furniture in place, the new house soon took on the feeling of home. With his new-found freedom from work, Grandpop was in his element painting and decorating various corners and crevices and especially so in the high ceiling and ample spaces of the living rooms. Here he put oak wall panelling and used gold trim to highlight the fireplace surrounds, all set off with various collections of objet d'arts from over the years for which there was now room to display – this had never been the case in Bow. All along, Grandpop's handiwork was to the fore and readily complemented the growing home like feelings.

'That'll look nicest – there – Pop' said Nan.

'Right, Mate – but I'll be adding a frieze to the surround, so we'll better see for sure later.'

'I think that the fireplace will look nicest with a little more gold piping – it's such a lovely contrast to the oak panelling,' Grandpop continued to enthuse.

It was such a wonderful warm feeling at home to see both Nan and Grandpop so happy and busying themselves on the decorating just like young people moving into their first real home – and with the same sense of excitement. For all of us there was no delay in Westcliff feeling like our proper home and there was no pining for Bow or for the life which we had left, willingly, behind us there.

Naturally, new for us then was the garden after the true 'back-yard' of Bow. Although our new garden was not over big, the main lawn and borders were enough to keep father and me both amused, plus the fact that we needed to buy various pieces of garden equipment or beg and borrow secondhand from the aunts. Probably that was the one and only time in my entire younger life that father and I did joint work and I was then in my twenty-second year. It was a remarkable and extremely strange experience for me in a father/son project – still, better late than never I suppose!

Of course, it was all such a novelty but the worst garden chore was the cutting of an enormous hedge which surrounded the whole property. The cutting, done about four times per year, was a major project in itself. Always done by hand (I suppose that electric trimmers were available and I do not know why we didn't have one – the cost I suppose!) with first the trimming then the sweeping up with endless bales of twigs and leaves for disposal, fortunately taken away, courtesy of the local council. It really did feel that, when the whole job was completed, it was time to begin again at the start – indeed, it was the Westcliff answer to the Forth Bridge!

Still, the work of the garden was but a minor issue which could not in anyway mask the sense of actual achievement I felt in finally having made the family move possible. To me, that gave enough answer to my own personal situation and dilemma of not by then having a steady girlfriend or settling down in the usual conventional way. I had helped Nan and Grandpop fulfil their dream and for the moment that was good enough for me.

New horizons had been achieved!

Chapter 11
Very Much The Good Life

As so much I enjoyed settling into our new home and the surroundings of living by the sea, there was the stern realisation of having to continue to work, then even more so to earn the money to fund the dream. With everything safely settled in and the family new home life on an even keel, all too soon it was time to return to work and to the corporate world. Father had gone the very next day to the move and so had pioneered the commuter spirit of our family.

'How was it, father?' I asked on his return the first evening. It was always 'father' when I spoke to him, never Dad or any other general terms of endearment. It all amounts to being proper I rather suppose.

'Quite acceptable, rather comfortable really,' he replied.

'Did the journey go quickly, were the trains on time, what views did you see, did you read?' My questions were coming very swift and fast and I noticed from father's stern brow that it was soon time to switch off the questioning if I wanted to avoid an explosion.

'You'll see for yourself when you finally make the trip,' and that was his concluding comment. The use of the word 'finally' rather sums up neatly his then attitude to my having a holiday for a few days!

Life at Bow had meant being less than half and hour from work, now, like father a few days before, I had the privilege of joining the commuting masses with a new overall journey time door to door of about 75 minutes. My days of enjoying a leisurely morning in the comfort of bed and getting up at 8am once the sun was up and the streets aired, were now well and truly over. 8am was now the time to actually leave home and, with the preparation and breakfast process, the actual getting up had to start an hour earlier. That was a small price to pay though for the opportunity of the new life.

Similarly it was much nearer 6.30 pm to get home in the evening and to have the gorgeous steaming dinner an hour later than beforehand. The thought of Nan's meal though certainly made for happy thoughts when sitting in the train. For father, the day was a little longer, although he would leave a little later than me; his return in the evening was about an hour later although his habit of evenings out did not diminish and fortunately the trains ran until very late! That service also helped me when having nights out on the town after work too.

My many commuting questions to father after his first trip were, as he had so succinctly put it, indeed 'seen for myself' when I 'finally' made the trip. The first days were a novelty, the trains generally on time and reliable but when doing the same trip five times per week in each direction there is a degree of sameness. It is of little wonder and perfectly understandable why the traditional London commuter is to be seen head down, engrossed in a newspaper or a book, completely oblivious to the immediate surroundings. Reading represented the best pastime and so presented me with a marvellous opportunity for keeping abreast of all the news, completing the crosswords and for making good and frequent use of the local library. Sometimes, I even took papers from work to read as well!

After the general chatty tones of people on the bus in East London, I was first highly amazed that on the commuter train everybody generally was so quiet, hardly any talking except softly between perhaps a couple of friends travelling together. Otherwise, just the rustle of the newspaper, the turning of the book page and occasional coughs and sneezes to disturb the regular noise of the train rattling along the railway track. Still, I could hardly complain, I was the very first person always intent on keeping myself to myself so why shouldn't others have exactly the same luxury?

Ever since my driving lessons and the coming of my car, my interests in railways had rather quickly waned in any case. Travelling daily in the commuter train, and especially with winter delays, any possible lingering interest was then forever extinct. The only possible exception to that was to be 'Disgusted of Westcliff' when writing to the local paper about the state of the train service!

Every day, on my journey to and from work, I was in the 'fortunate' position of passing the Bow area as the train sped along on its final run into London. If I really stretched up from the seat, I could just see the roof of our former home. If all that wasn't enough, the railway line passed such familiar landmarks as Devon's Road, our former home shopping street, and even right past the hospital, that Victorian edifice, where 'it all began,' the place of my very roots!

Being so comparatively close to London and with my natural feelings of continuing to be part of London and to enjoy all that the City had to offer, there were a number of occasions when I would drive in as well, especially at weekends. On such times I would actually drive along Bow Road and right past the former house.

Nan and Grandpop were often with me and all we could do was to smile most happily, breathe deeply with contentment of having finally made the change for the better.

'Can you imagine,' Nan would say 'we lived there for all those years, and you, love had over 20 years there.'

'Well, you had over 10 years more than me, Nan,' I replied.

'I always believed we would get away, Mate,' Grandpop said, 'now we've done it. Do you feel upset, Mate?' he continued.

'Oh, Pop, me – upset . Never. I hated the place, couldn't wait to get away,' Nan replied. 'now that we are once again living in the Southend area, it couldn't be better! How can Bow compare to Westcliff?' she concluded.

'You are so right, Mate,' Grandpop replied 'How can Bow compare to Westcliff indeed?' he continued in very deep and meaningful thought.

With that, I knew that it was worth all the efforts to get away, it was worth having the life as I then had it and Nan and Grandpop were so happy. All was indeed good.

The dramatic changes in our former home area had begun well before we moved away and once being finally set free and without the natural home instincts any more, it was truly appalling to see the area with fresh eyes and to witness what was happening. All that could be seen were soon even more high-rise houses, and the demolition of the traditional and well-known houses, shops and sights had created an overall air of dereliction and depression, all very sad in fact. It was even more difficult to imagine the place as a former home territory, such was the change in the style and character.

Here I was then seeing in reality the many mistakes that are continually made in the development of our inner City areas whether it is London, Manchester, Glasgow – wherever. During my early years in Bow, up until finally leaving in the mid-1960s, I had seen the very many fine buildings with potential life still left in them, which one by one were destroyed rather than enjoying some renovation and enhancement. Since those times there have been some improvements in some areas of East London like Docklands and Wapping, even parts of Bow becoming 'sought after' but at what price. Crazy, inflated prices for supposedly 'superior dwellings' but at what cost to once local people who neither have the chance nor wherewithal to even be able to consider purchasing such properties as potential homes. There seems to be no middle way for the majority of the population who have to make do, for example, with the awful flats as the only way for them to stay in their locality.

Even with housing improvements, though, there is one thing surely missing and unsolved. That is the matter of area infrastructure – people are enticed to pay many, often hundreds, of thousands of pounds for a property and, taking the present Bow for example, what does the area itself offer other than close proximity to the City and West End? The place itself is not one to frequent at night, and even if it were there is nothing immediately on hand to do. The park areas once safe in the day are no longer so. True there are supermarkets and a range of do-it-yourself and furnishing stores on the orbital road but the latter are hardly essential for everyday living. The local shops have gone and with them any sense of community spirit. The true heart of the place had gone forever.

All in all, I had absolutely no regrets for no longer living then in my former home area, it was becoming increasingly unrecognisable in any case. I knew what Nan and Grandpop thought about the whole issue, but with father it was more difficult to tell. Whilst on the one hand he aspired to the better life, in every respect the good life, he always seemed so totally oblivious to his immediate surroundings; I believe living very much in some make-believe world. For him, the time in Bow was a time in his mind when he was living in a big London town house, irrespective of the actual location. In his mind, the 'Bow' bit of the address didn't seem to have mattered; it was the London postcode that was the key.

Never do I remember father offering any opinion about the changes going on around us in Bow, never commenting about the less good and disappointing nature of things.

'I have really not noticed or thought about that,' was his usual stock answer when I raised the issue with him.

And I believe that was really true – his world was so within him and so closed down. There was little wonder why his relationship with his Canadian friend, Elaine, floundered – father's make-believe world simply did not stand up to the reality or probably to Elaine's scrutiny.

Thankfully, I had the enjoyment from my opportunity of those earlier years in Bow; I don't regret them for being at the time or style that they were. On the contrary, I in fact felt then pleased and proud to be part of East London. It was a most wonderful experience to have been able to enjoy the very best of the old and established times before those periods were consigned for ever to history.

No matter what for me though, even after the family move to Westcliff, I continued to feel and to consider myself as a Londoner and to look upon London as my true one and only home town. My weekday regular trips to London for work and my continuing association with London life for many pleasurable activities, all made sure that I kept my feelings and contacts with London when even not actually living there. In that respect, I was thoroughly different from my father's family, the uncles and aunts who having moved from Bow to suburban Essex, very much remained encamped in the suburbs only to make extremely rare visits to London.

Of course, they did use to make some visits to us in Bow but obviously that ceased when we moved away, so their connections to London became even less. They were not into the life of theatres or other attractions of the big City and I suppose that they did not miss the place in any way. Being also from that side of the family with closed emotions and never ever discussing personal thoughts and feelings, the matter will always be a mystery to which I shall never know the answer!

* * * *

I was indeed very happy with my Westcliff double life which was extremely good in every conceivable respect.

At home the sea walks, fresh air, pleasant shops and respectable surroundings, plus even a couple of live theatres and concert venues locally, which very soon began to have London shows. Especially so in the summer, I found it was a wonderful feeling to return to the fresh and clean sea air after the City, the highlight being at one point near Leigh where the train ran along by the sea and the tone of the long summer evening was surely set. All this and London itself only an hour away all made for a most agreeable and happy good-life combination.

Of course, in many ways more than the question of good ozone, the move to Westcliff was a breath of fresh air. The happiness and relief for both Nan and Grandpop was evident for all to see. They both seemed to becoming several years younger and had an endearing vitality and enthusiasm for making the very best of their new home. All the time they spent making improvements, Grandpop especially in painting and renovating, tapping here and there, adding bits, removing items that didn't seem to be appropriate any longer, simply always just tinkering and absolutely enjoying their newly discovered life to the full.

'Please don't overdo the work and over-exhaust yourselves,' I would frequently say to them when I returned home in the evening to find yet another room being painted, or new curtains being made for another set of windows.

'Don't talk daft,' they would reply, endearingly. 'We're not museum pieces yet! In any case, we are enjoying the fact that finally we have somewhere nice to live and a decent home to look after. We're in our element. It's when we don't work that you should start to worry!'

And that statement well and truly summed the situation up perfectly. Nan and Grandpop were such happy and strong characters that the only solution to all the troubles that they had experienced in life was to keep on going. It was the same now; they wanted to keep going, to enjoy life and to keep doing their best. That was the true East London spirit too that was instilled within them.

On top of all the decorating and home improvements, they too were running the house and doing all the home chores, cleaning, cooking, all the shopping, everything, in fact, bar the garden. I did feel worried, both Nan and Grandpop were approaching their 80s, but they really seemed to thrive on all their activities and from the sense of their achievements. Then I just hoped that they could keep their health, keep well and to be able to enjoy their new-found happiness.

Remarkably too, for me, as a result of our new life, father also became more human and from then onwards I began to have an altogether better relationship with him than ever I had experienced during my younger years. Still, there was some distance between us but at least we could talk more often and his absolutely terrible habits of sulking and not saying a word for days on end became rarer. I could only give thanks for that because I could never learn to accept that character trait – it was most awful.

As for my aunts and uncles – well even they became more human and far less severe personalities – or was it, perhaps, that I was mellowing with my 'advancing' years! No, I think not, it was them all behaving differently.

Without any doubt, the problem with father and that side of the family generally was their absolute inability to be really human, to relax and be themselves, always living behind a mask of ultra- and above it all respectability. I had experienced this so often and it was especially noticeable during my childhood and younger years when none of them could really relate to me other than to be officious. As I grew older, and started work, everybody became completely different and consequently I wanted them to think that the times we met were because it was mutually wanted rather than out of a general sense of duty. Perhaps I was living, like father, then in some sort of dream world in that respect but the fact was that I did then enjoy an improvement of family relationships equally with father and his relatives.

Perhaps, also, the fact that I saw more of the relatives on home territory in Westcliff was because of the inescapable fact that a day by the sea was a far better prospect for them than having to go from leafy suburban Essex to Bow! I couldn't blame them if that was the case.

'We live by the sea, drop in next time you are passing!' a very pertinent phrase for the time. Saying it once to Brenda and Dick was perhaps a bit pushing on my part, especially so when I noticed father's thunderous facial expression. Fortunately, though, sulking didn't happen as a result. Who knows, he might have had very similar thoughts!

So it was in Westcliff that I had a far greater sense of being part of a family and, most importantly for me, the family always then included Nan and Grandpop as the hub, together with the aunts and uncles. This was the very first time in my life, and by then I was in my early 20s, that I could really say that I was experiencing the true family unit. It is little wonder, then, that I was myself such a late starter in the personal emotional stakes!

The various aunts and uncles would come to us for a day, usually on a Sunday, and Nan would prepare one of her fabulous traditional Sunday roasts, with all the fabulous trimmings and a huge pudding to round off the meal. In the afternoon we would walk the seafront (we would need to if we were to have some appetite left for tea!), perhaps sometimes go on to the pier, but always being sure to collect the prawns and cockles for the traditional Sunday tea.

In return, and even more miraculously, all adding to the family unit feel, we would all sometimes drive to Wanstead and Buckhurst Hill for the return visit, itself very much a 'first,' but in any case essence of the spirit of true family gatherings.

It was hardly imaginable, but after all those years father's family had finally accepted Nan and Grandpop as being part of 'my' family and included them to the arrangements. I was very pleased for that alone.

Several of my colleagues from work, and two of my best friends from school days, lived in the area so I had a greater network of friends in the Westcliff years than at any other time beforehand. We all frequently met and had a lot of good times – all fairly free and easy and, 'boy-girl' wise, still very non-committal. Still, I especially was extremely immature and a thoroughly late developer on relationship issues, a true emotional invalid in the vein of my father's genes. Fortunately it would somehow change for me but not for very many years yet to come, so any relationships in the Westcliff years were purely platonic and nothing 'would come of it.'

This was very much to the dismay of my immediate family of my Nan and Grandpop. Father never did question nor raise the subject, but Nan and Grandpop often asked, as they had already broached the subject in the past:

'When are you going to bring your friend,' meaning girl, 'home?'

'Oh, maybe not yet, Nan,' I would say.

'Well, you cannot leave it too long – I want to see you happy,' Nan went on to say.

'I am happy, Nan!'

'That's not the point,' Nan would reply. 'We mean we want to see you settled with a nice girl, to make a proper home for the future. You must settle sometime with somebody and we really want to know you are going to be happily married.'

Truthfully, at that time, I was happy and the thought of leaving Nan and Grandpop alone was honestly something I did not want to contemplate. In any case, if I had not been at home then they would never have been able to afford to carry on living in the house and the consequences of such a change were too cruel to even honestly consider. They had brought me up and had always been there for me, looked after me and sacrificed all else during their advancing years for my well-being. Then I felt it was my turn to be there for them and to look after them even though, in reality, they still did everything at home.

I do not regret my decision or the destiny for my life at that time – the fond memories that I have and will always hold are a true testament to that. I do, however, accept that the pattern of my life was somewhat strange and different from the norm, but then we are all individuals and that's me and I've always been used to being in a different category to many other people!

For the time, my mind was very much made up. I had much to thank for the Westcliff home move, the style of life and its overall contribution to what for me then was, unquestionably, very much the good-life.

* * * *

As I was then enjoying all that the life offered to me at home and the absolute pleasure of living happily by the sea, then so too, I would say with 'age and experience' I was at the same time enjoying even more the life at work in the City. Naturally, too, by then having been in the same company for some four or five years, I had a good circle of friends, some still working as colleagues whilst others had moved on to other jobs but still in the City. So forged a tradition of meeting up on a regular basis in the evening after work.

'How are you, for next Tuesday evening?' would be the first indication of an approaching evening out.

'Well, I'm fine. I'll check with David and let you know,' I replied.

'Good, I'll call Bob and with a bit of luck we should make up a good little group.'

That's exactly what happened and so being sure to take the tea-lady's advice and have a good supply of milk in the afternoon, we all met together at the 'Bunch of Grapes,' a fine old hostelry in Aldgate High Street for the first of the evening bevvies! With a bit of luck, the freight boss from work would be in their having a few 'snifters' before heading home.

'Ah, my budding bunch of protégés,' he would cry out. 'Here, the first rounds on me,' he continued, happily and very happily for us too since that first round on him became more likely the first of two or three rounds! A fine old pub atmosphere was enjoyed – in the winter-time with a roaring log fire and in the summer-time to spend some time in the garden courtyard at the back with the sounds and bustle of the City noises kept well enough at bay beyond the high walls.

Our pub itinerary kept mainly around the City, at least for the first part of the evening and certainly until it was time to get something to eat. For that, there was only one place where then to head – to the East End, of course, and to one of the various Chinese Restaurants around the Whitechapel Road. By then, we were all very much in need of food and I for one was usually feeling ever so slightly wobbly by that time, with that overall rather misty sense of where I was and what was going on around me.

'We'll have the set menu for six, with all the assortments possible,' one of the more alert members of the group would confidently order.

'Yeah – that's right, a taste of everything,' was the assembled supporting reply.

Duly, a massive bowl of rice appeared, together with steamed vegetables, bean sprouts, various sweet and sour dishes, some Peking Duck, beef curry, crispy sea food bites and prawn crackers. Unfortunately, we would also select some lager and even rice wine as the accompanying beverage so by the time we had finished everything, the sense of earlier mistiness had by then become a real pea-souper London smog. Oh dear!

Quite late in the evening, we would stumble out and head back into the West End for a last 'jar' together before we all finally went to the station and our separate ways home. I suppose that it was a bit unfortunate that most lived south of the Thames, so we always ended up around Victoria, after which I then had to make my way back to the City on the underground and to Fenchurch Street for my own train home.

What an assortment of poor souls used to be on the midnight train to Southend! If there was in the past no talking nor much noise on the normal trains, then on that train there was certainly the sound of snoring, grunts and general shuffling around in an effort to get comfortable. Often in winter-time, the train was really warm and after the last walk to the station, a happy and acceptable lull fell over me and that, together with the 'clunkety-clunk' of the wheels on the track, I would soon fall into a most happy sleep. Once or twice it was too good a sleep and I would only wake up in a daze well after my own station at Westcliff – once so happily a snooze was I in that it was the train cleaner that woke me in the railway sidings at Shoeburyness, some six miles beyond my right station!

'You can't sleep here, 'Aint you got no 'ome to go to?'

'Pardon, well, yes, uh, I must have slept passed my station I think,' I somehow was able to reply.

'I think you must 'ave, too – come on then, get out before I lock up!'

Which of course I did. Thankfully, even if I was the only one that night, then it must have been a regular enough occurrence because there were always a couple of taxis at the station ready to deliver waifs and stays to their proper homes.

'Come on then Governor – where is it *you* want to go to to-night?'

And off home I was duly taken, fumbled with the front door key, a quick wash and change and snugly in bed by about 2am after all those adventures.

Next morning, with the aid of good black coffee, a various assortment of Alka-Seltzer's, and I was ready to set off for work almost as if nothing had happened.

'You can't go out like that,' Nan commanded. 'Have a good breakfast first, that'll set you nicely up for the day, a bit of fried bread, a couple of eggs, sausage and some good, honest streaky bacon'

'No, thanks, Nan,' I said as kindly as I could as I dived off to the bathroom! Oh, never again – well, not at least until the very next time!

* * * *

One of my main friends at work had, quite naturally by that time, become very friendly with one of the girls in the, then evocatively called, 'typing pool.' He got very 'serious' and was keen that we should go around as a foursome which I found a bit of a major step given my lack of emotional and relationship development. The matters were brought very much to a head by the upcoming Christmas time and the firm's Christmas Dance, which was going to be held in the West End.

'Come on,' said Nan, 'That's the chance you've been waiting for. It's the chance we have all been waiting for,' she added with enthusiasm. 'There must be somebody in the same office that you could ask to take to the Dance.'

'Well, I suppose so,' I continued without too much sense of conviction.

'Go on, then, ask her, and Pop and I want to know all about it,' Nan concluded.

The fact was that there was a girlfriend to my own friend's girl so perhaps my own chance was made easy. Anyway, I thought about it for several days, and spent the whole morning on the appointed day of asking, rehearsing in my mind what I could possibly say. Never had that journey to London appeared to go so quickly and before I had even thought about and prepared the first sentence, the train was already in Fenchurch Street!

At the office, I put off going to the typing pool for as long as possible, although very mindful that my friend, Chris, was desperate for the answer. Oh, the pressure!

I couldn't put it off any longer and so, just before lunch, popped my head around the door of the typist's room, saw that the girl, Sophie, was at her desk, not too many others were in the room and in any case there was quite a din from all the office machines working all together in unison.

'Sophie,' I called, 'Um, I was wondering, um, just thinking, really, er perhaps, um, considering, well I was, will you, er, would you, rather, perhaps, well – I mean – like to go to the Company Dance, I mean, that is if you have no other plans – um, we could go with Chris and Val, if that's all right – I wonder what you think?'

It was a pretty duff performance on my part; it would have been alright in I was in my mid-teens rather than mid-twenties!

'That's lovely, I would be delighted to go with you,' Sophie said, and so it was all set. I had, somehow, managed with much pushing and fluffing to have arranged my very first date!

Chris was pleased that he had his wishes for a foursome; of course it may have been that he too wanted moral support but he was rather more outwardly worldly than me but inwardly probably just as little boy lost, in fact.

Come the day of the Dance, it was work as usual for Chris and me, but the girls had the day off to prepare. Amazingly, I found out that Sophie lived in Leigh on Sea, just three miles from me in Westcliff, although we had never seen each other nor met on the train. Frankly, I was scared about that as I thought that a one-off dance was one thing – a more serious relationship that could develop from regular train travel and associations within the same town – well that was something totally different! What in heavens had I let myself in for?

* * * *

Rushing out from work on the day of the event, as usually precisely on time, and with the train performing well, there was just enough time to get ready, cleaned up and suitably in all finery to set off once again back to London.

'Be sure to enjoy yourself, have a wonderful evening. Pop and I look forward to you bringing Sophie home as soon as you like, we'll make her very, very welcome,' Nan called out as I rushed out of the house for the important first date.

I had arranged to pick Sophie up from her home and we would go by car up to London for the Dance. It was only a ten-minute drive to Leigh and, strangely, Sophie lived rather close to the former house where Nan and Grandpop had lived in Leigh in the 1930s. She was all ready and, I must say, very unrecognisable from the person I saw so regularly in the office. No doubt she thought the same about me, although for me, finery, really meant simply a better type of suit and extra-combed hair!

The journey up to London was reasonable enough, I became just very slightly a little more at ease but otherwise made very stilted conversation.

'Nice evening, pretty clear and mild for the winter-time,' I said. How's that for an opening line for a romantic evening?

As the journey progressed, we talked more about our lives, the workplace and some thoughts for the future. Or, rather Sophie did. I kept fairly quiet about my inner thoughts – that would have been altogether too progressive for me to divulge too much soul thoughts at that time.

'How long have you been living down here?' Sophie asked, 'I hadn't realised that you lived this way, hadn't really thought – never seen you around though. What train do you catch,?' she continued. The questions were coming rather too thick and fast for my comfort! I only mumbled some general replies, never giving too much away.

Finally we reached the West End and I found a place to park the car only a few hundred yards away from the Lyceum, the hall in Covent Garden where the Dance was being held.

'You certainly know your London,' Sophie exclaimed, 'I could never have found my way around all these back streets and then to park so near to the place too. Most impressive,' she concluded.

'Well, yes, um, I'm quite used to the area,' I replied, mumbling in my usual way, not terribly sure as to how to deal with a compliment from this girl.

At the Hall, we met up with Chris and Val and I immediately felt a good deal better, more secure – safety in numbers, I suppose. How strange that whole evening was, strange enough to be on a first date and to cope with that experience. Equally strange though to see all the work colleagues with their various wives or girl-friends, all, like me, looking somehow different and even the more elder ones, who must have experienced that same sort of evening over many years, but still looking out of place, very ill at ease and unsure.

Of course, that was it. Everybody turned up for the work 'Do' because they felt it was a duty, they had to be there. The heart wasn't in it though and, in that respect, we all felt the same. Work was for work, the balance of work and social activities just did not mix, it was all so false, all such a case of misplaced bonhomie. It was an evening when the staff manager made some pretty silly jokes, embarrassingly so; the Chairman looked very much as he wished that he wasn't there at all; the Chairman's wife looked even more uncomfortable, with a fixed and unconvincing smile; when office advertising posters looked so out of place in a Dance Hall, even though the whole hall had been hired for the private event.

Once the band started, then it was time for the dance floor. I had very much 'two left feet' and completely forgot all the steps that I had practiced with Nan's help. Somehow, we got around the floor and I was very pleased when within a few minutes virtually everybody else had got up from their seats and was on the floor as well. The place was then so packed that it hardly didn't matter what steps each and everybody was doing. It was then more a case of trying to avoid bumping into the nearest neighbour and to being absolutely sure at least to avoid colliding or crashing into the Chairman's wife!

'How's it going between you and Sophie?' Chris asked.

'Oh, nice enough,' I replied, probably very unconvincingly!

'Val say's she's enjoying herself and Sophie was telling her that she was so pleased that you were actually living in the very same town,' Chris continued.

'Yes,' I said, 'I found that amazing too.' 'Gosh,' I thought, what will this lead to? For a first, it was a nice evening but I was really in a state of bewilderment, almost shock and somehow couldn't even think of the possibility of anything developing or more coming of it.

The dance finished at 2am and as we stood outside the hall on what had by then become a very cold December night, it was men's gallantry to the fore as coats and jackets were offered to the ladies to help them keep warm whilst we all returned to our various cars. Fortunately for the ladies, who were not driving, they had been able to enjoy plenty of drinks, courtesy of the Company. For us men, it was an altogether different story, by then completely sick of orange or pineapple juice. Come to think of it, that was probably why the Company gave the party, knowing that the male staff couldn't drink and they would save on their alcohol bill accordingly!

Sophie continued her chatting, endlessly I must say, all the way during the drive home. Rather too much, frankly for my liking but that was me being too inconsiderate. I dropped her off at her house and properly escorted her to the front door. We shook hands – yes, really, she put the key into the door and with a 'thank-you for a really lovely evening,' she went inside.

'Thank you, too,' I said as I went back to the car, got in and very relieved that the evening was over, I drove home.

The next morning, Nan could hardly contain herself in asking question after question.

'How did your night go, how did you get on with Sophie, is she a nice girl, when will we be seeing her, when are you bringing her home here?' and so Nan went on.

'It was a nice night, it was nice to be with everybody that I knew from work,' I said, which was not entirely true 'And, yes, it was nice to be out with Sophie,' I continued, again not really wanting to admit that I found the whole evening a bit of a trial.

'No plans yet for Sophie to come here,' I continued 'but we'll have to wait and see – it's early days yet!'

'Well, don't leave it too long – be sure to ask her our again very soon and then bring her home,' Nan said. 'I'm really looking forward to meeting your first girl, well the first girl that I have known about,' Nan continued wryly.

At work on Monday, of course, we all met up again and, just as before, I had not seen Sophie on the train. I did see her as soon as she came to the office and, remembering Nan's recommendations, I asked her if we could meet.

'Perhaps we could meet up for lunch during this week?' I asked.

'Yes, please,' Sophie replied. 'What about if we go as a foursome with Chris and Val?'

'Fine,' I said, 'let's do it on Wednesday, oh, if that's alright with you, of course,?' I carried on.

That arrangement was fine and so began quite a regular series of 'foursomes,' but always during the lunch-time and the occasional evening. None of the outings was completely successful and it was always noticeable that Val and Sophie would always bond together, leaving Chris and me to do our own thing and get on with it!

The fact was that, for both of us chaps, nothing would 'ever come of it' as, unknown to both of us at the time, both the girls had joined the company with one thing in mind. That was to transfer to the sea-staff and to start work as assistant pursers on the ships! The call of the sea then was so very much greater than any association with Chris and me! So the end result of my first date was for the girl to run away to sea – there must be some lost moral in that story!

I suppose that I must say I was very relieved. I liked Sophie's company, but I was not ready for anything more than an occasional odd friendship, much to Nan's disappointment. She so wanted to have a special tea at home for 'my girl,' but then was not the right time.

*　*　*　*

For the first years of the life at Westcliff, I didn't actually take an actual holiday away from home. That wasn't to say that I was a dedicated workaholic, which most certainly wasn't the case. No, simply, I did take each and every due holiday day from the work but preferred to enjoy the time at home rather than to go away.

There was always so much to do, and a two-week holiday period gave me just that fine opportunity to do the things that I liked the most. Long local sea walks, enjoying the town, the local theatre, concerts and the arts generally, time and freedom to purposely enjoy my favourite London sights and attractions, to meet with friends and to happily relax, the freedom of life without the work commitment.

Time spent too by having lengthy drives and exploring the immediate areas of East Anglia and the South East. This gave me endless pleasure with the realisation that there are parts of Essex that are very much underrated and are pleasantly rural, indeed most attractive. That Essex I discovered was a world apart from the docks and industrial areas by the Thames and the huge urban sprawls nearer to London.

During the first few days of one of those holidays, my old school friend, Trevor, came to stay. Trevor was, like me, a born and bred London boy who had moved away from London when starting work to be near his job in Birmingham. We had not therefore met up for a couple of years, so initially had a lot of catching up to do. There's nothing like a brisk walk along the Southend seafront or on to the pier to catch up on all the news!

'Well, Trevor,' I said, 'any luck with girl-friends in Birmingham?'

'Actually, yes,' Trevor replied, 'in fact, I'm thinking of getting engaged this Autumn. And what about you, there must be plenty of waiting opportunities in the City?'

I told about my time with Sophie.

'Don't give up just like that, go to sea yourself,' was Trevor's recommendation. Well, at least that was a new angle to the 'girl question!'

We continued to talk about life, about our old times at school, remembering 'bat-man' and colleagues. Life was obviously changing and my own slowness in romantic development was even more evident as Trevor was himself soon to get married and we both knew of others from school soon themselves heading up the aisle. Certainly a thought and a concentration for the mind.

During his few days with me at home, Trevor and I took a few exploration rides around about, we said to enjoy driving, probably though to seek out local pubs and places to enjoy. Like me, Trevor was very agreeably surprised with the area's pleasant countryside.

One day when we set off, beginning in the area nearest to Southend, the coastal Essex, we drove a few miles north to the very pleasant landscape of the River Crouch. Burnham-on-Crouch is the main sailing centre and is a town with bright-coloured cottages along the quay and with some rather fine Georgian and Victorian houses along the main street.

A quick stop in an old, said to be, Smuggler's Inn, lucky Trevor able to sample and enjoy the local ale as he was not driving, we then set off north from the area to the River Blackwater and the truly charming old world town of Maldon with its steep winding streets and which was once the site of a battle with Denmark in AD 991. Plenty of pubs here too, but this time we settled for a delicious plate of local seafood. Maldon is well known for its culinary sea salt, but we just made do with straightforward salt and pepper!

Travelling on from there, next we reached the pretty village of Tiptree which, since it was famous for jam making, our stop there was for buns and jam and some tea – certainly a change, for Trevor, from the previous alcoholic experiences. Or was it that, perhaps, I was getting a bit upset of my enforced abstentions because of driving! Once again, suitably refreshed, we went on to take a quick look around the old Roman town of Colchester, before deciding in the late afternoon to start to set back home, but with a continued sense of exploration, by another way.

* * * *

We headed west and came to Great Dunmow, the scene of the 'Dunmow Flitch' trial held every four years to find a husband and wife who have not had a domestic argument for 'a year and a day!'

'This is the place for you,' I said to Trevor, 'once you are married – will you last a year and a day to keep the peace at home?'

'No trouble at all, we're win with flying colours,' was the assured reply. I rather think Trevor would probably be right, he being rather a placid type of guy. But it did lead me to wonder how I would fair in such a contest being calm enough often on my own but I knew I had a tendency to be abrasive especially after being too long certainly with some people and desperately then wanting just my own company again. A typical 'only child' syndrome!

Our homeward travels took us next to the pure 'chocolate box'- style memorabilia villages of the Bardfields and the crown of them all – Finchingfield, with its river, little bridge and beautiful village green, all surrounded by the very best variety of English village houses. All this complemented by one or two country pubs and tea-shops, as far removed from the everyday vision of urban Essex as could possibly be.

To round off the most pleasant day, I wanted to be sure to return by way of Thaxted, a magnificent small town with a timbered Guildhall from the 16th century and rows of half-timbered houses, many thatched cottages and plenty of friendly tea-shops. There are one or two good antique shops as well; rather ideal for Trevor then in the beginning throws of planned home-making and even from school times always with an interest in all things old. Grandpop's enthusiasm for bric-à-brac had also to some extent been instilled in me, so we both spent half an hour or so browsing around. Trevor found an old oil lamp, I picked up a two-tier brass candlestick; the stop wasn't wasted!

Frequently, on summer afternoons and evenings, the overall atmosphere in Thaxted would be enlivened by Morris Dancing and there cannot be anything more rural nor more English than that! It was the same on that evening but after all the driving and touring, the magnitude of different sights, though, we both thought that we had earned a thoroughly more refreshing and liquid break and headed for one of the delightful, old fashioned, thatched pubs in Thaxted. More orange juice – no, I think not, at least I had some ginger beer, gritting the teeth and letting Trevor tell me how absolutely delightful the local ale was, yet again. Oh, for the joys of driving!

By the time that we got back to the Southend area, it was well after ten at night and that meant there was only one thing then to do to round off the day – that was to head off to one of the many fish and chip shops along the Southend sea front. We were hungry and it all tasted even better than ever, if surely that was possible!

Trevor left for home the next day but his visit had once again brought into focus my own situation of still not yet having any steady relationship. Outwardly, I was not bothered, preferring to let matters take their course and still maintaining that my first duty was to look after the home and provide for Nan and Grandpop. Internally, though, I was worried and not entirely happy, especially when noticing how one by one the old school friends were all settling down in their various happily married lives. I really could not conceive then that a similar situation could easily befall me and I convinced myself I was doing the right thing, on the right track for me at the time. I think!

Any self-doubts, or negative thoughts, though, soon disappeared as I carried on with my holiday time. There were longer days and time to go even further afield, for which the whole of East Anglia was in immediate scope. To me the choice was endless and I loved to explore and find new places to visit. Having had an enjoyable holiday in Suffolk when living in Bow, from Westcliff it became easy day-trip territory.

One such trip gave me the chance to somehow rekindle the earlier relationship that I had falteringly begun with Sophie. Just before Sophie finally went away to sea for the first time, I invited her out for one of my day's 'rural rides.' That was a most happy day, and we got on then so much better then ever before which, I think, was simply because I then knew nothing demanding nor 'serious' was expected from the relationship, nothing would come of it. I was therefore much more relaxed, less stilted, being simply friends, enjoying each other's company and the day. So successful was it, that at the end of the day I felt really very sad that there was no chances to really then develop the relationship. Trevor's words rang in my ears 'you go to sea' – well I didn't know.

On that special day, we first took the main roads for swiftness and drove to Woodbridge bound for the coast My pre-booked special treat and the highlight of that day was for us to go to the old fishing town of Aldeburgh, the former home of the composer Benjamin Britten and the setting of the wonderful summer concerts in the nearby concert hall at Snape. I was fortunate in having got two tickets for an afternoon concert which we both so thoroughly enjoyed, the music and the very special atmosphere of the concert in that magnificent setting. Afterwards, we walked the long and thoroughly unspoilt shingle beach enjoying the sight of the colourful fishing boats pulled safely up on top of the shingle, away from the sometimes threatening North Sea, awaiting for another catch, another day.

I was determined to make the day as long as possible, the sort of perfect type of day that you never want to end. It was all going so very well and Sophie appeared so genuinely delighted and to be enjoying herself. So we then headed further north along the Suffolk heritage coast area, some parts of which have suffered from coastal erosion. Dunwich, for example, is a smaller village now than it was many years ago as a result of the erosion.

' It is said that the sound of the bells of the old church now swallowed by the sea, can still be heard peeling at certain states of the tide,' I said to Sophie, although I'm not so sure that she believed me, or even whether I actually believed the rather incredible story either.

Next, we set off to Dunwich Forest and to the many excellent picnic sites there and a chance to stop for some cakes and coffee which Nan had thoughtfully provided for the occasion, obviously ever hopeful of doing her bit to enhance the possible relationship! We went on to the village of Walberswick, from there taking the small ferry which operates across the estuary to Southwold.

Knowing Southwold from that previous holiday time spent there, I had booked dinner for us at the old Crown Hotel and what a delightful place it was too to round off the main-part of the day. Sophie was leaving for sea, then, within a couple of days so after dinner, there was then nothing for it but the short ferry trip back to Walberswick and then the drive back to Southend. A drive of a couple of hours to talk, think of the day, and what might have been had the sea life not beckoned for Sophie, for me especially to wonder what life could have been at that stage for me in different circumstances.

By the time we were back in Southend, I certainly didn't know any of the answers to the many questions going around in my head. And Sophie – she probably was quite set and secure in her own plans and it was not just bravado that she talked so long and excitedly about her coming life at sea. Of course, she had enjoyed the day and seeing aspects of her native land really quite new for her, but her life was most obviously set for the wider world and her eyes consequently focused, very literally, out to sea and to distant horizons.

At that moment when we said 'Good-bye' – it really was just that, and in fact our paths were never to cross and we never did meet again.

I continued for a few days thinking deeply about that day out and about the relationship that was no more. I sorted out my thoughts with some long sea walks, decided that there was no question of my going off to the sea, to chase a dream relationship or to tempt fate. I preferred looking at the ocean from the assured surroundings to me of the Southend seafront!

In any case, I still had a few more days' holiday left and that was not the time to be sad, I told myself. I had made the decision upon my life that I felt the most comfortable with and now was the time simply to get on with it and to go on and enjoy it.

Over the last few days of my holiday, I so wanted to take Nan and Grandpop with me for a couple of my excursions and exploratory trips, feeling still very much in the need of company and not to be too long left in my own thoughts. I was so happy that they agreed to come and so began another of my now becoming famous 'rural rides!'

As much it is a sea county, Suffolk is even more a vast country area, so that was the choice for the first day trip. The drive began by making first for Sudbury which is itself a pleasant enough market town, but to be really charmed we then went on to Lavenham. This village can trace its history from the wool trade of the 14th and 15th centuries. As a result, there are numerous well-kept half-timbered houses and thatched cottages, a fine Guildhall and a Wool Hall. At the edge of the village is the local church with its 141 ft high tower made of knapped flint, very typically East Anglian.

That area abounds with numerous other quaint villages and hamlets with evocative names like Thorpe Morieux, Kettlebaston, Maypole Green and Bardfield St Clare, all to delight the eye as indeed it did to us all that day as we drove the winding and very pretty lanes.

No matter how beautiful the countryside and the immersion in 'rural rides,' we all had the need for some town life to address the day's balance. So next we headed to the area's main centre of Bury St Edmunds where the 18th Century Angel Hotel was the scene of the meeting between Mr Pickwick and Sam Weller in Dickens' 'Pickwick Papers.'

'Time for tea then,' I said to Nan and Grandpop, knowing full well that the answer would be 'Yes!'

So in my imaginary Pickwick guise, we went into the Angel Hotel and enjoyed a very traditional English tea with cucumber sandwiches, scones and jam and fruit cake. All very respectable, and all the much nicer for that.

The town of Bury St Edmunds itself has many fine buildings and is said to retain its original 11th Century street plan. Moyse's Hall dates from the 12th century and the Guildhall and Cupola House are both of 15th Century origin. The town boasts excellent examples of Georgian architecture including the Theatre Royal and the main street shops.

Time then for the return journey which then began by heading back south firstly to Long Melford, one of Suffolk's most impressive villages with a 15th Century Church and many fine houses. Next we headed west to the village of Cavendish, still reputed to be one of Suffolk's showpiece villages as, indeed, is correct when seeing the abundance of half-timbered thatched cottages. The next stretch of the route surely delights even more with first the village of Clare, an ancient market centre on the banks of the River Stour. Stoke-by-Clare follows and there houses date from the 15th Century, many being plastered and decorated with chevrons or fish-scale patterns. Grandpop was in his element with so much interesting architecture to enjoy so our journey was rather delayed there!

Our homeward journey then continued through the well-trodden byways of North Essex with the car by then well laden with fresh produce from the numerous farms and market gardens passed along the way.

Considering my Norfolk connections from my unknown paternal grandfather, with a 'good head of steam' in the becoming older car, that county was not too far away for a day trip. So for our second trip during the final of my holiday days, we chose to head for the county capital of Norwich. The City's welcome sign says t 'A fine City' and indeed it is, being both an excellent shopping centre, with a marvellous extensive daily market, and much of general interest to complement.

Norwich Castle originates from 1130 and the Cathedral is one of the finest in the country. The Cathedral precincts are particularly attractive and the grounds lead down, pass the cricket grounds, to the River Wensum where Pulls Ferry and the Bridge Inn are reminders of the City's antiquity. My favourite Norwich landmark has always been the delightful Elms Hill area with its cobbled streets, pretty and crowded with courtyards and ancient shops, including a superb coffee shop and home bakery. Central Norwich too has a host of narrow streets and alley-ways to delight the eye, each corner throwing up something different and always a variety of specialist small shops such as the Coleman's Mustard shop.

If all that is not enough, it is said that Norwich has a pub for every day of the year (and a church for every week!). Our own favourite and for which we again duly made for on that day, was the 'Adam and Eve' near the Cathedral. Quaint, and with a wall made from traditional Norfolk beach pebbles, the pub was a real delight, as was the whole day's visit and a suitable conclusion to the 'rural rides' of my holidays.

I have always enjoyed driving and touring around an area by car, generally exploring in depth and the splendid and invigorating feeling when really getting to know an area, in all seasons and especially lovely in the long days of summer. You can guess, then, that it was a real thrill for me to do this and so wonderful that Nan and Grandpop came along, equally revelling in the experience.

The beauty too was that wherever the trip, we had the pleasure of a return home to Westcliff rather than back to the inner City of Bow. It really was a special and star quality time of my life and in no way do I regret having spent that time how I did. Similarly, I was happy to spend my holidays in that way, in fact there was never enough time to get all I wanted to do into the schedule, so what would have happened had I actually gone away for two weeks?

* * * *

Then the crowning beauty of all this renewed years of home life location wise – why London, of course, only an hour away from Westcliff. I always wanted to remain true to my roots and to London and never wanted it not to be a part of life, of my being nor of my leisure surroundings. Thankfully, this was always important for me.

Whether to go by myself, with various friends, with Nan and Grandpop, even sometimes with father, and that, in itself, was with a sense of the growing maturity and each other's final acceptance of some sort of relationship, although never to be deep or respected in what is a traditional 'father/son' sense, as such. In whatever circumstance, the value and enjoyment of London to me was always the same, always the most happy and positive experience. Moreover, it was an experience from which I would never tire.

Always, how magnificent it was to see the Changing of the Guard at Buckingham Palace, the beautiful uniforms, the helmets glistening in the summer sun or the resplendent heavy coats in the winter, always accompanied with the uplifting sounds of the marching music. Sometimes, there was a long period of time passing before re-seeing the event, which would then only add to the thrill of a re-visit. That ceremony and tradition, so easily taken for granted, but equally so easy to forget its wonderful value and contribution to life.

So often, too, the greatest delights for me came when visiting with friends who had either never seen the spectacle or, if they had, so many years before that it was a feint memory. Then I benefited from seeing things afresh through their eyes and perceptions as well.

'I never remembered it to be this good,' friends would say, and we would stay for as long as possible to fully savour the atmosphere. It was always the same.

So it went on. The realisation about the beautiful parks right in the very centre of London. Many times to make the lengthy, almost country-like walk, from Kensington Palace, through Hyde Park with a chance to look round the Serpentine on the way, often stopping for a coffee whilst sitting by the lake. This ensured that we were suitable rejuvenated before the brief moment back to reality with the traffic sounds of Hyde Park Corner. City noises, though, didn't last long as next it was into the mighty spaces and tree-lined walks of Green Park, then to cross the Mall and so into St James's Park to admire the birds and ducks enjoying the lake - not to forget the Pelicans. How amazing, too, to see the squirrels scampering around in the Park, ready to be fed from passers-by, and right in the centre of the City!

That particular walk would normally end for the day at Parliament Square, time then to once again admire Big Ben, Westminster Abbey and the magnificent buildings of Parliament itself. A truly spectacular end to a very special day in the heart of London, friends were thrilled, visitors were thrilled, not to mention that no matter how many times that I had done it, I was more than equally thrilled as well!

Even if there wasn't time on that day, a time would be soon made another day to continue on from Westminster by taking the river boat to Greenwich. Then, I was in my element, giving a commentary almost to rival the efforts of the crew – and all that without me actually passing the hat round for 'voluntary contributions!' Doubtless, though, somebody would take pity and friends would buy me lunch afterwards – there was, after all, a method in my madness. This was me very much in home territory – it was just a pity that the steamer service to Southend was no longer in operation so that I could have continued on home in fine tradition.

Or perhaps not. I think that by then I would have probably bored all my friends once and for all!

The fact that I worked in the City didn't detract from my including those sights also as part of my leisure tours, It was always different, anyway, to be there in one's own time, free of work time constraints or any kind of restrictive timetable. Then it felt to be a completely exciting area, when it could be enjoyed solely for its sights and to be wrapped up in its history. So then it would be seeing through tourist's eyes the City locations, the Tower of London, Tower Bridge, always a favourite with accompanying friends, then on to St Paul's, the legal centre and the buildings of Temple Bar and the Law Courts, all to add to and supplement the delight.

Cultural London couldn't be forgotten either – it was essential to me and was always included in visits for the benefit of friends too. Always a chance for a look into the National Gallery or the Royal Academy and then an opportunity to admire the Burlington Arcade nearby, even if the shops' prices were rather too high for our pockets! Similar thoughts too about the buildings and shops in and around Bond Street – lovely to look at but out of our price league!

There had to be time, too, for a re-look at the museums; the British Museum, the Victoria and Albert Museum and, whilst in Kensington, hoping that there would be a concert or performance at the nearby Royal Albert Hall to really complete the day. Days and programmes were always so very full, never time for boredom, never time to rest, just to fill the mind and rejuvenate the spirit with so much activity.

'You certainly know your London,' friends would say, probably both excited and sometimes exhausted from the 'Cook's Tour'-type experience!

'Well, I should do, it's my life and it's inbuilt within me,' I would often reply, and that in itself was absolutely true. An analysis of my character would probably involve an analysis of London itself, we were so intertwined!

Had London itself changed?

A question, that, over the years, I would very often ask myself. A question that would seem all the more relevant when there with friends who, although from the area themselves, had moved away or who had never been as involved in the place in their formative years as I had.

Frankly, I do not believe that it had changed very much at all by the mid to late 1960s, especially as far as the centre or 'Regal London' was concerned. To me, it was all refreshingly the same, everything comfortably in place and all exactly in line with what my cherished memories told me. That was the beauty of ceremonial and traditional London, the parts of Central London and the City, and it was so comforting to me that it was just so. To be part of and to witness the heritage and traditions.

London to me, naturally from all my childhood years and years of upbringing, also meant East London and in particular, Bow. Over time, then, a return visit to the scenes of so many formative years was then most inevitable. That was a different London, a not especially nice London but nothing could take away the fact that it was my place of birth and a place which had been home to me for over 21 years. Like it or not, it was surely the place of my roots.

Any such visit would always prove to me, if further proof was indeed necessary, how much Bow had suffered from unfortunate re-development and how in later years it looked so desperately sad and forlorn, even when compared to my own time there. Or was it that I had viewed life there through rose-coloured glasses, never seeing the place, nor admitting that it was as bad as it obviously was?

It wasn't the case, though, that everything had changed. The old house was always there and looking still the same even if it appeared that nobody else had ever taken over the caretaker's living accommodation that had been our home for so long.

Had we been the last of that particular line? It certainly seemed to be so and the end of our period of living in that house had also seemed to have marked the end of anybody actually calling that place 'home.' Somehow, it seemed especially fitting and very much right that this should have been the case. Proper to think that the living dynasty had ended with our departure.

Still the same, too, was the fine old church still standing imperiously in its central island position on the main road, with increasing years even more traffic passing to and from and thus meaning that the Church oversaw a permanent traffic jam. Only my 'trolley-wires' for so many years were missing!

Overall, though, that was about all that was the same. Gone were all my very well-known streets of the good, classic, Victorian terraced houses, gone were most of the former so well-known shops of Devon's Road and even many of the old, traditional pubs. No more was my 'famous' former Dairy, off Bow Road, with its disappearing, phantom shop assistants – all of them now a thing of the past. And what had replaced all these buildings? Something better? No, absolutely not, just rows and rows of awful blocks of flats with endless, dull and rather sinister-looking concrete pathways leading all around and between the wretched buildings.

What always appeared before me on these return visits was to see a well-known place with its soul ripped out, a place no longer with any conceivable identity, all so totally strange and in most ways alien. Always such a sad sight but for all that, one which was very necessary to see time and time again, to remain acquainted with my roots and in memory of all that was my past

Any visit back to Bow could never be complete without the walk along Bow Road and to the location and place of my old school, to re-live the thoughts and years of 'bat-man' fame. Not only for me, but also for old school friends when we made the 'pilgrimage' together, this was an especially haunting experience. The school establishment itself had actually moved away, in fact to the leafy suburbs of Essex, but the building itself remained, intact, and home to a completely different school.

'Do you remember,?' either I or one of my friends would say as we stood outside those gates, the gates through which we had gone through in such a variety of different circumstances over so many years.

Of course, we remembered, all too clearly as if only yesterday. The bell and its rule over our then lives, the team of the various 'bat-men,' the frights, the fun, the discipline, the control of our early lives, the mere fact that one building had been such a major and controlling element of life over so long. For that moment, when actually standing outside again, it was so easy for any of us to forget that we had all moved on, and away. So easy it was to think that we were students once again, waiting outside for that wretched bell to ring to announce the beginning of more classes. It all felt so unreal, weird, and totally strange. It was then always the same, a desperate urge to move away, enough was enough, to then turn around and put our backs firmly away from that place – our own, personal 'House of Horrors!'

In a way to balance that visit, we would all go once again to the pub by the side of the school, the one to which we had rushed for lunch on that very last day. It was, for us, a sort of balance to the day, a balance to ensure that the visit would at least conclude on a more happy memory as that very final school day had been for us all! It helped, too, that the publican had changed and so we were completely incognito!

Strange as it can be to say that any visit to the old school area could be positive, the square immediately close to the school provided that inspiration. The square with its very fine mix of Georgian and Victorian three- and fout-storey houses had become very gentrified, houses neatly renovated and painted, wrought iron entrance gates, well manicured gardens – and even well kept flower beds and magnificent trees in the central gardens of the square.

Just think, after so many years, that I could actually be saying that any visit to that area could, indeed be, 'positive!'

How, though, it made me think of what could have been done with the rest of the former houses in Bow. That square was proof itself of all the potential.

The nostalgic visit was over – time to return to a real life, to go home to Westcliff but to feel benefited from once again having spent some time immersed in one's own roots. Friends would have exactly the same sense of emotions – glad to visit, very glad to have seen again but equally glad to get away.

Bow, an important place from the past, indeed a most formative place, but a place no longer as home, consigned very much to the realms of history.

Chapter 12

Really Here And There

No matter how much I would have wanted it, life for me, as for nearly everybody else, could not be based just on leisure and pleasure. Maybe mare's the pity for that but there wasn't much that I could do about it and, unlike my Grandpop, I didn't even do the football coupons! Grandpop had remained unsuccessful of any wins at all so any such thoughts along those lines of easy prize money remained very much a distant dream.

I needed to do much soul-searching too about myself and where exactly I stood at that point of life, perhaps very much having reached the mid-20s with little personal direction or real result. With Sophie by then well away at sea, probably with suitable boyfriends in every port, let alone with various eligible officers on board ship, any thoughts that I may have had, even if only very elementary, were in a similar dream-like capacity. Come to think of it, I didn't even receive an occasional postcard from exotic places – I was very much a thing of the past as far as that romance was concerned.

Of course, I kept telling myself that was exactly how I wanted it to be – but, inwardly, I wasn't entirely convinced that to be the true case. More and more, various friends were one by one getting married, more and more I would be sitting alone in the church and rather awkwardly at the reception afterwards. Can there really be a male version of a 'wallflower?' Maybe, and, if so, then I was fast becoming that!

Matters came very much more to a head when Chris, my friend from work, even he too announced his marriage. Like me, he had the experience of his association with Val, Sophie's friend, who had also run away to sea. Chris then set about new conquests and very soon had met up with another girl, also from work.

'Be careful, Chris,' I had warned. 'You know what it is about this place, its not you or me the girls are interested in,' I tried to continue, wisely, or pretending to be a man of the world. 'They are only here with one thing in mind – you know, to run away to sea!' Of course, this was a very cynical statement to make and rather too symbolic of my own then very jaundiced view on personal life.

'Oh, no?' Chris replied, 'Sheila is different. Alright, she may have thought about the sea, but not now. We really have an understanding on this and we want to be together.'

And 'together' was just how it turned out to be. So, once again I was at a church, at a reception and drifting away afterwards within thoughts and mixed feelings about my own position and about life itself.

The problem with me, without doubt, was that I was an emotional invalid as far as female relationships were concerned. I was suffering both from my very closed upbringing of being very happy to be in the company of older people and of living such a life-style. On top of that, I had not, during my early life, been used to girls of my own age at any time within my family and then the 'icing on the cake' was surely the long school years at a boys-only school.

Others, more mature, more adapt at becoming world-wise and in tune with life, had all been better suited to develop from such circumstances but I had not been so inclined nor so fortunate. In that I only had myself to blame. I was insecure, unsure still in female company, with a tendency to be very nervous and very immature in the most silly and stupid kind of way. I was still, in such matters, a school-boy and should have had a cap to match!

This particular trait of my character was so very off-putting to any potential and possible firm relationship. Whilst, on an extremely superficial and non-committal level, it meant that an occasional, short-term small degree of friendship could work; it would soon become evident that anything more serious was not possible. I really think that had I carried on in my efforts of being a girl's boyfriend at that time, then the Merchant Navy would have been full of despairing girls who would have rather run away to sea than have a relationship with somebody like me!

* * * *

Whatever my emotional and relationship shortcomings, work continued to progress for me during the latter years of the 1960s, perhaps, in reality, as a substitute for anything else. I carried on working, hopefully diligently, with the same Shipping Group. In fact, such was the prowess in that respect that when a brand new company division was set up, to cover the new freight container concept, I was duly interviewed and accepted for a post within the newly set-up company.

Not only was this a most positive move financially and also a better job, it was also good for me because it meant a return to the real City again, an EC3 postcode address, in fact to that very St Mary Axe. A chance, then, once again to be nearer to 'my' bank to keep control of my growing funds – or perhaps I should say overdraft!

As the change of home was on a positive note, then I am afraid to say that the work style and the actual life within the workplace was also undertaking a change but of a negative character. The days of the friendly, almost jovial atmosphere which had been such a welcome for me to experience in my early work years, were disappearing fast This was, supposedly, because everybody was becoming more 'work orientated' although, in my mind, nothing in reality could be more further from the truth and it was a retrograde step.

These changing ethics were perfectly displayed in the closing years of the 1960s and early 1970s in the company. People had more so called 'meetings,' spending a massive amount of time just talking, or perhaps, more accurately, 'waffling,' with supposedly endless discussions but achieving very little tangible result. Nothing wrong with having meetings, I thought to myself, but everything wrong when nothing came of them, except to set the date for the next meeting!

Firstly, I felt myself as a casual observer to this but it was so easy to become embroiled in the philosophy too until realising the sheer futility of it all. It was a rude awakening calling for an immediate halt on my part and a personal campaign to return to old values. This was all accompanied with a supercilious air of importance and business power forming, all utterly ridiculous. In reality, far less seemed to me to be achieved in a whole morning, or indeed day, than had been accomplished in an hour in the past

Typical of the new working regime was that suddenly everybody begun to write 'Memo's' to each other, copying in almost everybody they could think of, including the tea lady at the same time! Was I working in a freight company or was it perhaps a paper manufacturer, anxious to boost their own sales and add to their own profit? I did wonder!

What exactly did all this memo writing mean? Of course, I thought, there was a perfectly logical answer. It must have been that everybody wanted the excuse to be able to go as often as possible to the 'Typing pool' in a chance to meet the ladies and the chance for a romance. 'Don't bother,' I should have called out 'they are all going to run away to sea, anyway – it's all a waste of time!' And, what a thorough waste of time it really all was.

All the useless memo writing was in place of just getting up from the desk, walking a few yards and discussing the topic with the colleague, getting an immediate answer and knowing precisely what exactly to do next. That was how it used to be – all over and settled in minutes, the problem sorted and the necessary action already under way.

And with the memos – what progress was that. Probably at least to wait two or three days, at a best estimate for somebody to be bothered to read it.

The document probably lying around with a mound of other similar such papers in the 'in-tray,' impressively piling up with other such documents.

'How's your in-tray today, looks that you are pretty busy?' was a common enough message forever ringing through the office.

'Oh, I must really get through this lot, perhaps stay late or take the papers home for the weekend,' would be the normal style of reply.

And that was it, summed up nicely. It was almost a status symbol to be the custodian of a bulging to overflowing 'in-tray,' to show that the person was important and of absolute value to the company. What complete and utter nonsense!

The dull and depressing inefficiency of it all just went on and on. Having done one's own bit and issued the memo, what next was there to do other than wait whilst a reply was dictated by the fraught recipient. Next for the equally frustrated and overworked typist to type it sometime, taking its place along with a mound of similar superfluous duties. Finally, the memo would then have to negotiate the office distribution system back to the originator who by then had probably forgotten what the original enquiry was all about!

Well, at least the 'tea-lady' would have received her copy and would probably be better suited to keep everybody on the right track! 'Milk and sugar with yours, luv – and what are you doing about all these low freight rates, it's an absolute disgrace. What type of biscuit was it you wanted?'

Glorious imagination, perhaps, but in a way reality. Nothing but utter corporate madness and pomposity, born in those times in the late 1960s and probably developed most 'successfully' ever since!

In these new business times and in the new world of inflated office ranks and titles, of course I couldn't be a humble 'clerk' anymore – my job description had been changed to 'executive' – same thing, same job, just supposed to have sounded better! Even the work duties were the same although, by then, my salary had increased and I was then – just – on a 'four figure' per annum salary. That, perhaps sounded impressive but, of course, expenses had risen similarly so there was very little difference in the reality pocket, that glorious actual 'take-home' pay.

I looked upon all these changes coming so quickly within the workplace as bad enough but, unfortunately, that was not all. Something altogether and personally more alarming happening at the same time was that the actual working hours were becoming worryingly longer. As if that wasn't bad enough, it was not the official 'paid' hours that were affected – they stayed the same. No, the extra hours arose from the unofficial 'unpaid' overtime periods of having to get in early and leaving late. These were the hours when people thought it was necessary to be seen by the boss, and others, hard at work, so called 'toiling' at their desks in what was, after all, their own 'private time.' All that they were doing, probably, was just planning and answering those stupid and unproductive memos!

What a completely crazy corporate world, a world which I, as a relative lowly clerk, alright, 'executive,' could really only observe and pay lip service to. I didn't like it but felt too insecure to stand up against it, choosing rather to 'go with the flow.' That didn't stop me from regretting and fretting about it, all the time cursing rather too mildly but always under the breath. I saw, I commented mainly to myself and I was not the stuff that revolutionaries are made of, unfortunately! By this time, though, my feelings of business discontent were well and truly planted.

As a balance to all this negativity, there was one positive change in the workplace at about the same time. Positive in that everybody then called each other by their Christian name, from Directors to the tea-lady, with the exception of the Chairman and the Main Board. It really didn't, in my mind, mean anything, a false 'friendship,' only 'show' and, as such, unsubstantial.

I began to realise that perhaps I should have been born 40 years earlier than I actually was, so at the time then to be ending my career rather than advancing it! Having enjoyed and experienced the old practices and lifestyle of business in my first years at work, it consequently made it all that much harder to accept those latest, retrograde developments that I really abhorred.

In a rare sense of parental bonhomie, but becoming more the norm with growing maturity on both sides, I talked with father about these changing working issues. It seemed at the time that the Civil Service, his work, still then remained firmly routed in the old traditions and was carrying on doing things in exactly the same way as they had done for years. Perhaps that was what could be expected from a government service, but at that very moment it certainly had a good deal of appeal to me.

'You must stick with your job, see the changes through, assess how they will work and, you'll see, in the end it may just as well be for the better,' father advised. I couldn't make my mind up if father had really believed in, or meant, what he had said or was it just a case that he was fearful of me quitting my job in favour of the Civil Service. Perhaps he was simply scared if I did just that would then have found out rather a lot of father's very heavily shielded double life. Who knows?

From our conversation it appeared that it was just the City corporate image which was in the process of change. There and then I could have called myself a 'pioneer' but the fact still remained that I didn't especially like it. There wasn't very much that I could do about it – retirement in the early 20s was not an option!

'Grandpop, what about the Pools – can I do a row? perhaps not, I would be disillusioned if not winning within the first couple of weeks. Bingo? – no, not that either. Knuckle down then and get on with it!

Being more than somewhat 'pleasure-bent,' I felt a little bitter too because the uncertainty of the finishing hour at work meant that I couldn't plan with confidence any evening theatre activity in the week and that was a disaster. By then I had become so used to the pattern from the early years of being off from work on the dot to join the theatre queue that it came then as a disappointing shock. Bad enough to have to adjust to new working practices but when that had an impact on personal life too, it all became rather too bad. I didn't 'live to work,' but rather 'worked to live.'

It also had an even greater effect on my most fledgling romantic life and it was virtually impossible to arrange any 'date' with certainty.

'Sorry, darling, I left you standing outside the restaurant for an hour and a half, but I was busy doing some memos!' Hardly terribly romantic nor an especially helpful introductory line and, given my awkwardness in the relationship field, it was a situation made all the more harder by the new working regimes.

I think everybody at home was beginning to despair of me ever being able to 'find a Girl.' Nan and Grandpop were both most distressed at my singular inability in that respect, but as usual and time and time again, father didn't touch the subject, probably being far too busy himself with his own romantics to even think about me!

Still, I was most thoroughly mixed-up and unready for any romantic steps.

* * * *

All this new-found and so-called 'professionalism' in the work place soon meant that the company jumped on the idea of various business courses for the staff. Marvellous, having by then been away from school for over six years and having consigned my educational frightful memories to the dustbin of life, it seemed that once again I was to be faced with the 'delights' of the classroom.

In one year, I was 'lucky' enough to be selected for no fewer than three such courses, that I really began to feel that I had been transported by some time machine straight back into the realms of 'bat-man.' I suppose that there were degrees of maturity about the fellow students, perhaps even me, although I very much doubt that. Nevertheless, it was time spent in a classroom and the atmosphere was un-unnervingly all too familiar and alarming.

Usually, the 'school' was for a session period of two or three weeks at one time and since it was held in Bedfordshire, some 60 miles north of London, it was, of course, residential. That, in itself, was a completely new experience and was, I suppose, much more akin to a college or university type of life, which I had so chosen to avoid following my school years. In fact, apart from the period of classes and copious amounts of evening work and make-believe group sessions, it was all rather gentlemanly.

Off then on a Sunday afternoon from home, trying not even to think of the loss once more of precious personal time. That, at least, could always be the personal excuse as to why I was still single! Or, rather, that's what I thought as I drove so importantly up the M1, me and the little old car so very much itself in the big world. Once at the place, it really was rather nice, or as nice as any learning establishment could possibly be in my eyes.

Accommodation was all rather respectable single rooms, very much like the style that could be found in any number of reasonable 3/4 style hotels. An extremely positive note was that the food was mostly rather excellent and very plentiful with all the potential 'gentlemen of industry' dining in the evening in a very smart and candlelit main hall.

Nothing, there, then to complain about but whilst the non-curricular activities were very adult, the classroom style was absolutely no different to my school experiences. It really did feel like having gone back in time to those awful and thoroughly despicable years of school.

'Who is that talking, I don't know who it is but I will not have it,?' so said one of the lecturers.

'You are all really quite hopeless – learn, learn and learn again – You don't leave this room until you have all learnt it.'

So it went on – and on. The only conciliation was that the commands were not directed singularly at me but rather to the group as a whole. I took some comfort in that at least!

The days were long; the going overall was rather tough. It was strange too for me to be back in the 'boys-only' environment after the years of the mixed workplace and all that added to the sense of my once again being back in school. But because we were all so busy 'learning,' the time on each individual session went remarkably quickly and since, as a group, we got rather used to each other, there was a degree of bonding and help to those less fortunate in being able to quickly pick up the course's message. Amazingly, and wouldn't 'bat-man' be surprised to hear it, but it wasn't always me that was lagging behind either! That, I suppose, is what could be called real 'teamwork' and, apart from the subjects themselves, was what could be deemed a positive result from the whole experience. Otherwise, the positive result for me personally was that the workplace, as changed as it had become, didn't then seem such a wholly bad place when once again returning there from the exile period 'in class.'

* * * *

By the late 1960s and then with some six years of shipping experience behind me, plus the resounding success of my having attended those courses, I suppose I was becoming more use as a worker to the company even if I personally did not like the changes in business culture. Anyway, I made progression and became an assistant manager as opposed to executive or clerk – luckily, there was some money in it too. Most significantly also was that I then qualified for a turkey at Christmas!

That was such an excitement that I barely noticed that the wretched thing wasn't nearly enough sufficiently frozen with the result that it began to drip most wildly during the trip home in the train. Yes, British Rail did actually keep their trains reasonably warm in those days too. The poor lady suffering from a trickle of moisture of dubious quality from the said turkey which I had placed on the overhead luggage rack did not exactly act in the true spirit of Christmas!

It was very fortunate for me that with the added work responsibility came a widening of my own horizons and with it the perks of some business travels. That may all sound very grand but it was amazing, come to think of it, that there hadn't been anything previously other than frequent visits to the London docks, given that I was working for a shipping and transportation company. Now though things became different and the immediate North Continent of Europe came within my scope. I was bound for more far-flung locations, to the harbour areas of places like Bremen, Rotterdam, Antwerp or Zeebrugge. Hardly, I suppose, very exciting by the mere sound of it but it was considering that apart from a school jaunt to Norway and occasional visits to France, any sort of European travel was a novelty to me.

There was something very grand, almost colonial like, about these trips. I couldn't help feeling somewhat like a former Governor in India or someplace because on arrival at, say, Rotterdam airport there would be at least one or two officials to meet me. My name was held on a placard, and me feeling most important, still very much the wide-eyed 'little boy' in the big man's world. Then whisked off in a very lovely car, so often a Mercedes, not any comparison to my old Standard back home, normally to be taken to a rather swanky hotel, the officials always doing their best and trying their utmost to please. I wondered often whether they all thought that I was some company owner rather than a comparatively lowly 'assistant manager!'

During the evening, whether it was Belgium, Holland or Germany, a very good meal in some of the area's finest restaurants was normally arranged, everybody being most hospitable and never a question of my having to pay for anything. Me pay? – that wouldn't have been strictly correct in any case as I would have filled in my appropriate expenses form which had the evocative name 'swindle sheet' within the company!

Apart from the working aspect, and that, of course, had to be done otherwise those back in London would ask questions, the trips were great fun. Of course, any harbour is very much the same, cranes, lorries and ships, but I thoroughly enjoyed the life aspects of the various cities. The glorious coffee and cakes in Belgium and Holland, the accompanying Genèva with the coffee in the Dutch cafe, the succulent sausage snacks in Germany, there was always something to look forward to.

This all sounds very much at variance with my negative comments about the new working ethics and practices. But then, why not enjoy those trappings of pleasure; I was, after all, away in my own time on many occasions in any case. How often the visit would mean setting off on a Sunday afternoon or not actually getting back until late on a Saturday. And, apart from those coffee shops, and the chance of buying some 'duty-frees' at the airport, there wasn't much else in the way of leisure. Of all the times that I was in Zeebrugge, I didn't get the opportunity even for a quick look around Brugges.

Very occasionally, if one of my more senior colleagues was sick, I did get the chance for a visit to one of the Mediterranean ports but, once again, only ever seeing the harbours but with the chance this time to enjoy coffee and cake in a sunny piazza, which made a welcome change!

The North Continent was handy, though, in that I was frequently able to use the air services to and from Southend Airport. That was an 'adventure' in itself in that it meant using extremely 'historic' planes, the sort that were built to carry freight or cars as well as passengers. Seats were normally right at the very back of the plane where you could hear the creaks and groaning of the car and cargo restraints! This was really the style of pioneering aviation, long before 'business class' was invented, almost an embarrassment to turn up at the airport to check-in. Even more so when being delivered to the foreign airport by the officials in the Mercedes, a need to say quickly 'Goodbye' before they could see the means of departure.

For me, though, it was a fast 'door/door' transit, far quicker than flying into London and then having to take the train back home. The other advantage was that at least, as the planes flew so 'roof and wave top swimmingly' low, you could see the whether the tide was in and the lights of Southend Pier and home from a very close distance!

It wasn't just the Continent that was then the scene of my working activities. The developing work and expansion of the company into all aspects of transportation, rail and road land arrangements in addition to both short sea and ocean shipping, all resulted in operational centres being established in key cities all around Britain. These locations too became in my orbit, part of 'my patch.' Until then, very much a 'Southern Boy,' location-wise, not railway! (anyway, that by then really was a thing of the past), I quickly became introduced to Birmingham, Liverpool, Sheffield, Newcastle and our base in Scotland at Coatbridge, just outside Glasgow. Again though, invariably, this just meant the immediate depot areas and very little else and at the risk of offending anybody, in most cases this gave a very poor introduction to most locations. I really couldn't help but so terribly miss London and the City when 'out of town,' although that wasn't the case when on European escapades, obviously rather revelling in seeing new life!

As a consequence, the working weeks came anything but routine and, for my liking. I was far too often away from London and my once cherished evening theatre visits were then certainly a thing of the past. So often, there were frequent, and often hastily arranged, visits to be made here and there, to me very often without thought. Why, I often wondered, could there never be any proper business planning with a consequent saving of both time and money? Really, it was most crazy to be told to rush to Glasgow by air for a day trip on a Thursday, back in the office on a Friday and then:

'Oh, by the way, we need to take a look at another operational issue – you had better fly up to Glasgow on Monday again and we'll discuss the result when you are back in the office on Tuesday morning!'

These 'day trips,' by the way, were a very 'efficient' use of my salary by the company given my standard payment for an eight-hour day! I would have to leave home around 5am, catch the train to London, then the Underground to Kensington and (then) the airport bus to Heathrow, the flight to Glasgow and at least there someone would meet me for the drive to the depot. All this would be reversed in the later afternoon and evening and I would be home by about 10pm - some 'eight-hour' day! The rail trips to the North of England were hardly much quicker so over those times my unpaid 'overtime' bill was indeed excessive.

Trips to Birmingham were another case in point. I usually travelled with a colleague in his car. He lived in South London and always thought that Victoria would be a good place to meet up – at 6am! No matter how many times I tried to point out that a 'good way' from South London to the M1 Motorway would be via Tower Bridge and 'right past Fenchurch Station,' my own station is from Southend, my remonstrations always fell on deaf ears. Nothing for it, then, other than to take the very first train at 4.30am to London and the tube to Victoria to await the 'chauffeur's' arrival – at least he was usually on time.

'Morning, how are you,?' he would say 'not asleep yet' – that was some joke!

'I think it would be good to have some breakfast,' he would continue and then, as a let down 'but let's get some miles behind us first.'

'What time did you get up?' I asked, hoping for a reprieve.

'Pardon, oh sorry, the traffic was a bit noisy then, what did you say?' he continued. Oh, it didn't matter.

'Nice morning, isn't it,?' was my feeble comment.

And we really then proceeded to get 'some miles behind us' as we roared up the motorway until he decided to stop after nearly two hours at his 'favourite' service station at Watford Gap. By then it was around 8am, I had been up for over four hours and I felt absolutely starving , so much so that even the usual motorway service station breakfast tasted good.

After the day's work in Birmingham, it would be then the return journey to look forward to, probably leaving just after 5pm, nicely to be involved first in all the rush-hour traffic out of that City and then to join the heavy traffic on the motorway and head south.

'Better keep going,' was my colleague's tactic 'We don't want to be too late home so don't let's bother to stop for anything to eat.' With that my heart sunk!

'I'll drop you off at Victoria, then – ok? he would continue.

'Why yes, um, unless you feel up for driving via the City . . .,' I tried to reason thinking of how nice it would be to alight from the car at my own station.

'No, it's so much easier for me through Victoria' – so that was it settled.

At least out of the car at Victoria, I could call in a favourite pub for some refreshment and food before tackling the final part of the journey home where I usually reached around about 10pm. Not a bad day of 18 hours all for the price of eight hours pay!

I did find the idea of the business trips to Scotland quite exciting having by then spent plenty of winter's evenings watching 'Dr. Findlay's Casebook' on the television, in itself rather a sad reflection on what I sometimes did at home in the evening! I suppose that it passed the time whilst waiting for the ever elusive, and always expected, letter to come from Sophie on the high seas. Some hopes for that though. The novelty to me of Scotland was first its obvious different use of the English language and the inescapable feeling when there of actually being almost in a 'foreign' country.

Whilst I didn't see very much of the country during my first visits, and the part of Scotland I visited, the heavy industrialised areas of Glasgow and the Central Lowlands, was, even to try to be polite, hardly photogenic. However, on clear days I always did marvel at the mountain scenery as the plane flew in. I even saw Loch Lomond from the air and this was a mental note to visit Scotland at leisure sometime, given my love of mountains and lakes nurtured from that school visit to Norway.

That time of business life was certainly a hard pace and very demonstrative of the changing business attitudes that I had personally experienced over the six or seven years of my career so far. My mind would often return to those times of the gentlemanly pub sessions and subsequent efficient business deals plus the happy memories of that mad rush by everybody to get out of the office promptly at five. Those really were the days!

* * * *

At least though to balance all that corporate activity, I had my precious weekends at home in Westcliff and by that to have the chance of theatre visits back to London on the Saturday evening, so all was not lost! Even by my mid-20s, I had still not grown up emotionally and most of the family almost regarded me as a lost cause as far as any romantic life was concerned. Still then, I was the so called 'home-boy,' seemingly perfectly happy, within the constraints of work, to come home for dinner, sometimes even to spend the evenings at home or, at most, have occasional evenings out with friends. Indeed, I was not completely alone and there were still some contemporary single friends, although it was rather the exception to the rule.

Still, I felt the responsibility to look after Nan and Grandpop, help to maintain and finance the home arrangements. Never did I even then feel comfortable about the thought to leave them because I knew that father could never be relied upon to finance nor look after them. But I didn't feel stuck, nor did I feel sad by my lot. In fact, I continued to feel very good that I was able to provide for them and to be living the life in that way.

The jingle of extra coins in my pocket meant too that I had graduated, car wise, from the Standard Pennant, which I sold when it was over 12 years old to a chap on his first car and it moved on to an equally loving and cherished home! I then bought an Austin A40 (not good!) and so quickly changed it within a couple of months to an Austin, A60, known as the Austin Cambridge. That was a real tank of a car, completely solid and reliable and was soon a sight on the highways and byways of East Anglia and the South East as I continued with my exploring hobby and the famous 'rural rides.'

Often, I needed the car for business too, as in those days 'company cars' were mere distant dreams. My Austin Cambridge filled the business role very well either sedately sitting in the underground car park at the company office in the City, or in hosting those overseas visitors, of Mercedes fame, in driving around to company depots! Many times, I felt like asking them to compare our cars but then thought better of it – not a good idea, no matter what I thought of my car.

Probably in a couple of years I clocked up around 50,000 miles giving a grand total on 'the clock' of over 100,000 miles – all with the same engine, same gear box – in fact same everything except of course for tyres and a few small spares. It was a fantastic car and I would run out and buy an A60 again if they were still available. It was a real shame that tried and tested cars like that A60, or even the Morris Minor, were not simply been updated over the years rather than just scrapped. Perhaps I should have transferred to one of the company's overseas offices in India and been completely at home as those cars are still made and are running around there!

Despite my enthusiasm for the car, I did, however, fancy a change and so as a toast to the approaching 1970s, I scraped some more pennies together, then talked nicely to the man at the bank in St Mary Axe, by which time I considered I was by then a long, loyal and trustworthy customer.

Suitably financed, I then set about the car hunt, spending endless hours, days, evenings and weekends hunting high and low through all the car shops in and around Southend. The routine was so precise – the local paper on Thursday, time then to tick off possible options and see first on the Friday evening, remembering, as Grandpop told me, always to say 'I'll think about it and come back to-morrow.'

'Look, boy,' he said, 'you must make the dealer work, don't be too enthusiastic, and make him think that he's got to lower the price!'

It was hard advice to follow, especially when having seen what I thought was a dream car! It was, for all that, good advice though because most of the local dealers were 'rather suspect,' to put it mildly. Why was it that the car I wanted to buy was always 'a fine example, just one careful driver?' Yet my own car I was trading in to sell was always 'a bit run-down, obviously been hard worked,' or 'chequered history, by the look of the log book.'

'Well, you didn't say that when I bought it from you,' I once said and to that there was no obvious reply!

Nevertheless, a deal was finally done and I bought a four year old Rover 2000 which was – in one word – fantastic!

After a car purchase, I always did a very strange thing – took it to the local garage which had trustily looked after all my previous cars, and asked them to give the new car a 'once over.' Most people would have done that through the Automobile Association before committing themselves to the car, but I had to be different!

A Rover 2000 – how proud I was –I had arrived – where, oh, that didn't matter. The car was painted in gleaming light grey with red, real leather seats, a sporty and swift gear shift, a purring engine, perhaps a little bit greedy on petrol but I wasn't so worried about that fact - it was the car I wanted and that was the pleasure of it all. Even my friendly local garage gave it a 'reasonable' bill of health which was just as well as the cheque had been handed over by then. What was it Grandpop had said to me about not getting too enthusiastic?

With my new pride and joy, I even occasionally forsook the train and just went to work by car – no, not to show off and in any case when not being involved in company business I had to park the car in a nearby car park so nobody was any the wiser. Simply, it was all the fun and enjoyment of the drive. In those days even the traffic wasn't so bad and the door-to-door time by car was hardly any different than by train. But what a sense of enjoyment it gave me!

Even more then when there was an opportunity offered to use the car for work connections, I jumped at the chance! A trip to Birmingham was still often on the agenda and I loved that chance to travel that far in my 'motor,' not least because it meant I avoided the unseemly early morning trip to meet my colleague at Victoria! And I could stop and enjoy my breakfast earlier too!

The Southend Arterial Road was fine, but the M1 to Birmingham was better!

* * * *

Having visited Scotland several times in a business connection and bearing in mind my geographical thrill of all things 'lakes and mountains,' I felt for a holiday there. Given my enjoyment for driving and for the idea of touring generally, obviously the idea was tailor made for me and my car. In any case, during the Westcliff years, by then already five years there, I had not actually taken a holiday away as such because there was always so much to do at home and in the area. The Rover 2000 era though made a change of mind and a thirst for greater car adventures!

So that was it – the seed of an idea – and to make it extra special and by way of a big 'thank-you,' I wanted Nan and Grandpop to come with me. They wanted to but first insisted that I should go with friends. Even though there were still one or two uncommitted, but I wouldn't have it – I wanted this treat for them especially as they had both recently celebrated their 80th birthdays.

It was therefore fixed. Maps were consulted, routes planned and hotel arrangements all made. The big expedition was arranged for June and I booked 2½-weeks off work, which was an event in itself.

I made sure to resist the request from my then Boss:

'Just pop in to the Glasgow Office on passing for an hour or so.'

'Oh, sorry, but I am now not going in that direction,' I replied, even though I knew I would virtually have to pass the door. For me, it would have completely spoilt the whole holiday though and I was sure that one simple visit would soon run into a full blown day – at least!

I think that Nan and Grandpop were probably as thrilled as I was when the time came to set off, the Rover purring gently as the bonnet faced North! It was a superb and a very bright June morning as we headed through the familiar Essex countryside northwards towards Cambridge and then on further to join the A1 near Huntingdon. That territory was so familiar to me and I had to 'pinch' myself several times to fully realise that I was then embarking on a much longer trip. Before long it was time for a breakfast break which we had when near to Peterborough. The first part of the journey was safely accomplished.

With the miles of the A1 ahead of us, the faithful Rover then really came into its own and the miles quickly flew by as we went, without any hold-ups, through Rutland (still a proper county in those times), next into Nottinghamshire and then through the various Ridings of Yorkshire. The increasingly, for us, wild and open countryside and edging hills of the Yorkshire Dales were a fine sight, all a magnificent kaleidoscope of ever-changing scenery as we went south to north. Next, we were soon beyond Scotch Corner and into County Durham before finally leaving the A1 for a spot of orienteering and putting my map skills firmly to the test I had planned that our route north would then be by way of smaller roads so that we could get into the spirit of the countryside and get a feel for the North – all very dedicated and a past reflection of my years of geography at the school – 'bat-man' would have been proud of me!

With my new found sense of adventure, we headed next to Bishop Auckland by which time a stop for lunch was called for. In memory of those pleasant City lunches, a pub lunch was called for, although, I had to make do with ploughman's without the ale. Grandpop enjoyed his pint though as did Nan with her Gin and tonic!

The afternoon was a meandering change from the morning's fast main road driving and most enjoyable for all that.

Now the route was enhanced by the magnificent scenery first of Northumberland around Corbridge and Hexham and then the Northumberland National Park area itself. As we continued northwards through the Border Country my enthusiasm for hill scenery was well catered for as also was a general appreciation of the wildness of it all. The afternoon was capped as we stopped at the glorious look-out point at Carter Bar, immediately on the border point between England and Scotland. We were lucky to have had such a glorious and clear day and so were able to admire the scene for miles around and made good use of the directions map at the site.

So, we were then for the first time driving on Scottish soil and soon were in Jedburgh where we stopped for tea, in celebration of that most English of traditions! Next the drive took us on through the Scottish Borders country through St Boswells and Lauder and into the Lothian's before finally reaching

Edinburgh and our journey's end for that day. Before finally checking in to the hotel, we did drive around to see the immediate sights of the city including Princes Street and the Castle, just to get acquainted. Amazingly, none of us tired after our day and enjoyed the city sights just as if it had been the first outing of the whole day!

I suppose that the overall journey from Westcliff to Edinburgh had taken about ten hours, but we had proper stops and sightseeing so I think it was a reasonable achievement. It was a holiday after all and I always think that the journey itself is there to be enjoyed as an essential part of the holiday – and the car had performed well! I was pleased, too, that the drive had included some backways rather than just a mad main road dash. The experience of the many humped-back hills through the Borders had been an absolute pleasure and taken well in its stride by the wonder Rover!

We had a couple of nights in Edinburgh and thoroughly enjoyed the city, which was a completely new experience for me as I had never visited the city before. How different I found everything as my business connections to Scotland had only been to Glasgow so the whole trip would be one of discovery. And what a discovery I found Edinburgh to be. Nan and Grandpop hadn't been to Scotland before either and so were as excited as me in our expeditions. So, too, with our subsequent tours through the Highlands over the following two weeks – a good holiday, but still happy at the time to return home.

Soon we were back once again in the familiar countryside of North Essex and without sounding too parochial, I must say that it felt good to be back on home territory and to realise that 'our' particular area of the country had countryside not only equal but in many respects superior to many of the places we had seen.

'It's a lovely feeling to be back in home territory,' said Nan. 'It's been an absolutely marvellous holiday for us both, nopefully for all of us and I wouldn't have missed it for the world,' she continued.

'That goes for me, too,' said Grandpop. Few words, but said with such honest conviction and sincerity.

The golden rays of the summer evening certainly added to the attraction and finally we passed the sign announcing our entry to the 'Borough of Southend-on-Sea' – we were home – and London was only 40 miles away too!

It was wonderful that Nan and Grandpop enthused and enjoyed their holiday as much as I did. It was a positive and happy experience for them and so much a true and proper, happy celebration of their 80th birthdays. This too gave me so much pleasure at their being and a feeling of happy contentment with life at that very time. It was significant and very much a highlight point of life, always to be remembered and always to be cherished.

Chapter 13

All At Sixes And Sevens

It didn't take too long to get back once again into the home routine after the holiday, to go back to the regular daily commuting routine and to once again get into the corporate swing. I do admit, though, to frequently sitting in the train and dreaming of the beautiful mountain and loch scenery of the holiday, comparing it most favourably with the factory scenes and urban sprawl approaching London through suburban Essex. It did bring a degree of soul searching and thoughts about the overall direction of life. The sort of 'what is it all about?' type of question, although nothing could take away from me my more positive feelings once I was once again immersed in the feel of London itself.

I thought that it would have been rather nice to have been able to spend the first moments back in the office after the holiday in having some pleasant discussions with colleagues about the trip. That would have happened in my early days in the City, almost a tradition to all sit around over coffee and 'compare notes.' Not any more!

'Glad you're back – this happened the day after you went away and we had no idea how to contact you' ('Good,' I thought!). 'Better take a look at the problem now and bash off the reply as soon as possible.'

'Welcome back,' I continued to dream 'Did you have a good holiday?' – as if!

'By the way,' another of my colleagues continued 'There's quite a problem on this,' showing me a wad of unintelligible documents 'You had better get up to Liverpool in the next few days – what about to-morrow? – it needs sorting out!'

'Well,' I thought, 'if it's that urgent then why for heaven's sake didn't some other soul 'get up to Liverpool' pretty quickly some days ago whilst I was still away.' As if I was the only one in the company, or, more likely, the only mug who could be put upon to run around. That gave me the idea that, if I was so vital to the company's success, then I must remember my importance when the next pay review time came – then my 'value and importance' would be on a completely different level!

I was soon overwhelmingly disillusioned and I suppose that, by mid-morning, I had almost forgotten that I had been on a holiday and that if things continued at that pace then I would be ready for another holiday by the end of that week! Those days away had made me see with even more clarity the craziness of the gathering corporate world, the false sense of rushing around in ever decreasing circles but at the same time achieving absolutely nothing other than personal stress.

'Why don't you all 'look at yourselves in the mirror,'' I thought as I got even more annoyed and frustrated at the sheer futility of it all.

'Welcome back, indeed!'

* * * *

There were also some quite dramatic changes, to put it altogether rather too mildly, then about to happen at home, too. After almost 20 years of his being a widower, of living his single life without any commitments, it was so that finally father had come into a stable and settled friendly relationship with a lady – Margaret – whom he had met at work at the Tower of London. That very fact in itself had the most very romantic connotations, the thoughts of which rather made my mind run wild!

Father and Margaret seemed to get on well together and Nan suggested that father invited her home several times to Westcliff both for weekends and longer breaks.

I can see now the strangeness of the situation, it being father coming home with the 'girl' when it should have been me in that situation! Perhaps that was why Nan and Grandpop so initiated the meetings when they had always said and always indicated that they longed for me 'to find a girl.' This must have been at least a substitute.

Margaret's visits to Westcliff were really rather happy events. Often we would all have trips and outings together, the usual 'rural rides' and visits to the theatre and concerts in Southend. Naturally, we would sometimes all meet up in London and Margaret became indoctrinated with our family's way of life. That, in itself, was a difficult enough experience for her and I couldn't help but notice that father did little to make life easy for her, being just as remote and non-committal as ever. I felt it was left to me, Nan and Grandpop to compensate with endless conversation to which, fortunately, Margaret reciprocated. Yet the relationship seemed to flourish, making me think that, if father could do it, then there must be some hope for me too!

Margaret was a few years younger than father, and was herself divorced, although that was immaterial. She had two grown-up sons who were living away from home. Would that mean, I wondered, that in one fair swoop, our family would be considerably expanded, so much so that I would then have 'step-brothers,' if there is such a term. 'No,' I thought, that would never be the case in reality; father was such that there could never possibly be any inter-twining of two separate 'Family Houses,' so to speak! I was confidently assured of my maintaining my 'only-child' status – any character reformation was duly saved!

At the time they met, Margaret's home was in North London and she and Nan and Grandpop immediately had a rapport brought about by their joint backgrounds, a co-incidence in itself. Their reminiscences about all their joint old sights and times were a joy to hear:

'Do you remember … ?'

'Oh, yes, that was how things were'

'We used to have to go all the way to Manor House just to get the bus!'

'Such a shame that the area of Tottenham has now changed so much – I remember those houses where you were brought up, nice houses too. Not many of them left now, though, all gone and replaced by endless tower-blocks.' Sounded just like Bow!

There was never a loss of conversation when we were all together even though, interestingly, father seemed happiest just to let Margaret do the talking! Still, that was father all the time, not to get too deeply into any part of the conversation, aloof and never, ever wanting to get involved lest he would need to show or display some emotion. Rather unkindly, I really wondered what exactly attracted Margaret to him, what surely was the hidden personality trait within my father that had remained so invisible to me in all those years. Perhaps it was me, I continued to think, that brought out the very worst in father and yet, and yet in these new situations he really did not seem any different. In fact, he often appeared to be as sharp in his discussions with Margaret except it was so noticeable that she didn't seem to bother, simply just to ignore him during his more difficult moments. In fact, just like I had been doing already for some years – we both had the right answer in the way to deal with the persistent problem then!

Without doubt though, Margaret was good for father – she had a happy sense of humour and rather scatty way of life which was totally the opposite to him but nevertheless did seem to gel all the same. Fortunately, in time she did even have a positive effect on my father and very gradually he even began to change, to become almost more human. He would talk, he would very occasionally laugh, or rather it was more a nervous giggle, but a reaction nevertheless. In all quite an outstanding change slowly came over him, so much so that it was even difficult for us to recognise father when seeing them together.

Then, he was so different, but it was good. Fortunately for me, it enabled me to very slowly replace some of my earlier negative perceptions of my father with something altogether much more pleasant. That didn't take away the fact that he was never there for me when I most needed him through the usual trials and tribulations of all my younger years and especially after the early death of my mother. But I couldn't really complain because I could never have wanted for, or ever had, more better 'parents' than my Nan and Grandpop and for that I was eternally grateful. Still, seeing the 'new' father character did make me realise just what I had lost throughout those early years.

The approaching domestic changes for father occurred at about the same time as, for him, some significant changes in his working surroundings too. I do remember that he had enjoyed his time at the Tower of London and after all he had met Margaret there, not to mention Elaine, the lady friend from Canada before that! It must have been a magnificent place in which to work. But for him, a posting for the last few years of his working life was an even more impressive job location when in 1971 he was transferred, still within the Civil Service, to an administration role in the Department's office at Buckingham Palace.

That was a true and deserved accolade to my father, as a 'proper' person through his life, to be working there and to conclude his career in such a role. The job and position was one he cherished and in fact the whole family cherished equally and very deeply.

Father's job, father's new found relationship, made his life then so positive and he gained in confidence, which may seem a strange comment about somebody then in their late 50s! With all the new happenings, none of us at home was therefore in the least bit surprised when one day in early 1972 he finally announced his intention to get married. In fact, rather charmingly and so typical of father again being 'proper,' he actually asked Nan, Grandpop and me if we would accept and agree! Most naturally the answer was a resounding 'Yes!'

Of course, in reality we were all happy at the prospect, especially for father, as difficult character that he was, there was probably no escaping the real truth that he had been a very unhappy person through most of the years that I had known him. I tried to be most magnanimous in my thoughts about him and tried to forget how uncaring and almost unkind he had been to my mother and also such a hard person towards me.

So it was with a very great sense of celebration and the cracking open of the champagne all round when Margaret came the very next weekend to Westcliff. I must say she seemed totally calm at the marriage prospect and even though father was now positively different, I couldn't help but wonder how the relationship would work out.

'You're going to have a step-mother, now' Nan reminded me. Whilst that may have been the reality, I quickly decided that I was too old to ever view the pending relationship in such a way. There was only one mother figure to me in substitute for my own mother and that was Nan.

'Margaret will be 'Margaret' to me,' I replied 'and I am going to be sure that from the very start there will never be any step-mother question.'

Uncharacteristically for me, when remembering my usual level of communication with my father, I said to him right away how I thought about not regarding Margaret in a step-mother role and that, to me, she should be 'Margaret.' Most amazingly, father nodded complete agreement and didn't challenge my ideal in anyway. Goodness that was the first time any decision of mine had been accepted by father without an argument or be followed by a period of his most awful sulking and complete close-down of communication channels. A change indeed!

The proposed relationship arrangement was equally endorsed by Margaret herself and so everybody was indeed happy and I especially was most relieved that it should start in that way. The portents for the future in that respect seemed rather good and we could all settle in preparation for the wedding.

'It's your turn next,' both Nan and Grandpop enthused, I knew that was what they most wanted and for me to be settled and happy. It also made me rather sad to think that probably one reason why Nan and Grandpop kept raising the subject was that because they both wanted to see me settled before they were much older. They and I too, were conscious of their own mortality.

With that, I blushed and stumbled a muttered 'Oh, we'll see,' or something equally non-committal!. This whole situation was not one that I could readily face. I didn't want to think about it and I therefore erased such thoughts from my mind, my natural approach to any issue or problem without a discernable solution. 'Think about it' – me – no, never!

The occasion of father's 'engagement' was perhaps the only time for a general family celebration which we all enjoyed together and which father instigated. A Spring wedding was fixed and the immediate outcome for our family unit was the final major change and break-up as father would be leaving 'home' to live with Margaret back again in North London. I wondered how he would feel about that after spending some six years living by the sea.

'Oh, I don't know about such things' was his rather evasive reply.

'I thought that perhaps you might both wish to live in the town here,' I continued 'especially as Margaret seems so much to like to be away out of London.'

'We haven't really discussed that,' father said, 'and in any case it is much easier for me to go and live in her place when it's available.' Of course, that was it too, father had notoriously all his life somehow never had any money and probably could not have afforded to set up home of his own. Going to Margaret's place was the only possible answer.

So this was indeed a time of major change but it was not one that would immediately affect me given that father was not so very often actually at home at evenings nor weekends. But there would be a space in the regularity of life which would take some getting used to - and it would seem strange to actually have to go 'and visit father.' For Nan and Grandpop, it was very much an end of a long era; they had all lived with father in their house for over 30 years.

Even though father had few possessions, certainly no furniture of his own, the preparations for his final removal were hardly different for somebody going away on a holiday. Just clothes and a selection of books were about all that he had to think about. There was nothing more to it than a couple of runs in the car up to North London. That, I felt, to be rather sad and not much to show for almost 60 years of a life. Father, though, would have none of that sort of discussion.

'Don't be stupid' was the less than friendly reply that I got when I realised the issue with him. That was more like it – father reverting to type! But, of course, it was most likely father not wanting to show emotions nor to talk about any private or personal matters. Margaret would need to work on him and influence him still much further before there would be any more significant change in that respect.

Even with most of his possessions moved into Margaret's, father continued to live on at Westcliff during the period up until the wedding time and life went on in very much the same trusted way. However, before our attention could be centred entirely on the approaching nuptials, there was something important and very necessary that had to happen. Margaret had the obvious difficulty to endure of being introduced to father's sisters, my aunts, and I do know that is was not a pleasant experience!

Brenda, always so protective of her brother and 'the family' (on 'her' side!) especially took the role of a suspicious parent and subjected father's future wife to the 'third degree' treatment. In fact, father was himself so afraid of the potential encounter; he invited both Margaret and Brenda, neither knowing about the other, to meet him for afternoon tea in Selfridges's café in Oxford Street. Margaret arrived first, to be met by father showing her to a table for two! When Brenda arrived, father coughed, drew up another chair and then said to Margaret:

'This is my sister, Brenda.'

'Nice to meet you' Margaret replied, never having an iota of an idea that she would have a future sister-in-law. Over tea and scones, father somehow completed the introductions.

'Well, my dear,' Brenda said, always using the term 'my dear' as a form of superiority, 'This is all a very big surprise and I don't know what to say,' and neither did anybody else, so there was silence all around!

It is easy to imagine that there was a hot telephone line from Brenda around the remaining family members so it was easier when father took Margaret to Wanstead to meet Ethel and Bill.

'Welcome to the family,' Ethel said to Margaret.

'Very nice to have you at our home and to know that you are a becoming sister-in-law,' Bill continued in a pleasing theme. I'm sure that visit saved the day for Margaret who had suffered seriously from the unexpected meeting with Brenda.

With that introduction difficulty out of the way, the final plans and thoughts to the wedding day itself finally got under way. Only Nan, Grandpop and I, from our side, attended the wedding which father had grandly arranged at Caxton Hall in Westminster. Margaret's two sons and their wives came, it being the first time we had all met up together. Trust father to keep everybody apart! The ceremony was followed by a reception at a local restaurant, all very properly arranged as would be expected of father in one of his better guises. It was a happy day, and after the reception they headed off for a short honeymoon in Bournemouth.

Nan, Grandpop and I returned to Westcliff and to a strangely different house. It wasn't as if you could really say that you missed my father, there had been too many times in my life, especially in the early years, when I was mostly even unaware of his presence. No, it was more, to put it bluntly, as if a well-known piece of furniture was actually missing from the house, something that you felt should be there but in fact no longer wasn't!

As often in life, changes frequently happen together and in many ways and an equally major and quite fundamental change was about to happen to me.

* * * *

What was soon about to happen to me was nothing short of severe and utter madness, even more so when it was blatantly self-inflicted! The changes would also lead to a general instability of my life, something for which I was ill-prepared and changes that were so much in direct contrast to the immediate past years which had been so perfect and which I had so thoroughly enjoyed. It was also the start of a chain of events that would have significance to so many aspects of life and the effects of which would be all too evident for rather too many years to come. Instigated the madness and because of this, I had nobody to blame than myself, which only made matters worse.

To begin, I did rather allow my disturbed feelings about the general working practices and the workplace to go very much to my head. Of course I allowed my hallowed dreams of how things used to be in the mid-1960s to cloud and prejudice my judgement. But the fact was that I experienced in 1972 a strong anti-job feeling, I was fed up both with my work and with what wrongly I perceived as an immediate lack of career enhancement, especially given the diverse nature and world-wide presence of my then company. Had I been sensible enough to work on my negative thoughts and overcome the difficulties, thus deciding to stay, I am sure that working circumstances would have been enhanced and my job experience would have been valuable as the company grew.

But that certainly was not how I saw it then and I began to look around to seek alternative employment. So began a ritual with the usual checking of the job pages every Thursday and Sunday in the broadsheets. Most weeks I found something which was both suitable for me and for which I believed I had the required business qualifications. This all added fuel to the fire that I was creating.

'Of course I am doing the right thing,' I simply told myself, because on paper it would seem I could apply with confidence for each and every job opportunity. Then I made myself believe that the most dis-quietening aspect of the whole exercise was that, at least once again on paper, the pay prospects appeared to be generally much better than my own current position offered. This reason alone, foolishly, set my resolve and was the ultimate driving force to make me carry on with the crazy and thoroughly misplaced exercise, all to my future detriment.

Suitably excited by the prospects, I applied for a position as marketing manager in a road haulage company. Within a couple of weeks I got an acceptance of the application and duly attended the first interview. No problem there, the office seemed rather respectable, much quieter than I had been used to and without the degree of madness that so annoyed me. I compared the interview with that I had some nine years before for the first job and felt comfortable with the experience by comparison.

It obviously went well as I was asked back for a second interview, which was followed very quickly within a few days by an offer of appointment. However, this was when I should have allowed the 'alarm bells' to ring, the actual location for my new job was in doubt in view of some company changes soon to take place. Since I had to give a month's notice at my old company, I foolishly said:

'Oh, that doesn't matter, I'll tender my resignation now and will be ready for you by the time you have decided the location.'

Crazy?

Absolutely. All I must have thought about was the 'carrot' of the increased money; everything else went to the wind! The new company must have thought that their lucky day had come with somebody so obviously naive and gullible, like me sitting in front of them! So it was all settled, I accepted the job, signed accordingly and without absolutely any sure idea of where the location would be – but expected to find out before the first day to start then only a month away!

It was little wonder that the staff manager in my old company looked somewhat bemused when I went to hand in my resignation.

'You've accepted a job but you don't know where it will actually be?' he said with an understandable degree of incredulity.

'Oh, yes, I know that, but it doesn't bother me,' I said truthfully as I had no reason to believe other than that the only problem was where there would be office space in London.

'Well, it's your decision and I can only hope that you know what you are doing,' the bemused staff manager continued. 'I'll set the papers in motion and you will now be required to work your full four weeks period of Notice as from today.'

'Thank you,' I said, with the usual degree of understatement that I was prone to in such circumstances. I duly left the room as fast as possible as even by then I was beginning to get a sense of nerves about the situation, especially as so many of my colleagues at work had voiced a similar cautionary exclamation.

I had naturally told Nan and Grandpop at home about the pending job and they knew of all developments except . . ., except I had told them and father that I was waiting to hear whereabouts in London the job would be based. That 'whereabouts in London' was no more than a figment of my imagination; the new company had never said that precisely. But that was what I wanted the result to be and somehow I had brainwashed myself, foolishly, into believing such an outcome.

The time absolutely flew by during those four weeks, more especially so when all the both outstanding and pending jobs needing to be done in the far-flung places such as Birmingham and Liverpool, all seemed to land very much on my plate. For those four weeks my feet hardly seemed to touch the ground and such was the pace of activity that I didn't once have time to think about my coming new job nor, more importantly, of its phantom actual location.

Within what seemed a mere flickering of the eye, the time arrived for me to finally leave the company where I had been for nine years, in fact since beginning work in 1963. I suppose that in many ways it was reminiscent of that final day at school, as much an end of an era, rather in more ways than one as I was soon to find out when I started at the new company the following week. For that moment though, I have some happy memories of a social round of very pleasant lunches with colleagues during the final week all enjoyed without any sense of my actually doing the wrong thing. Overall, it was so nice then to experience the City life as it used to be, as I best remembered it from those most early years, the carefree pub lunches and the friendly, almost laid-back atmosphere. Still, then, I had no reason to feel concerned, I was merely moving to another area of London and to carry on with the same style of work and life – with more money. That thought alone cheered me. If only I had known otherwise, my spirits upon leaving would have been considerably different.

So with the customary clearing of the desk, the final handing over of the various jobs and tasks outstanding to the person taking over from me, that was it – time to leave. Final 'good-byes,' 'Keep in touch,' 'Do let us know how you get on, where you are and what you are doing,' 'come back and see us anytime, we're all still be here!' – All very friendly, in fact and I did have some sad regrets at that moment about leaving. Still, the deed was done so it was then off to the usual journey home and for a relaxing weekend.

* * * *

The next Monday I returned to London in the usual way, but this time to the headquarters of my new company, which was in Marylebone, which meant taking an additional Underground train and probably added about 20 minutes each way to my travelling day. Of course, it was not to be for me the City life any more, rather the West End. Of course, I knew the area well although had never worked there and that in itself would take some getting used to, but, nevertheless, it was still London after all. Still the money was good, I told myself!

On arrival at my new office, I immediately noticed a rather restrained atmosphere in the building, no smiling Commissionaires, rather huddled groups of various people looking somewhat serious, all speaking in hushed tones. People barely looked at me or noticed me even though I wore an obvious 'new boy,' or rather 'little boy lost' expression. I felt immediately strange, insecure with a realisation that dramatic changes in working life were really most unsuitable to my character and I felt a most uneasy feeling.

Although I had attended the office a couple of times for interviews, I had not really studied the building as such. That morning, alone in the entrance hall, I suddenly realised that the building was very grey, altogether too functional, an almost cold and austere feel. There were none of the beautiful features of the original City office or even anything as near as warm colour schemes of the other offices where I had worked. As for the finer points of decor such as beautiful paintings and majestic chandeliers, of those there were most definitely none. I felt strangely unhappy but realised that this was not the impression to give when supposedly starting a brand new and 'dynamic' job. There was nothing for it other than to make the best of the day and at least to announce that I had arrived.

The reception desk was unmanned but there was a sign by the side of an internal telephone 'inviting' callers to dial an extension.

'Hello, I want the personnel department.'

'Hold on, I'll transfer you,' was the less than welcoming reply. A silence of only a few seconds followed but it seemed very much longer.

'Yes, can I help you?' to which I introduced myself and was then asked to 'come on up to the third floor.'

I felt immediately better on seeing the personnel manager as it was a face I knew from the interview time, somebody I could connect with but, nevertheless, strange that he seemed totally unprepared for my arrival. I couldn't also help but notice that he seemed very odd, almost unfriendly and completely pre-occupied with other thoughts and issues other than me or my imminent beginning appointment with the company.

No wonder. Following the first awkward silence then one or two inane and completely off-the- point small talk comments, the personnel manager then informed me, after a bout of some nervous coughing:

'I am afraid that I have some rather dramatic news for you – the company has decided upon its location plans and the division to which you have accepted to be appointed is being moved in about two months to – how can I put it – um – is going to be moved to Scotland!'

'To Scotland – really – whereabouts?'

He mentioned the name of a town that I had only vaguely ever heard of but soon realised that it was a location in the Central Belt of Scotland between Glasgow and Edinburgh. The only then thought to pass through my mind was that wherever the place was, it certainly wasn't London. That was a devastating enough thought in itself! At that very moment I was incapable of taking the information in or of accepting the situation then opening up in front of me.

As if to add insult to injury, the personnel manager continued 'Oh, it's not all the company moving up north; most of us will be removing to other locations here and there.'

'Here and there,' I replied 'Well, where, exactly?'

'Oh, it hasn't been finally decided yet, but some of us will go to other buildings in the suburbs, I think. But anyway, that's us, not you, your division is moving, as I say it's Scotland bound for you'

'Do I have a choice and can I maybe go to the London suburbs as well?,' I hopefully asked.

'Oh, no, I'm afraid not,' was the most definite reply. 'That is not an option open to you,' the Personnel Manager continued as I lapsed even more into remorse.

I felt absolutely unwell and with a horrible sinking feeling, in fact in a complete daze. I merely mumbled some words to the personnel manager, was told in return that of course they would help with all relocation costs but in the meantime 'go off now to your new department and begin all your new tasks with vigour. Yours is a key role to the company's future and we expect great things from you,' he concluded without probably realising the enormity of the situation for me. Or perhaps not really caring, I was merely just a number in the corporate workplace, a chess piece that could be moved at will. And 'being moved' was certainly what was about to happen! My name would simply be a flag on the personnel chart as 'being moved' and would then sometimes appear in the box marked 'Scotland office.' That was no matter of corporate concern.

The rest of the day was nothing other than a blur. I took some papers from a file and began to at least appear to read some outline work details. At least in that building I did have my own office which would have felt really very grand if only the situation had not been so temporary. It did mean, though, that I could keep to myself, be in my thoughts, and try to think how on earth this problem could be resolved. I was too much in my own thoughts to naturally realise that so many other people were involved too and their lives so similarly affected.

It suddenly occurred to me why there was such a subdued atmosphere when I arrived that morning in the entrance hall and I suppose that I took some comfort from the knowledge that I was not alone in the ordeal. But there was no comfort from the fact that the situation was purely of my own making and never needed to have happened at all. At least all the others in the company probably had the chance to negotiate a good leaving package if they didn't want to move – I had only been there an hour so that option didn't even exist And as I had indicated my willingness to move at the time of the interview, the fact that I thought that would just be within London was no real excuse.

What had I done?

Matters were made even worse because I had been hired to start work on a new project and I didn't really have any work colleagues at the time as such. On top of that, with all the dramatic goings-on in the company, most others seemed to view me with a certain amount of suspicion, probably thinking, in fact, that I had been brought into the company as an architect of the move!

That was certainly not the case and that point I made very clear to anybody that I felt confident enough to approach. About the only thing to unite us at that moment was the thought of the impending move, which apparently had been announced to the other staff on the previous Friday, that sort of news that is guaranteed to ensure a 'happy' weekend!

Any thoughts that I might have had of re-instating the idea of the happy City lunch in this new job were quickly dispelled for that day. It was good enough at lunch-time to get out of the office, the wretched building in my mind, and to walk some West End streets, rather oblivious though to the bustle of life going on there. So preoccupied I was that I didn't even realise that I was in the vicinity of so many well-known sites as Oxford Street and Regent Street! Absolutely everything that day seemed so alien and I just didn't feel to be any part of my life.

Finally, at the end of that awful day, I began the journey home; and I simply could not get my thoughts straight at all. What was I to do? How could I possibly move away to Scotland? Why should I? I was a Londoner, loved the London life, liked to live in Westcliff. And what about Nan and Grandpop? What would they say, how was it all going to affect them? Endless questions, endless uncertainties, nothing making any sense. Station after station rushed past my increasingly blurred vision until the train finally reached Westcliff – I was home and the time to face up to the realities was very much at hand. My legs and feet were like lead as I walked those well trodden paces from the station to home, absolutely dreading the thought of entering the front door, something before that occasion that I could never imagine to have such a negative feeling.

'Hello, love – how was the first day – come and settle down, I've cooked a special meal, you can tell us all about the day as we enjoy the dinner,' Nan said, obviously thrilled and readily excited to hear about the new job.

'Well, boy, it doesn't take so much longer to get home even with the tube,' said Grandpop. 'It looks that you have made a good decision – well done, boy.'

If only they knew.

I tried to eat and tried to appear to enjoy the meal, even to attempt to become involved in the friendly talk and banter but I was no actor. I pushed the food around the plate, I didn't really taste anything much. The situation was unbearable and I just couldn't put off the inevitable any longer.

'Look, this is very difficult, but there's been an awful disaster about the new job,' I began. Nan and Grandpop looked at each other, looked at me, seemed very concerned, as well they might, I thought to myself.

'What is it, love?' Nan said 'I thought there must be something when you hadn't telephoned us during the day and now I see you are hardly eating your dinner – now I know there must be something radically wrong!'

'Tell us, boy, nothing can be that bad,' Grandpop added.

'Well, it is – in fact it couldn't be worse,' I said.

'The first thing I learnt when I got to the office today,' I continued 'was that my division in the company, not all the company, just my 'bit,' is moving to Scotland – my job is going to be in Scotland – and in two months.' It all came out in a sort of garbled nervousness.

'Scotland – did you say Scotland?' I think Nan and Grandpop virtually said the same thing together.

'Yes, that's it – Scotland. There's no question about it, no choice. I don't know what to do, what have I done?' I blurted on without much sense.

'Now, listen here, boy' Grandpop spoke. 'There's no point getting in to a state about it, you must see how things go over the next few days, talk to the others at work, give time to consider before making a mess of things.'

'Pop's right,' Nan said 'don't be hasty. There's too much happened for one day, you must let the dust settle and then see the way forward more clearly.'

'Another thing, boy,' Grandpop continued, 'whatever happens, Nan and I are behind you, you don't have to worry about us, we're here and we will sort it out together.'

The chance of discussing the situation at home obviously made me feel somewhat better and I realised that my immediate worry of breaking the news to Nan and Grandpop was dealt with, although I had no idea of what the solution to the problem could possible be. Phoning father produced a non-committal kind of response, almost a 'I told you so attitude' and who was I to blame him if that was what he felt. He was right, after all.

I felt happier knowing that we could now face up to and discuss the issues together but overall it was a most difficult situation. Without doubt, I should have immediately resigned, gone back 'cap in hand' to the old company or looked around again for something else. There should have been absolutely no question of my considering the option given my feelings about London and my life in the area, my own home life and the circumstances that I felt about being at home to look after Nan and Grandpop. I had played my part extremely badly from the start, remembering my:

'I'll be ready by the time you have decided the location,' my foolhardy statement at the time of the job offer!

By saying this, I had indicated my willingness to go wherever and could hardly then turn round and say 'No!'

There was nothing for it other than to prepare for the inevitable. Letting the issue rest for a couple of days as Nan and Grandpop suggested, at least gave time to think through the various options but the major question for me concerned Nan and Grandpop. If I left Westcliff they could not afford to pay for the rent of our house, especially so now that father had also 'flown the nest.' It would be so very cruel if at that moment, because of me, that they once again had to leave their seaside home as they had once had to do almost 40 years before. I could not forgive myself. What could possibly be that elusive solution that I so desperately sought?

I could think of only one answer to my immediate dilemma – ask Nan and Grandpop if they would come with me?

'What do you think?' I finally asked them one evening, rather in the style that somebody would ask if you fancied going out for tea! It was little to wonder that there was a stunned silence until Nan said:

'Well, I really don't know about that at all – we would have to think about that, we can't say right away but certainly Pop and I wouldn't be able to afford to carry on living here anymore, we both realise that!'

Of course, that was the real problem and it was the very situation that I dreaded and which I just did not want to face. There was little more that could be discussed that very moment but the seed of a thought had been planted? We all had the happy memories of our holiday in Scotland and as such perhaps the idea was not too ludicrous after all. What I didn't think, and if they thought, they didn't say, was that there is a world of a difference between having a short holiday somewhere and actually living in that place which is some 400 miles away from your natural territory. My then thoughts, decision, and our decisions, were being made for all the wrong reasons almost in a sense of panic and without considering the issues through.

One thing was most certain – time wasn't on our side. Each hour, each day brought the inevitable that much closer. The issue couldn't be put off, we all knew that, and yet such was the magnitude of the problem that we all somehow 'played for time.' Perhaps I was hoping for a miracle, perhaps it was all a bad dream

to which some magic solution would miraculously appear. Or, rather, I might wake up!

A couple of days later, still in that dreadful week, when I got home from work, both Nan and Grandpop were waiting to discuss the issue, even before dinner which even in itself underlined the seriousness of the situation!

'Listen, love,' Nan said, 'Grandpop and I have been thinking and here's what we propose. We say that we are prepared to come to Scotland with you, leave here, provided we get a proper home. Then let's all give it a few months and if it doesn't work, then we must together decide what to do next – you stay on, or look for another job back here and we can home again.'

I was stunned, not really understanding that an outline resolve to the problem was in the offering.

'Do you really think you are prepared for this upheaval?' I replied.

'Well, it would be wrong to say that it is our personal choice,' Nan continued, 'but we both realise, Pop and I, that you are in such a state over the issue. We can't let you go off alone at this moment, perhaps in a few months, we can all reconsider, but for now, we're with you, we're in it together and we are prepared to give it a try.'

'There you are, boy,' Grandpop said, 'problem immediately solved!' I certainly hoped that he was right, but even then I couldn't help but think that it was simply a case of problems mounting upon problems. But at least it meant that our own family was not going to be split and I was most relieved about that. Once again I was in a position of being so ever grateful to Nan and Grandpop, they always put my welfare and well-being first, even ahead of their own thoughts and considerations. There was really no more to say and I certainly then owed it to them to really make the best of the bad job that I had created.

I phoned father that evening and told him of our decision and wasn't in the least bit surprised that he voiced no opinion either one way or the other.

So it was then that Spring 1972 saw us returning to Scotland, not this time for a holiday, but with the mission to find somewhere to live. Once again the weather was fine and so it seemed that the 'sun shone' on my efforts, literally! The business location was in Central Scotland, that rather bland and immensely dull semi-industrial 'bit' between Edinburgh in the east and Glasgow in the west It would be impossible to imagine an area that could be negatively more different from our Highland holiday. As for comparison to Westcliff –I wouldn't even bother to consider that issue!

We all felt immensely down – me especially when realising the whole exercise was my responsibility. Back at the hotel that evening I poured over the maps trying to find an answer, there was no way that it would be of any use for us to live in Central Scotland. The dullness though had its effect and concentrated the mind to the problem and in itself directed the subconscious overnight to a solution.

That was it – of course! – the fact was that for London I travelled 40 miles each day to work so what about a radius of 40 miles from that industrial heart of Central Scotland!

That was the answer!

Within 40 miles from the office location was the southern part of Perthshire and Perthshire meant hills!

Of we went the next day to a point no more than 40 miles from where the office would be and began the search all over again.

The one positive thing to emerge from the exercise, and believe me I was desperate then for something positive to happen, was the fact that house prices in Scotland in 1972, especially in those rural areas where we were looking, were only a fraction of those in the Southend area. I could afford to get a mortgage and buy a house rather than rent as we did then in Westcliff. At least, too, that meant that if we then decided after a few months that the whole experiment was a waste of time, the we could move back 'home' and, hopefully, benefit from a house sale profit as well. Surely, I thought, surely this didn't mean that there really was light at the end of the tunnel at last!

In fact it only took us two days to find a suitable home, a new bungalow in the final stages of being built. I had to admit that it was all rather idyllic and my spirits lifted considerably.

'I can't believe how lucky we are,' Nan said, 'after all this time, Pop and I are going to live in our own bungalow again – it's too good to be true!'

'Oh, Mate,' Grandpop replied, 'this is wonderful. You see,' he continued, turning to me, 'every cloud has a silver lining and this is certainly our silver lining!'

Certainly, I accepted that at that very moment it did really seem that the outlook was so very much better. That was it then and, as had happened six years before in Westcliff, I signed on the dotted line that same afternoon and the deal was done, a solution to one problem. But rather than thinking of it as a place to live, I thought of it as a place for a holiday, perhaps a rather long holiday maybe, never as a place to be a home.

With everything settled, we returned back to Westcliff. What had seemed horribly desperate at the beginning was then beginning to look much better and I suppose that we were really excited about the prospect of our new house. Nan and Grandpop, especially, were absolutely enthralled by the idea of a bungalow home again and, amazingly, they really didn't seem in the least bit concerned about moving away to an area so much distant from the real 'home.' 'Our four walls and our own things, the furniture, our belongings, they are the things that most matter to us,' Nan said to which Grandpop nodded his agreement. 'So wherever we are, as long as that's secure, then we're happy.' At least I was pleased about that and considering they were both then in their 80s, it was a remarkable positive attitude, an attitude which I could do nothing but to absolutely admire. But then, of course, as they became older, Nan and Grandpop naturally spent increasing amounts of time at home and their feelings perhaps were understandable.

For me, however, my immediate enthusiasm was only of a temporary nature, probably borne out of relief of a solution to an immediate problem. It did not disguise the fact that the whole exercise upon which I was embarking was thoughtless and one of complete madness.

* * * *

Late spring 1972 was therefore a time of house packing once again and one with such a major move in prospect. Fortunately, we only then had to give a month's notice to the landlord of our house to terminate the rental agreement and that was completed without problem.

Remarkably, given the happiness of the last six years in Westcliff we didn't initially overall feel too sad about the packing up. I suppose that the key to the issue was the fact that, as in the move from Bow to Westcliff, and as Nan and Grandpop had both themselves said, our possessions and furnishings were going with us and that was always the most important thing rather than the framework of the house. What I then did not appreciate was that a complete change of location, indeed even country, culture-wise, was a thoroughly different prospect altogether.

Of course it was a major undertaking and, dare I say, totally foolhardy. For me, it was so often bad enough my being away from the home area of the South East of England for a few days or a two-week holiday, the first thing I would then want to do is to get back to London to immediately become re-acquainted with all the things I held dear, to once again see the sights and to walk the treasured streets. I was like a little boy lost without that real element to be always in my life.

What was happening then?

I was moving away completely – even if not 'for good,' then for probably some considerable time. I busily reassured my self that I would be frequently back in London because the company had said that 'probably' (and isn't that a word with very heavy meanings!) with the relocation of the office in which I worked to central Scotland there would be a 'regular' need for meetings back at the then headquarters in Marylebone or in whatever London location was finally decided upon. That thought somehow compensated me, although I must have lived in some sort of strange illusion if I was to believe anything that the new company ever said or promised.

Then there were still all the relatives in suburban Essex and father and Margaret then living in North London, so on a family level there would be the need to maintain regular trips. I was off to 'exile' but that, I kept telling myself, was only to be temporary and London was and would always be my home. Of course, nothing could change one's original hometown but I had not realised the magnitude of what it would be like to live so far away from one's natural base. I fully admit, too, that I had never researched or properly thought about how it would be to actually live in Scotland. I should have realised that I was a Londoner and nothing could be more different.

In complete and utter comparison to the move from Bow to Westcliff those six years earlier, which had been a thrill and a culmination of a dream, now the feeling was becoming completely different. Each day added to my sense of anxiety and foreboding; my inner feelings told me that what I had done was completely and utterly crazy and each step forward that I was then taking was simply another step away from the tried, tested and therefore cherished lifestyle, and from a place where I felt totally comfortable. This was a move towards the abyss.

Purposefully, I made sure during the final weeks, then days, to retrace steps to all my known haunts and places that had meant, and continued to mean, so much to me. Naturally, that included the majority of the main London sights, the heritage and traditions, visits to as many theatres and concerts as possible, many times, often nightly! Each visit was filled with the same re-assuring thought – simply saying that my being away would be only temporary and that I would soon become re-acquainted with my cherished experiences again soon. But there was the hidden, sinking feeling that I was en-acting what was surely an end of an era. I was really saying a rather lengthy 'good-bye!'

I even went back to Bow – Nan and Grandpop, understandably, didn't want to do that. I spent a day trying to see as much as possible of what had been my home for 21 years. In many instances, I didn't like what I saw and for the same reasons of seeing the terrible changes for the worst that had already begun to take place before we had finally left Bow. The place had become increasingly unrecognisable to me and for the most part it wasn't really the same place anymore. Only our old house and the church were the reminders in the immediate area and so, as such, it was very much a past era of memories. Nothing more.

In my mood then, though, the reality of change didn't matter, I just wanted to see it because it was myself and the surety of the past which I was seeing at a time when I was to embark on such a major change. There was comfort to me in that and I was therefore glad to be there. I even went back to take a look at my old school, which in itself highlights the state of my feelings then when I took 'comfort' from that memory too! Perhaps it helped that by then the whole school had itself moved away so there was no chance that I would come face to face with 'chief bat-man' or indeed any of the others!

I lingered long in deep thoughts, thinking I heard again the school bell, the noise, the chatter, the visions of the school friends, the 'bat-men,' all manner of thoughts from my past, my very own heritage that I was about to forsake. It was almost as if everything from those past years was in a momentary kaleidoscope happening again, there and then. It felt all so real, so right. Of course, I told myself, it was right – this was me, this was my past and my place. It made the thoughts of what I was about to do even more unreal and even more distressing.

But then, what was the sense of such remorse. Once again, I considered that I should take the example from my Nan and Grandpop. They had the spirit, the sense to make the best of whatever episode and whatever their innermost thoughts, they were both not only prepared, but more than willing to embark on this new adventure even though they were over eighty. That was the example that I should take – get on with it, make the most of it and then, if, or rather probably, when the whole scheme failed, come back 'home' again, but with dignity and head held high.

It would be wrong to say that I walked back to the Underground with a spring in my step, but certainly I did feel considerably better!

* * * *

As the final weeks became days, the memory path became even more hectic as there was an obvious need also to visit all the aunts, uncles and to see father and Margaret as well. Amazingly, both father and Margaret had become rather supportive of the whole idea. I believe they were like that because my distress at the path I was carving was so obvious to them, and they were more perceptive and therefore more understanding as a result. Anyway, the change in father had been so favourably great since his marriage to Margaret that almost for the very first time in life I was experiencing a true father/son style relationship. That, in itself, was a big enough novelty to me.

He emphasised to me that I could always look upon their home as a London base and we could all come and go as often as wished.

'And you and Margaret will come and visit us in Scotland, won't you?' I replied, in what was for me a most unusually friendly tone to speak to my father.

'Most certainly, and we'll both look forward to that and rather soon too,' father replied. How's that as a change from the usual 'We'll see' which had been his standard reply to all my requests throughout my childhood years and beyond.

The aunts and uncles were neither here nor there about the issue, but then that was hardly surprising as we had become less deeply involved in recent times. Probably they thought me to be completely mad and not worth their thinking about, in any case! In reality though they must have been dismayed at the prospect of missing out on their regular trips to see us at the seaside but they never said. My aunts especially would never, never show their true feelings! Their 'distance' and 'aloofness,' always made it impossible to really get to know them or to be in anyway close.

From the final days to hours and that meant a rush around Westcliff and Southend and more whole hosts of 'good-byes!' We had only lived there for six years but it was a friendly place. Nan and Grandpop, especially, had got to know quite a lot of the neighbours and I certainly knew some too from my regular trimming of the hedge sessions. Such a display of friendliness soon brought upon me once again that awful overwhelming feelings of sadness to which I was then often prone. The reality and enormity of what was then happening really hit home to me and I freely admit to having had more than several 'lumps in my throat.'

The whole situation then became even harder to bear with the beautiful Spring days and evenings which really showed the area at its very best Always to see the busy fishing boats, the sailing boats restfully at anchor, the sparkling sea and, of course, it suited my memory at that time to always see the tide in!

And I was leaving the place – by my own choice – how stupid! And that was about the only comment that I could possibly think as being appropriate to my actions.

On a personal memory level too, to add more insult to injury, the Southend local paper announced that in early June, just one week after our due departure, the steamer service to London was to be re-instated after many years! Given my wonderful childhood memories of those trips, I think that alone more than anything brought home to me in a most cruel way what I was giving up and what I had brought about on to myself by my own foolishness. I should have been on that sailing and it would not be possible. Oh, to be sailing up the Thames instead of driving to work in some unknown territory of central Scotland!

Everything had gathered at an ever-increasing pace and there was nothing else then for it other than to get on with it. I cherished everything of my life during the very last week in Westcliff, enjoying and watching every moment of my regular train trips to and from London, as if to commit to memory and my mind all the sights so that I could flick, at will, those 'memory pages' whenever the need be. Those thoughts definitely put an entirely different emphasis on the daily toil of commuting!

It wasn't only the case of packing at home. Similar arrangements were going on all the time in the Office too. About a total of 20 others were also making the move to Scotland but at least half of them had already stated their intention to only go for as long as it was necessary before finding another job – back in London. They weren't even moving house either, such was what they really meant by 'temporary.'

Such had been the pace of change since I had joined my new company, plus the very circumstances of those days; I had hardly got to know anybody during my short time in the London office. Even the colleagues who were also coming at least in the short term to Scotland were little more than names to me. It was all so unreal, made even more so because I was employed on a new business division in the process of setting up. There was hardly any need for any real business contact let alone any social niceties.

I took the opportunity of going back a few times to my old office and had some good times seeing again the various trusted colleagues, saying 'good-byes' and once again having the most awful regrets. In my heart I was hoping, almost expecting, somebody to say 'come back here' – and I would have – immediately – but nothing was said. I wondered why? What had I perhaps done wrong? Well, in reality, nothing but like many companies, my old one too was experiencing some difficult trading and simply were not considering much extra recruitment. I really would need to go ahead with my 'imposed exile!'

Removal day finally came and went off smoothly. None of us spoke much, went about robot like, cleaned up, took a last look around the house that had been our home for six years, admired again all the beautiful decorating that Grandpop had done to further enhance the rooms and which made the house 'home.' That was it then, to close the front door, return the key to the agent and get in the car at Westcliff for one last time – that was, I told myself, until our return. Almost without looking back, we began to move away.

'Perhaps it's just as well that we are going, boy?' Grandpop said.

'Why?' I said, rather surprised that Grandpop should have made his statement so firmly.

'Well, the hedge looks as if it will soon need cutting,' he quipped, thankfully adding some much needed light relief to the most difficult situation!

* * * *

First, after leaving Westcliff, and travelling along the old faithful 'Arterial Road,' we drove back to London. It was totally impossible for me to leave the place just like that and without the chance for a longer look around once again. We went to stay for the night with father and Margaret in North London, immediately taking up their offer that their home could be our London base! I rather thought there and then that we could easily become the most frequent visitors, so much so as to be part of the fixtures and fittings.

That was a night of memories, especially for Nan and Grandpop, and was the first time they had sayed overnight in their old territory of North London for close on 40 years or more! All of us first went back to the pub where Nan and Grandpop had first met – 'The Jolly Boatman' in Tottenham and that was a very special start to the evening of nostalgia. After that happy start, there could have been only one place for us to spend the rest of that memorable evening – that, naturally, was in London itself.

We drove everywhere - we saw everything – of course all the major sights and no matter how many times I saw them, I never tired of it. To me it was like an injection of life, a very necessary and needful experience for me at all times. Throughout the West End we drove, stopping occasionally to take a walk here and there, around the Royal Parks, the Mall to Trafalgar Square and to Westminster. We were then by the Thames, seeing some tourist boats in the early summer evening, I wishing there was time for a short trip but rather thinking that such an experience would only add to my woes!

The Thames-side route then took us to the City and to what I considered to be the site of my real business world. As always was the case in the evenings, the streets were deserted, most places closed but ideal for all that to be able to drive up and down and to criss-cross in all directions. All the territory of my first business years came vividly to me again during the course of that evening tour, the various offices where I had spent time or visited, St Mary Axe and my first bank, Houndsditch Warehouse, Leadenhall Market, the various cafés and, of course, those much loved and favourite City pubs. My mind was full to overflowing, taking everything in, to keep an accurate and vivid picture to be stored until the next visit – which would have to be so very, very soon!

Even though they first said no, Nan and Grandpop finally said:

'Let's go back to Tottenham via Bow.'

I didn't need to be asked twice – the longer that the evening tour round could last, the better!

From the City we drove through Whitechapel and the East End until we finally reached Bow. We drove along Bow Road, down Devon's Road, talking of memories all the time, all joining in, very amazingly too , father included, with thoughts and reminiscences.

'That's where the Dairy used to be!'

'Pop, do you remember that place before the war and the night of the air-raid?' said Nan. We all joined in with more memories and re-caps.

We became increasingly deep in thoughts and I especially.

What about simply resigning there and then – what about the house I had bought – it was then still only a deposit – but that was sizable – well sell it! – Give up the whole idea – get a 'fresh piece of paper' and start again! Thoughts rushed through my head – do anything but prevent this wretched move!

No such actions were then possible – in reality it was already too late. The next day there was nothing for it other than to say our 'good-byes' to father and Margaret, to get in the car and finally go.

'Remember,' father called out, 'come back whenever you like, anytime – it's very good that you should all think of this as your London home!'

'And you both come and see us, very soon,' we all called out, in a very rare display of any emotions within our family. If anything at all had been positive about this whole wretched life upon which I was then embarking, then this rekindles family relationship was it!

Now, once again then, the Rover was heading north, this time, although surely momentarily, in a one way direction. This time its passengers very much quiet, very much unsure and reflective. A major change in my life was then occurring – that I knew and I also knew that it was probably not for the better.

How much life would change and how much life would be most difficult, I was unaware and perhaps for that moment it was just as well!

Chapter 14
A Time And A Place

The sunny, early April morning, the familiar Thames-side buildings with the Royal Festival Hall just behind me and the Savoy Hotel and the Shell-Mex building across the river. Ahead of me the Hungerford Railway Bridge and the rumble of the trains crossing the river to the now more modern, almost inspiring, glass dome of a renovated Charing Cross station. Basically, though, it was all such a very familiar scene to me, almost timeless, in fact. At that precise moment, only the huge wheel of the London Eye, just seen beyond the railway bridge gave to me the sense of another time. Otherwise, so very much the same place though in all other respects.

Here, thronging the familiar riverside walkway of the South Bank, a mass of people, a variety of both young and old, from a variety of places and times, all forming a long line stretching as far as the eye could see. A line being joined by more and more people all the time, now going into the distance behind me further back along the South Bank towards Southwark and, who knows, even beyond. Some say that soon it could reach almost London Bridge as it did the previous day.

Slowly, very slowly, the line moves forward and I shuffle along in steady pace, still aware of the Royal Festival Hall and remembering the very place and my being there as the scene of the Festival of Britain nearly 51 years before. If that same steam engine that so enthralled me then had still been there now, I wondered, would I now have been so excited? Most probably not, I honestly considered, although no doubt had there now be another kind of exhibition then there would have been something else as equally as exciting to see.

As the queue moved slowly on, I was soon passing under Hungerford Bridge as another train headed off from Charing Cross. How many times had I crossed that very bridge, coast bound, full of delightful thoughts as heading to Folkestone and filled with marvellous holiday dreams? Here was a familiarity, the sense of belonging, of memories, very much personal but also, because of the occasion, very much apart of very much the reason for the National mood as well.

Having moved beyond the railway bridge, and with the line of people moving ever so slowly, I had ample opportunity of seeing a part of the London skyline which was so very new to me, the London Eye. For all that, a magnificent sight, so huge and so almost awe-inspiring as a tribute to modern technology. Somehow, it looked right, not out of place even though so very different and so very much in contrast as compared to the distant view of Big Ben and the Houses of Parliament. That was still remarkably the same, reassuringly so. I could have been transported back in time to my childhood with that scene alone. Well, that is apart from looking to the right of Big Ben and to the rather new parliamentary offices of Portcullis House; that was a sure reminder of a new era in what was otherwise a well established scene.

Overall, though and, most remarkably, there was not so very many changes, at least not outwardly. Standing then by the mighty wheel of the Eye, looking immediately to the left, the buildings originally known to me as County Hall, the home of the old London County Council, seemed very much the same, just perhaps a little cleaner than I had remembered. The fact that the building was now a hotel, with even a Burger Bar, was only apparent on closer inspection but that, in itself, was again most re-assuring. Here was a sense of maintaining the old, the heritage, even in times of change. This, the very essence of London, all again so apparent once again before my eyes, the very good feeling of tradition that had been the comforting factor to me in so many circumstances of my London life and experiences.

How busy the river was – even in early April, full of tourist river boats and various other equally interesting assortments of bustling barges and water traffic generally. Surely there were now more piers, I noted, even one right by the side of me at the London Eye itself, as well as the well known landing stages at Westminster and Charing Cross. But – that was new, I thought, there was now then even a regular river-boat service, very much like a 'water-bus,' with announcements of departures up river to Chelsea and down river to the new areas of Canary Wharf as well as to Greenwich. That seemed such a marvellous idea, a fine means of travel as well as an alternative to the congested buses and tubes. How I would have supported that in my earlier London days, I thought, when remembering my enthusiasm for all those childhood river trips!

There was then so much for me to take in, to remember, that I was almost unaware that the queue was once again moving, so in good order I took the pace along as well, moving ever closer to Westminster Bridge. Whilst the focus of attention was to the buildings of the Houses of Parliament themselves and especially to Westminster Hall, so tantalisingly close then just opposite across the river. I, and all the others in the queue, knew that destination was still some two hours away in time. Everybody knew too that our route still stretched ahead of us, away from our destination. In fact, on first towards Lambeth Bridge before winding across the river and finally back along the North Bank, through Parliament Gardens, to Westminster.

The crowd on that day were all brought together by the sense of respect and feeling at such a sad time, the recent death of Her Majesty, Queen Elizabeth, the Queen Mother. In itself there was so much reason for collective national thought and reflection, let alone it being the time for my personal memories. So many, then, wanted the opportunity to pay respects at the Lying-in-State in Westminster Hall and the fact of the enormously long queue paid testament to that fact. The lengthy time taken was rather immaterial. It didn't matter; more important was to be there, no matter how long it took, to be part of the day and the occasion, to be in thoughts and to remember.

That sense of occasion was completely overwhelming for me too, not just from the National sense, which was important enough, but also from the chance of a personal rediscovery, a time to inwardly recall and remember.

After so very many years of being away, of course it felt good and completely right, to be in London, to once more feel and to be a part of the London scene and life, as a very natural course for me. This, after all, was my rightful place and there had been too many years for me away from that very centre of my life. Of course, I had been back on very many return visits, a combination of various occasional days and much longer stays, but to be a visitor even to one's roots is never the same feeling of actually living. Although once again I was not actually living in London I was, as in those Westcliff years, living in the South East and therefore close enough that London was once again just a short enough journey from home.

Those Scotland years had, incredibly, lasted so very much longer than I could have possibly imagined. Those years had too been the scene of so very many life changes, so many difficulties, some unhappiness as well as, conversely, some more happy life's changes and developments too.

Now, though, I was back to were I belonged – and to where I should always have been.

How too, this was so much like the London I remembered and wanted always to remember. Complete strangers chatting and talking to each other, so reminiscent of those childhood scenes for me when travelling on the bus with Nan and our bags full of the fine foods for my birthday party. Here, again, was that very same so re-assuring spirit with people willingly sharing each other's picnic nibbles.

'Here, have some of our sandwiches or crisps – and what about some chocolate, we've got plenty, more than enough for us, plenty to go round,' all said with an infectious laugh.

'Are you alright for tea?'

'Will you kindly keep my place a moment whilst I dash over there to the sandwich kiosk – oh, yes, perhaps I can collect something for you whilst I'm there?'

Keep the place – of course the space would be kept, everybody's kind and good humour would make sure of that. This was not the time or place to jostle for a place. This was a time for the best of the country, good humoured and orderly. Nothing made that fact more obvious than the so few police around, especially when thinking of the thousands of people who were in line. And the police that were there were more intent on making sure everybody was content and alright, all so proper.

On the queue moved once again, slowly but steadily, now being directly opposite the Houses of Parliament itself, with a fine, clear view of the Member's forecourt immediately overlooking the river. A perfect spot and a perfect view, just the right place to make yet another quick mobile phone call to my wife at home. Such a shame that she was unwell just at that very time and couldn't herself make the journey with me.

'Hello, love, everything all right with you – are you feeling any better now?' I asked as soon as her cheerful voice answered the phone.

'Thanks, yes, my head's quite a bit less painful now and I'll be perfectly alright in a short while. It's just a pity that it had to happen like that today, I would have so much liked to have been there with you.'

'I miss you too,' I replied.

'Me. too, likewise. Anyway,' my wife continued, 'I've just heard on the news that the queue is now right back towards almost Bermondsey I think they said. Where are you now?'

'Directly opposite the Houses of Parliament, such a glorious view,' I replied.

'Oh, how lovely – and you're quite lucky then,' she began to reply.

'Excuse my interrupting you, love, but do you know what I've just this moment seen,' I said.

'No, what, some celebrity, somebody I may know, what exactly?' my wife enquired.

'Nothing like that, love, no I've just seen a cormorant dive off a nearby barge – there, there it is' I continued as if my wife was standing next to me. 'It seemed as if it was trying for some fish but I think that all it got was some small piece of wood – better luck next time.'

'That sounds an almost unreal sight for central London, a bit like the squirrels we see in St James's Park,' my wife continued and so very lovely to be involved in the sights and sounds of the day even when not actually being there.

'I suppose that the whole waiting won't have taken so very long, after all?' my wife continued.

'About and hour and a half or so left now, so no more than three hours overall, which isn't too bad,' I said as once again continuing the steady walking move and getting ever closer to Lambeth Bridge.

'Anyway, love, I'll let you know how the rest of the day goes and it's certainly lucky with the weather being so dry and quite comfortable in the Spring sunshine. I'll call you when I know which train I will be catching home. Be good and hope you continue to feel quickly better,' I concluded.

'Right, dear, see you soon,' and with that wish the mobile clicked off.

Now, I thought to myself, thinking of the convenience of the mobile telephone that is certainly something that makes the present life so much easier. Even although my wife wasn't able to be with me on that very day, the frequent phone calls possible at least gave the sense of being together to share thoughts and moments of the day.

Lambeth Bridge and yet another memory from my past on this day so full of such memories. How I had spent occasional times there when my father used to work at Lambeth Bridge House. Now, just a short distance behind me was the familiar sight of Lambeth Palace but as for Lambeth Bridge House? I looked around; no for sure that building didn't exist any longer. That, in itself, was most symbolic because, likewise, my own father had died some 20 years previously and with him, those personal associations of his London too. Thoughts, though, lived on and when looking back across the Thames, that view, naturally, was exactly the same. It was as almost if I expected to then hear my father's sharp and determined command:

'Get along, hurry up, there's no time to wait now!'

Uncannily, that what was then happening, the whole queue moved forward rather quickly just at that moment, going all the way across Lambeth Bridge without almost actually stopping. Almost within only a few minutes, we were weaving the line through Parliament Gardens getting ever nearer to Westminster Hall. The closer the queue got to Westminster Hall, then the quieter and the more subdued the whole line of people became. The cheerful banter stopped, as did the regular exchanges of names, addresses and life stories, the focal memorial purpose of the day was then immediately on hand with first the chance to sign the Book of Condolences.

The final steps past the House of Lords and then to the entrance door of Westminster Hall itself. Then, it was only the need for and the sight of the modern technology of the security scanners that really put a present-day date and time to the period. Otherwise, as I followed the fellow queue members into Westminster Hall itself, it could have been almost any time in the many years of history of this great building and the part it has played in our heritage.

Within less than half an hour, I was outside once again, this time in Parliament Square and very much aware of all the preparations taking place in readiness for the Queen Mother's funeral itself, to take place the following day. With time then for another phone call home to my wife and to be involved together with impressions, thoughts and recollections of the day. Next then to make my way once again to the station and begin the journey home, less than an hour and a half away.

Importantly, this was the very essence of being part of London life and the feeling to be in the right place, to be rightfully where I belonged. It was a day so full of so many featured memories, almost a review in a nutshell and a consequent kaleidoscope of my very life.

* * * *

As I had rediscovered London in the fresh eyes of, thankfully, once again living in the South, then so too I had felt the similar need to go back to Bow. Well, I was anxious in the first instance to see the place again as it was by then some 35 years since I had actually lived there, probably getting on for some 20 years without having seen the place, it was even more necessary, I felt, to go back. To return alone, to see everything again, to memorise and for a personal rediscovery.

So then, in the early years of the 21st century, I was once again back in the very centre of my once most central universe – there in Bow Road, again.

In some directions that I looked I saw nothing changed, which altogether surprised me given that I had experienced so many changes during those earlier visits many years ago. Of course, now I was only remembering selectively, seeing only what I wanted to see and what at that moment seemed right. 'Rose-coloured glasses' again? – I very much think so.

I saw the old house which was my former home, the church, all very much the same. It was almost to me as if I would then buy a paper and find it to be the mid 1960s rather than 2002. For that very moment it suited me to think that way but it was not an overall considered or subjective view.

For a long while I stood outside the former home, looking at the house, with the same entrance steps and pillared doorway, even that side door leading directly to our flat was there. Before long I was remembering the scenes of my childhood and early adult years all flashing through my mind. I couldn't help but gazing at all those windows, remembering the tale Nan and Grandpop had told me about the war-time blast I smiled at the thoughts of that story once again. I thought of all those old offices, all those multitude of cleaning duties, the carrying of endless buckets of coal that Nan and Grandpop had worked at for so many years.

And then what about our own fairly basic basement flat which was nevertheless home and the scene of some very happy childhood times and parties. Now, the flat still looked as if nobody had ever lived there since us, everything seemed so derelict, dirty and uncared for. What would Nan and Grandpop have thought, I asked myself, if they could have seen it then so run-down and neglected? They would both have been devastated when considering how hard they worked, almost against the odds, to make the best of the home, even though really it was nothing. And yet, on the other hand, I thought, it was right that, after our leaving that house, there should indeed have been nobody else to actually live there. By that, our departure had been so marked as very much the end of an era.

Along from the house, amazingly, the old favourite pub was still there – I went in and, although delightfully Victorian and very well kept, I didn't really recognise it from my past I even found it difficult to conjure in my mind the thoughts of my Nan and Grandpop actually being in that very place although as I sat quietly there, I heard their laughter and their voices running through my mind.

'What are you going to drink, Mate, the usual port and lemon or are you celebrating to-night, we've finished all the caretaking duties for one night? What about gin and it instead?' I imagined Grandpop saying.

'Oh, pop, you know me – gin and it, only for very special occasions. No, port and lemon will go down nicely, thank-you very much. And even if we haven't finished the fireplaces yet, I could do them much quicker once I've had one or two of those,' and with that Nan would have let out a glorious giggle. Their evening would then be set!

Dear Nan and Grandpop, themselves so very much an essential part of London, of Bow and with that special East End spirit. Equally, though, so very happy and at home when we had finally made that move to Westcliff. And what had I done to that – made a foolish work decision that meant we had all moved away and they had consequently spent their last years away from their own East London and Southend roots in Scotland?

At least I was lucky, I had the chance to finally return and once again be back in the area that meant so much not only to me but to them as well. The time when we moved North was the last that they would ever again be part of their home territory. So much I owed to them and yet somehow I couldn't help feeling that I had so let them down with that untimely and completely unwarranted move. It was a life's event without sense or proper foundation and should never have been. It was a grave sadness for me which I found so hard to come to terms with and none more so than that time of life's memories.

My thoughts then so overwhelmed me, sitting in that pub, concentrating too much on everything that was bad. Of course, that wasn't entirely the case and that had for me, and us all too, been some better moments too. I was immediately grateful to be happily married and with such a kind and lovely wife, with such tremendous intelligence and spirit. What a pity, I thought especially when sitting in that pub of so many memories, that Nan and Grandpop had never known my wife, both having died well before we met.

'You must get a girl, we want to see you happy.' How often they had said that to me. Well, the answer to both questions was firmly positive – I did 'get a girl' and I 'am happy.' It would be good for them both to somehow know that now.

Back once again in the main street, I soon realised that there was, indeed, so much more that had changed.

I was prepared for negative thoughts concerning all the bad re-developments once again, especially all the horrible flats and concrete passages. But I wasn't prepared to find that, indeed, some sense had prevailed and that some of the flats had gone, even if they themselves were no more than about 30 years old, to be replaced by new rows of individual houses, reminiscent of the Victorian terraces of my young years. I thought to myself that my thoughts had been vindicated and that I should have been an architect after all! Excitedly, I wondered what my wife would say about the result of my particular earlier vision, rather getting carried away with the situation.

Bow had certainly become a place of contrasts. I could barely believe my eyes when I saw on one side of the street a car showroom selling Porsches and Mercedes! That didn't compare with the old second-hand car lot that used to be on an old bomb site in Bow Road in my time. I was intrigued to see mention on various buildings that they were part of 'The Bow Heritage Trail.' My enquiries revealed that there was indeed such a planned trail taking in many of the fine Victorian buildings that were left in parts of the borough. Another triumph for my thoughts, the situation was almost becoming too much to take in or to fully comprehend!

The sight of the old Devon's Road shopping area soon returned me to reality. Everything so terribly run down, boarded-up and empty shops, very few people around, a real inner-City soul-less type of place, especially with the buzz and former market-excitement sounds gone for ever. Just an eerie silence, paper blowing about the almost empty streets merely added to the overall unreal feeling of what had once been such a bustling and bubbly place in my life.

And then, by contrast, almost unbelievably, in the far distance along Devon's Road, the unmistakable outline of that very hospital where my life had begun, getting on for almost 60 years before. That I could just not imagine being true, the place was a decrepit Victorian edifice on the day I was born so it was impossible to even begin to think what it must be like now. I didn't want to know and quickly turned my back on that area, getting quickly back to the main street and not feeling entirely comfortable or even completely safe to be walking in that area anymore.

I had seen enough, I had relived the old memories that I wanted, I had seen some positive changes and had even seen developments such as the up-market car showroom that I would not have thought possible. But this only a memory lane, that place was no longer me, my life's situation and my thoughts had changed too much for that. Life had simply moved on and whilst I so welcomed the opportunity to see around, I realised that I was seeing something that wasn't anymore me and it was something with which I could no longer identify.

Time then, to go back home to my wife, and to a life which was of that present day and time. With the sense of change, I made my way to leave Bow from the new Docklands Railway station which had been built in the very Bow Road and only a few yards from the old home. That was symbolic in itself.

* * * *

The pattern of life, as much built upon roots and memories for me as on the new and uncharted times. For so long I had been away from the place of my natural roots, as much out of regular contact with London as out of contact with my inner self. So much had happened to me in those years away, so much that had affected every aspect of my life, my being and my very character. As a result I found it hard to connect the stages of life into any coherent pattern, so great had been the effect of those years, the period that I call 'my exile.'

That time up until leaving Westcliff when so many aspects of the life had been good overall, of course, even then there were times that I wanted not to remember, indeed forget, such as some of the school years but even they were entwined too with many better things. I had a generally comfortable and good home life with the security that knowledge brings. How, too, I had loved those first City years, the achievement of owning the first car and then the supreme satisfaction of finally securing the move away from Bow to 'somewhere better,' the long cherished dream of our family. An immense satisfaction had happened in those years in Westcliff alone, probably representing the very pinnacle of achievement in an early life.

By contrast, though, what I had done other than that ruined the ideal by my thoughtless actions in that crazy work and home move idea and from that I suffered far too many years as a result. There was really a before and after – 'before' and London representing the good and satisfying, 'after' representing the bad and distressing years away.

Perhaps rather a symbolistic overview, because some good things did happen in the 'after' years, those many years away, but in my own mind I only had positive eyes for my London connections. That is until now, the third stage where once again, centred in London, the good and satisfying once again becomes apparent in contrast to those middle years. The great shame, though, is that those middle years were all far too long and they have the effect of still affecting and casting their unfortunate cloud over the present times.

For all that, though, now also represents a time and opportunity for hope, a hope for the right circumstances to resolve all the issues long outstanding and affecting our lives. A chance once again to be able to rebuild and concentrate on the best facets on offer. This is and always has been, the hope and security feeling brought about by my London being, nothing short of a reconnection with my reality being, my past A comfort, most certainly yes, but also, as a result, an ability to help to come to terms with life itself.

I wondered, was my re-awakening to London all just a memory lane and did I simply hanker for the 'good old days,' or the good days and times as I saw and remembered them? Was this all that I was doing - trying to relive a dream and by that to try to re-connect to an almost unattainable past and time? Perhaps my return was to make up within myself for that ultimate wrong decision those years back when I had left the area and denied to Nan and Grandpop the chance to end their days in their home territory.

But surely, such thoughts are all wrong in themselves and I needed to learn to adapt and re-acquaint with life's circumstances in the new place and time. The need to learn from all aspects of life, the good and the bad, the mistakes and the successes, the culminating benefit of all life's experiences and heritage. Time, then, to move on.

Of course, all life had changed – personal circumstances, relationships, work, home – everything. But through all there was the one most essential and stabilising factor That I so needed, had always needed and I was sure that I had found my answer. The stabilising factor for me was London and it was this very experience that I was realising and re-living.

This was then not just the simple re-kindling of memories; it was the full and absolute realisation of the very significance of my own life, a question asked and a very real answer found.

The importance to me of London in general, the essence of my being and thoughts, the bridge of life from old to new – a tangible link, the London link.

The End